To Thomas Drayton Parker
Sans peur et sans reproche

CONTENTS

PREFACE
by Edward L. Beach Sr.

The fact that this book has at last been completed is principally a result of the persistent encouragement and actual material assistance of my very dear friend, Commander Thomas Drayton Parker, USN (Ret.). Its writing has taken place, on and off, for ten years. What I had originally intended as a series of anecdotes of my career, principally for my own interest and amusement since retirement, and possibly for publication in a periodical of some kind, has grown wide of the original mark.

I find that instead of only telling *what* happened, I tend to spend about half my time describing the background of events and, in general, telling *how* and *why* things happened. Writing, when I write, becomes intensely interesting to me, and I usually work at furious speed, with long dormant memories flooding in, and words pouring from my pen. As quite often occurs in such instances, I realize that the "tail has wagged the dog." This book is, consequently, less about Beach and more about the U.S. Navy than one would expect from an autobiography. In fact, I have described the growth of our Navy as I saw it from the 1880s, when, you might say, our modern Navy had its beginnings, to the end of the First World War, when our Navy was fast becoming the most powerful on earth.

I hope that what I have written may have some value. If it leads to a better understanding of the Navy, a more complete appreciation of how it operates, and possibly a more sympathetic realization that, after all, the men of the Navy are simply you and I—then I shall feel that Parker knew what he was talking about.

Captain Edward L. Beach Sr., USN (Ret.)
Palo Alto, California

PREFACE
by Edward L. Beach Jr.

Born in Toledo, Ohio, on 30 June 1867, Father was the second of four children of Joseph Lane Beach and Laura Colton Osborn Beach. Joseph impulsively joined the Confederate Army, and was wounded and captured by the North at Antietam. After discharge from a northern prison, he went to Toledo, where he married. In the early 1870s the young Beach family, parents and four children, had established residency in Minneapolis, Minnesota, and as a youth Father began to realize that his parents would not be able to finance a college education for him. He therefore applied himself vigorously to his high school studies, at the same time letting be known his intention to apply for appointment to the U.S. Naval Academy at Annapolis. In due course he won a competitive examination given by his congressman, and received the coveted appointment.

Mostly written during the early 1930s, during the period of my own preparation for this same competitive examination, I frequently saw Father hard at work in a nearby room. I won appointment in 1935, having been thoroughly prepared by Father's close supervision, and my last sight of him in this connection was that he was still writing, with his Parker pen, on a long sheet of yellow, ruled paper. Although Father's memory was excellent, I'm sure he reviewed what he wrote, and verified facts, using, obviously, the U.S. Naval Academy's annual *Register of Alumni*, which I've also checked. He made no mistakes as to names. For a smoother flow, I have deleted extraneous phrases and added known dates for specific events. Father identified persons according to current custom as he was writing. In some instances, I have more fully identified certain individuals, including classmates and shipmates who later became well known to the general public. Father's words have been mostly reproduced exactly as he wrote them; only very minor editing was done to clarify.

Although not discussed by Father in his autobiography, he published thirteen novels during his life. There were four novels in each of three series, plus one stand-alone novel. The Annapolis series (*An Annapolis Plebe*, *An Annapolis Youngster*, *An Annapolis Second Classman*, and *An Annapolis First Classman*) were published between 1907 and 1920, and detailed life at the U.S. Naval Academy. The Ralph Osborn series (*Midshipman Ralph Osborn at Annapolis*, *Midshipman Ralph Osborn at Sea*, *Ensign Ralph Osborn*, and *Lieutenant Ralph Osborn Aboard a Torpedo Boat Destroyer*) were published between 1909 and 1912, and detailed life as midshipman, ensign, and destroyer skipper. The four books of the Roger Paulding series were published between 1911 and 1914, and detailed life as an enlisted man in our Navy. Father's last novel was *Dan Quin of the Navy*, published in 1922. Two other unfinished novels about Dan Quin are in my house.

Father dedicated his autobiography to his close friend, Commander Parker, who for years had been strongly encouraging him to write it. I remember meeting Commander Parker once or twice when he called on us in Palo Alto, perhaps around 1930, when I was about twelve years old.

As Father's amateur amanuensis, however, it seems to me that he might have done a little more for my mother, Alice, his wife during the second half of his life. He met her in 1915, the year Lucie died, and they were married two years later. Lucie had no children, but Alice quickly presented him with three, of whom I was the first, born during his fifty-first year. John and Alice Jr. were born in 1919 and 1921, respectively. Early in the twentieth century, it may not have been the custom to dedicate books to one's wife—he dedicated none of the twelve books he published before she died to Lucie. When I would ask him, however, he always described the great assistance Lucie had been to him. His last book, *Dan Quin of the Navy*, published in 1922, five years after he and

Mother were married, bears dedication to Captain Leonard Cox, his second in command at Mare Island, Father's final duty station.

I have taken it on myself, in double filial homage, to add Mother's name in the dedication of Father's autobiography. Mother survived him by nearly thirty years. Like Lucie, Alice gave her best to him, and to the Navy. Hospitalized at the end, he died in Mother's arms in the last month of 1943.

Much of what Father wrote in the pages that follow applies nearly as well to me as to him. I loved all my time in naval service, as he did, and have tried to show this in the ways fate has made it possible to do, just as he did. There were of course a few bad times as well as the many good ones. But the picture we, he and I, want to present is that the U.S. Navy is a truly great career for anyone interested in serving his country, or, more poetically, the great world ocean we have all inherited.

Captain Edward L. Beach Jr., USN (Ret.)
Washington, D.C., 2002

From Annapolis
to
Scapa Flow

I

AT THE BOTTOM

Looking back to June 1884, and mentally crossing the continent from my home in California where this is being written, I see myself awaiting dinner formation on the lawn in front of "New Quarters" (demolished long ago) at the U.S. Naval Academy in Annapolis, Maryland. This was to me an exciting and fearful time. Age seventeen, I had just been admitted as a naval cadet—though in cadet language I was a "plebe," at the bottom of the human, or at least the U.S. naval, scale.

The evening before, three older cadets, scornful, cruel, and contemptuous, had welcomed me to the Naval Academy—forcing me to stand on my head, to crawl sideways like a soft-shell crab, to run on all fours barking like a dog, and to play the fool in other ways—all under a shower of abuse and of threatening imprecation.

"Brace up, mister! Look to the front and wipe that smile off your face! At last you're an officer and a gentleman! Don't you forget that! And the most contemptible thing in the Navy; don't you forget that, either!"

After these three terrible beings had left, I wanted to go home. My boyish soul revolted at the thought of four years in such a terrible place.

That night I had spent in a hammock on the old frigate *Santee*. The next day, one of glorious June sunshine—the day on which this narrative opens—witnessed the graduation of those who had finished what I was just beginning. But during this great occasion, we of the entering class were left aboard the old ship until noon; then we were marched to the New Quarters, where, huddled in groups, we were waiting for dinner.

The battalion came marching back from the graduation ceremonies. As I looked it was halted; the fours swung into line; and at the order of "Break ranks!" the orderly formation broke into a mob of joyous young men racing toward the spot where we stood awaiting dinner and whatever else might come.

One ran directly to me. I recognized one of my tormentors of the night before. To my amazement, his tone was friendly. "You'll get along all right," he said. "My name is Dutton. I'll spoon on you." (Meaning, "I'll be your friend.") "Come to see me any time."

I was too dumbfounded to answer. It seemed impossible that the ogre of the previous night could be this friendly young gentleman.

Graduation day was almost as important to the new third classmen, who for the past year had been suffering plebes, as to the graduates. During the period of duress they had endured not only the just and strict discipline of the Academy, but in addition had been hazed by the tyrants of the upper classes. Much of this hazing was pure fun, when understood; without malice; amusing at times even to the victims. The upper classmen had exacted an outward respect and obedience that Admiral Farragut of Civil War fame would never have demanded from his juniors. One of the theories of hazing was that it indoctrinated newcomers with the notion of authority; an opposing theory called it a result of artificial imposition of an alien rank structure. Whatever the reality, some form of hazing has existed in most armed forces since the beginning—and in other organizations as well. At Annapolis, though silly brutalities occurred at times, upper classmen as a rule disapproved of them. In extreme cases, a plebe might be ordered to drink ink or eat soap.

The system of hazing had prevented nearly all friendly contact between plebes and cadets of other classes—though this was not a hard-and-fast rule. Nonetheless, plebes were excluded from the Naval Academy dances, from certain walks and benches in the grounds, from sitting down in the presence of upper classmen, and from drinking milk at meals—this last without protest of the medical staff, although it involved the loss of needed calories. Many things were taboo. For an entire year, two hundred "special policemen" exercised unlimited powers in curbing the actions and speech of the plebes.

Suddenly all had changed. The downtrodden plebe of the day before had become a lofty third classman: in naval cadet or midshipman parlance, a "youngster." The scowling enemies of the past year now showed themselves as smiling warm-hearted friends. To be addressed as "Atkins" or "Reese" instead of "Mr. Atkins!" "Mr. Reese!" or, insultingly, as simply "Mister!" denoted a signal honor. The corresponding joy of addressing superior beings without the preliminary "mister" was deep. Traditionally, aside from that first year as a plebe, "sir" or "mister" were forever dispensed with between persons who had spent time together as midshipmen, whatever their respective graduation dates.

However, each of these new youngsters, as of that day taken into the fold, had been enjoined to "start the new plebes right" for the honor of their own class, and for the good of the naval service in general.

"The Navy will go to the dogs unless the customs of the service are observed." This was the cry. The new upholders of discipline, only recently lowly plebes, were wild to do their duty.

Naturally, therefore, the next person to address me said nothing about friendly calls. He was a scowling, thin lipped, high cheek-boned, blue-eyed member of the class just superior to mine.

"Mister! What's your name?" he snapped.

"Beach," I replied.

"Say, 'Beach, *sir!*' Square your cap! Heels together! Little fingers on the seams of your trousers! And wipe that smile off your face! Do you hear? When you speak to me, end each sentence with a 'sir!' Now spell your name with a 'sir' after each letter!"

"*B*, sir, *E*, sir, *A*, sir, *C*, sir, *H*, sir!"

How my soul loathed this tyrant! How little did I realize, as I discovered a year later, that he had a kindly, gentle heart.

Near me stood a tall raw-boned plebe. A third classman, or youngster, addressed him: "Say Mister! What's your name? Where're you from?"

"Wilbur is my name, sir. I'm from Dakota."

"Huh! Hereafter, when an upper classman asks your name, you will reply as follows: 'I am Magical Mike, the untutored Terror of the wild Northwest, the howling blizzard of the Great Desert. Pray don't look at my feet!'"

People have inquired where Curtis D. Wilbur, the former chief justice of the supreme court of California, and recent secretary of the Navy, got the nickname of "Magic" that was used by his intimate friends. The above tells where, how, and when.

Often names given in this absurd way have stuck. For instance, there was William Hogg: "Hereafter your name is 'Billy Pig!' Don't you ever forget it!"

And poor William Hogg never could forget it. For forty long years, except officially and to juniors, he was "Billy Pig."

One of my classmates was "Richard Montgomery Smith, sir, from Mineral Point, Wisconsin, sir." For purposes of identification he was officially required, like the rest of us, to print his name on the front of his white working uniform blouse, or "jumper." After blocking out my own name on each canvas blouse, I looked at the job he had done. On each jumper, in big letters, appeared, "Smith, sir."

Another classmate from Point Coupe, Raccourci, Louisiana, called himself "John Archer Lejeune." I have been told by army officers that if the Great War (World War I) had outlasted General Pershing, who commanded American forces in France, a major general of the U.S. Marines named Lejeune, from somewhere in Louisiana, who had been my roommate at Annapolis, might have commanded American forces in France.

As I write, the muster roll of my class jumps back into consciousness: Aiken, Alexander, Bassett, Baya, Beach, Behse, Benham, Beckwith, Beswick, Bischoff, etc. Their faces are all clear before me.

One was Harris, from Key West, Florida—Jeptha Vining Harris. A man named "Jeptha" can never expect oblivion. But there were other reasons for remembering Harris. As he told me later, he had read, a year previously, of some "brutal hazing" at the Naval Academy, for which twenty-two cadets had been dismissed at one time. While preparing in Baltimore for the entrance examinations, he determined to prepare further by learning to box. He took daily lessons at the boxing academy of Jake Kilrain, a famous pugilist who was then training to fight John L. Sullivan for the world's heavyweight championship. Finding Harris quick and strong, Kilrain became interested in him and trained him as if for a prizefight. In a month, Harris was having daily bouts with the professional pugilist.

On the evening of our first day at Annapolis, Harris and others were standing on the *Santee* wharf. Several third classmen approached; one named Hurlbut took Harris in hand. Not liking Harris's truculent manner, he lost his temper and slapped him. A moment later, he lay fourteen feet away, unconscious.

Then a slight, earnest-looking youngster accosted Harris. "My name is Wiley. What's yours?"

"Harris, sir."

"Will you fight?"

"If you wish, sir."

A ring was formed. Hardly had Wiley taken the position of guard when he was overwhelmed, like Hurlbut.

The other youngsters present hastily sent for Fitzgerald, the best boxer of the class, to fight as its champion. He lasted as long as his predecessors did— and no longer.

Some days later, several of us walking with Harris on the beach at Fortress Monroe met two third classmen, "Freddie" Moore and "Jonah" Cloke, both noted football players and good athletes.

"We'll have to fight," said Moore. "Mr. Beach here will be your second, Mr. Harris. I'll fight first. Mr. Cloke will second me. After you lick me, I'll second Mr. Cloke while you lick him."

Third classmen felt honor-bound to engage Harris, who, during the next few months, was constantly forced to fight, though always the winner. Wiley went up against him three times. Wiley was a bundle of grit. Eighteen months later he fought a terrific battle with Naval Cadet Gray—twenty-eight rounds. Gray was big and strong, and fifty pounds heavier than Wiley, whose face was battered into a pulp. But Wiley was like John Paul Jones. It was Gray who gave up and spent the next two weeks in the hospital, while Wiley never missed a recitation or a drill.

I, too, had a fight with Harris, over what I can't now remember. When I came to he was doing everything for me, and most earnestly apologized for hitting me so hard. Former Judge Jeptha Vining Harris, attorney, is now fighting for his clients at Key West, Florida.

In 1939, only a few months graduated, in my turn, from the U.S. Naval Academy, I found myself aboard the destroyer *Lea* in Key West, and obeyed Father's directive to call on Judge Harris. I rang the doorbell at his imposing brick house, the "southernmost house in the United States," stated my business to the woman who answered the door, and discovered he had died only a week or two before.

A year after I entered Annapolis, Wiley was court-martialed for hazing. He was convicted, and dismissed. He left for his home in Texas, and, by law, was forever disqualified for further service in the Navy. If Wiley had not been dismissed at this time, he would never, I believe, have become commander in chief of the U.S. Fleet. But that (as Kipling did not say first) is another story.

At this point, a reader may well ask, "How can someone dismissed from the naval service become commander in chief?" and "Why doesn't Beach tell the tale right here?" During the 1930s and 1940s, when Father was putting pen to paper, everyone in the Navy knew who Wiley was, as did many non-Navy people. To avoid altering Father's storytelling style, I will not interrupt with the tantalizing details. Rest assured that Father continues the story later.

The day after graduation, my class and the new first and third classes sailed aboard the USS *Constellation* on a practice cruise. After tacking down Chesapeake Bay, we spent several pleasant days at Fortress Monroe, where Jeptha had a few fights, and we all bought wonderful dinners for seventy-five cents each at the old Hygeia Hotel. "Wonderful" is no exaggeration. Few places in the world have equaled the Chesapeake Bay region of fifty years ago in excellence and profusion of food. Canvasback ducks were everywhere. Fine oysters in the shell were bought by the bushel; diamondback terrapin, by the dozen. Ten cents would buy all the soft-shell crabs a family could eat at a sitting. Turkeys, wild and domestic, abounded. Cellars were always stocked with Smithfield hams. And in spite of America's temporary condemnation of alcohol, I have happy memories of Maryland mint juleps, brandied peaches, and eggnog.

This portion of the narrative was probably written before 1933, when the Twenty-first Amendment repealed Prohibition.

But certainly none of this good cheer reached us aboard the *Constellation*. Here was discomfort, violent and sudden. We had to learn how to eat naval seafood and yet stay alive. Our meats were salt pork and salt beef (that we called "salt horse"). With these were served beans, hardtack, rice, dried peas, pickles, butter, sugar, coffee, and tea—no canned fruits or vegetables.

Drinking water was kept in rusty iron tanks, and after a shaking up at sea was a deep rich red, with a compound of all flavors. The worst of all discomforts was having only salt water for washing, since the few gallons of fresh water served to cadets for this purpose were appropriated by the first classmen, except for a little allocated to the youngsters for washing their teeth. We plebes got none whatever. Ordinary toilet soap used with salt water forms a sort of glue that fixes dirt and perspiration on the skin. This thin, sticky coating is unremovable, but it served one useful purpose. Mosquitoes would die in the attempt to pierce it; cockroaches would run from it; and other bugs, nameless here if not on the *Constellation*, would spare gluey sleepers.

My first impressions of ship life were far from reassuring. Sleeping in a curved hammock is not all it might be, especially if hammocks are slung in dense proximity. During the day it was "all hands on deck to work ship," and at night, "watch and watch"—meaning half of us on watch at any given time. After a day of incessant maneuvers, our rest at night would always be broken. One night I would sleep in my hammock until nearly midnight, go on deck for a cold middle watch, and sleep again from about 4:15 until an early reveille. The next night I would have only the "mid-watch" in my hammock, snatching what other naps I could on the windy deck.

The "turning out" of a watch at night was always accompanied by a wild uproar. Boatswain's mates with shrill pipes and raucous voices howled and bellowed, aided by certain first classmen. There was always a violent, sudden awakening, with cries of "Turn out! Turn out! Shake a leg! Out you get!" over and over again. Unless there were signs of instant obedience, some first classman, or maybe a "bosun's mate," was sure to crouch under my hammock, rise quickly, and turn my bed inside out. The air below at night was thick and nauseating. If a plebe was seasick, so much the worse for him.

The daytime drills included sail, gun, and instruction drills. Our appetizer before breakfast was a run up the weather (windward side) lower rigging, over the "futtock shrouds" into the "fighting top," and over the topmast, then down the lee rigging. This seemed perilous to me; but it was amazing to see the upper classmen run like cats to those dizzy heights, with no thought of a thousand dangers. At first I climbed slowly, painfully trying not to slip, squeezing tar out of each ratline as I ascended.

The futtock shrouds, iron rods supporting the broad "top" that one crawled upwards over back down like a three-toed sloth, until able to crawl over the outboard edge of the top and collapse on its platform deck, filled me with terror. Swallowing my shame, I would take the safer route through the "lubber's hole" (a hole through the deck of the top, close to the mast). After a few more painful minutes I would thankfully descend to the main deck.

We loosed and furled the sails. This required me to lay out on the yardarm, standing on the swaying foot rope, gradually edging out as the ship pitched and rolled.

Before the cruise was over I could run up the rigging of any of our three masts to the cross trees (far above the fighting tops) and slide down a rope to the topgallant yard as unconcernedly as a blue-jacket or a monkey.

The danger I at first feared was not unreal. On a later cruise I stood with a classmate named Campbell on the foot rope of the fore topgallant yard. He slipped; down he whizzed a hundred feet or more, striking an iron jackstay at the foretop, bouncing off, and landing crosswise on some running gear fifty feet above the deck, to which he desperately clung. Several enlisted men, always generous of themselves, jumped directly under him to break his fall; but their potential offering of their own bodies to soften his landing was not necessary. Another sailor gently "lowered away" on the running gear and although badly shaken, Campbell suffered no serious injury. Meanwhile I was looking down with intensity from the topgallant yard of *Constellation*'s tall foremast.

Another time, on a cold windy morning, Cadet Oskloosa Schley, a nephew of the afterwards famous rear admiral, Winfield Scott Schley, raced up the weather main rigging and up, over the futtock shrouds, to the cross trees. As he reached them the ship rolled deeply to leeward, and poor Schley was jerked clear of the rigging. He fell, struck the ship's side, bounced into the ocean, and was lost at sea.

Instantly the *Constellation* was thrown into the wind and the lifeboat called away. Seven men sprang into it; others, at their stations, started to lower away.

The after boat fall jammed, the boat went down by the bow, and a heavy sea completely swamped it. Though the other lifeboat was lowered, only two of the first crew were picked up. Six lives were lost in less than six minutes!

On these cruises we were instructed in making and taking in sail, in sending light yards up and down, in tacking, wearing, and box hauling, and in knot tying. I soon learned the difference between a "granny" and a "square" knot, and mastered the bowline, sheepshank, rolling hitch, and clove hitch. I also learned how to put a "monkey fist" into another cadet's hammock lashing, thus making the hammock impossible to use without an hour's fussing with a marlinspike.

The rigging seemed a bewildering mass of ropes: bowlines, buntlines, clewgarnets, clewlines, clewjiggers, reef tackles, downhauls, halyards, sheets, tacks, braces, brails, lifts, mast ropes. There were many of each kind at each mast. In tacking, wearing, or box hauling, the *Constellation* would spin around on her keel in a way dear to the hearts of officers and crew. For nearly a century (since 1797) she had been famous as a "smart working ship."

Although he did not address the *Constellation* identity controversy, it's hard to see how Dad could not have known of it. The ship in which he sailed those midshipman cruises was not the 38-gun frigate of 1797, but an entirely new ship, of the same name, built in 1854 under the guise of "rebuilding" the older one. The new *Constellation* mounted only twenty-two guns, instead of the nominal thirty-eight of the older ship, but they were of much larger caliber and very much heavier weight. The ship herself was considerably larger than the old one, in fact bigger than the 44-gun *Constitution* ("*Old Ironsides*"), the only one of those six 1797 frigates still in existence. Both *Constellation*s earned reputations as smart ships. The 1854 ship was the last all-sail–powered man of war built for the U.S. Navy. She is preserved in Baltimore, where the many differences between her and Boston's *Old Ironsides* can be examined by anyone with the knowledge and interest to do so.

At an "all hands" maneuver the boatswain would pipe the crew to their stations. Then there would be an interval of intense silence. Next came the sharp, staccato orders of the officer of the deck, and three hundred men would jump into violent action. Amazingly, there was no mixing of the thousands (as it seemed) of different ropes (mostly known as "lines"), all in use at the same instant. And the howling, shrieking, bellowing of the officer of the deck with his trumpet, the junior officers, the boatswain mates, the other petty officers, each responsible for some part of the evolution, was pure pandemonium. Sails were flapping, ropes swiftly reeving through blocks, men running wildly about the deck.

Our officers of those old days were excellent beyond compare in their perfect control of ship, helm, sails, and men. Lieutenant E. H. C. Leutze handled the ship and crew with an execution as swift, as delicate, as certain, as Paderewski's at the piano, or as Leutze's own father's on a mural; the lieutenant was the son of Emanuel Leutze, whose paintings are in the dome of the Capitol, and in the Metropolitan Museum of Art in New York City.

Gradually I learned the names and uses of ropes and of other things aboard ship: clewlines and buntlines were to haul up a sail; a sheet was to haul down its lower corners in the process of "setting" it; the flying jib was the furthest forward of all sails, the royals the highest, the courses the lowest, and the spanker the aftermost. I learned that the lowest yard on the mizzen mast is not the mizzen yard, but the cross-jack yard; that it carries no sail, and that "cross-jack" is pronounced "crojik." I learned that the "fore truck" is not a wagon, but the top of the foremast; that the "cat" is not an animal, but a rope, or "line"; that "reef earings" are not worn by ladies; that a "jigger" is not an insect.

Father also learned a naval limerick:

There was a young lady from Bangor,
Who slept in a ship while at anchor.
Through a port she jumped out
When she heard the Bosun shout,
"Haul down the main sheet and spanker!"

2

CHANGES IN WARSHIPS

During my early years in naval service, the Navy was in a state of decay. Most of its ships were old, built of wood, and used steam only as an auxiliary to sails. When under sail (as they usually were) their propellers could be disconnected to spin freely in order to reduce drag. Some had only two blades so that they could be pinned, or locked, with the blades vertical, directly behind the keel, where they would cause least drag. Some propellers, in fact, could be physically removed from the propeller shaft, although this was a difficult operation that often involved putting a few men in the water at the stern of the ship. Many of the old captains used coal only in emergencies, or when entering or leaving port. I vividly recall three weeks aboard the *Richmond*, late in 1888 at the equator, when during a continuous calm the captain would not order steam.

A year later, however, in the same ship, we were happily "rolling into Rio" when, ten miles from the entrance, the breeze died out. We began bobbing about helplessly in ugly currents, our masts describing huge arcs against blue skies. After talking earnestly with some of the senior officers, the same captain (he must have learned something from the previous experience) appointed a "board of survey" on a large quantity of bacon that formed part of our ship's stores. Soon thousands of pounds of this bacon, condemned by the board as "unfit for human consumption" were sizzling in the furnaces, and we were rolling into Rio on bacon fat, a splendid fuel.

If the material of our Navy was defective, our personnel still kept high morale. A tradition of victory is invaluable. The American and British navies (except when fighting each other), and the Japanese, have had this tradition almost continuously. During the campaign about Boston, in Revolutionary days, our infant Navy fed and clothed Washington's army by capturing British store ships. During the "undeclared war" with France, 1798–1801, American ships were victorious in eighty-four of eighty-five sea battles. In the War against the Barbary States, 1801–1805, our warships destroyed their piratic navies. In the War of 1812, our ships won fifteen of eighteen single-ship actions, and both fleet actions. Success is deep in the heart and soul of our Navy and Marine Corps, and dominates the thoughts and actions of their leaders, in solemn appreciation of the fact that the men of today must maintain the glorious record of our past.

The result is enthusiasm for studies, drills, target practice, and maneuvers, and thorough investigation of weakness or failure. This enthusiasm, the constant, strong effort to excel, the bitter intolerance of inefficiency, is the determining influence aboard our ships and at our stations. The rewards of success are great: not only promotion, but also the sense of accomplishment after intense effort. The fixed aim of every one of our naval ships today is such thorough preparation in every detail that the battle of tomorrow will surely be won.

It was this spirit alone that saved the Navy after the Civil War, when ships rotted, Navy yards were deserted, and promotion was almost halted. In this atmosphere of discouragement, the naval service never faltered in its effort or its loyalty.

As only a very few ships remained in commission, these naturally became overcrowded with officers. At one time the old *Lancaster*, with slow-moving engines that seldom moved, even slowly, had twenty-two "assistant engineers" on board. In port, engineer officers stood useless "cold-iron" watches.

At the outbreak of the Civil War, 303 naval officers resigned to "go south," and war needs had caused a large increase of numbers in each grade. Robley

D. "Fighting Bob" Evans, then but eighteen years old, was graduated from Annapolis in 1863 as a lieutenant commander.

Although born in Virginia, Evans had snared an appointment to the Naval Academy from Utah. When war became inevitable, his family expected him to resign and join the Confederate Navy, but he decided instead to follow a senior officer's advice to remain loyal to the Union. His mother thereupon wrote out his resignation for him and sent it to the Navy Department, where it was automatically accepted, requiring a telegram from his senior friend to set things right.

For many years after the war, senior officers were often little older than their juniors and there were few retirements for age; therefore, there was but little natural promotion. To make matters worse, Congress, impressed by the large ratio of officers to ships, passed a law permitting but one promotion for two vacancies in the next higher grade. It then took 256 vacancies in the grade of rear admiral (there being only six rear admirals in the entire Navy) to cause the promotion of one very junior ensign. Officers were age forty before they reached the lieutenant's grade, and seemed destined to remain there the rest of their lives.

This apparently hopeless stagnation caused hundreds of officers and hundreds of midshipmen, graduated but not commissioned, to resign from the Navy. Many of these became distinguished in civil life. Professor A. A. Michaelson, who graduated in 1873, enjoys world fame for his discovery and measurement of the speed of light. Not many are aware that Michaelson's work was done at the Naval Academy, and that he owed much to the unstinting support of its superintendent, the then Captain William Thomas Sampson, who later gained fame in the 1898 War with Spain. John Weeks, class of 1881, became secretary of war; my classmate Curtis D. Wilbur, secretary of the Navy. Frank Sprague, class of 1878, invented the constant speed motor, which increased the use of electricity a millionfold. Lewis Nixon, the number one man of '82, became general manager of Cramp's shipyard, near Philadelphia, at that time considered the best shipyard in the country.

These are only a few of the notable men the Navy sent into civilian life. Many others remained in the service, and gave the best they had in them to bringing the Navy out of the doldrums. Well known among these were Alfred Thayer Mahan, Sampson (previously mentioned), Bradley Allen Fiske, and George Dewey, and there was a host of others. The notable work of William Sowden Sims is mentioned later. During this great period of development in electricity, steam engineering, and other sciences, naval officers, almost as a body, threw themselves into study, experiments, and invention. We developed smokeless powder from Russia, "built up" guns from France and England, rapid fire and machine guns of our own invention, hardened armor plant, higher grade steel, the automobile torpedo, and the submarine. There were many other inventions and developments of naval engines and weapons, all of which we worked on eagerly. The whole Navy of this period was enthusiastically interested in the fast-developing technology of warships and the sea.

A "Naval War College" was founded by Rear Admiral Stephen B. Luce at Newport, Rhode Island. At this college, in the 1880s, Captain Mahan, whom Luce had recruited to become a member of the faculty, gave a series of lectures. In 1889 these were assembled and published in England under the title, *The Influence of Sea Power Upon History,* and their impact was like that of an exploding bomb.

The influence of this book was immediate and enormous. The British parliament at once adopted the "two power standard" (its navy was to be superior to any other two navies in the world). The construction of eight new battleships of the *Royal Sovereign* class, capable of an offensive power unknown before, was ordered at a cost of $55 million, and soon this was followed by another appropriation for the same purpose, of $180 million. The young German emperor, William II, went wild with the purpose of creating a great German navy, and ordered that all German naval officers study Mahan. Germany started building "*Royal Sovereigns,*" as did France and Italy; and soon the United States had joined in the mad race.

But to go back: in the 1870s and 1880s, American naval officers were fired with ambition and purpose. There had never been such developments in warships, in guns, and in ammunition, or in steam, hydraulics, and electric engineering. The "automobile torpedo," invented by Robert Whitehead, a Brit, was developed abroad. Dr. Jordan Gatling, an American, invented a machine gun firing hundreds of bullets a minute; Benjamin Hotchkiss, another American, produced the revolver cannon. In 1892, a U.S. Navy lieutenant, Bradley Fiske, invented the telescope sight that changed great guns into instruments of precision. It is due to this invention that modern sea battles are fought at ranges up to ten miles or more. In the battle of Jutland at the end of May 1916, at a range of eight miles, Admiral Franz von Hipper sank two of Admiral David Beatty's battle cruisers and put a third one out of commission, all within thirty minutes.

In the early 1900s, Sims, of our Navy, wrote a bitter criticism of our battleships, both as to ship design and armament, and then offered the design of what he called "the all-one-caliber, big gun, center line Battleship." This, like so many other things Sims has done, came like a thunderclap. The design, so different from previous battleship designs, carried immediate conviction. Our government hastened to get out plans for the *Michigan* and *South Carolina*. But the British, who believed that the life of their nation depended upon naval superiority, grabbed that design as a starving man wildly grabs food, and built the *Dreadnought* in one year. When the *Dreadnought* ran her trials, however, England also understood that the tremendous naval superiority of this one ship reduced Great Britain's naval advantage from many battleships to an advantage of only one. Although the new ship was clearly a vastly better one, both England and her arch rival, Germany, strove to turn their newly created near-equality into real naval superiority. For the British, this change in relative strength was hard to take.

With one stunning blow, Sims (or HMS *Dreadnought*) destroyed the continuing superiority of the British navy. He relegated Britain's great fleet of pre-*Dreadnoughts*, with their two turrets of four heavy guns and several sizes of smaller guns, to the second battle line, replacing them with four- and five-turret battleships carrying ten or twelve heavy guns on the center line that could shoot in virtually any direction. The change was revolutionary. Ten or a dozen big caliber guns hitting a distant target, dealing devastating damage before smaller guns were even within range, would obviously hurt an enemy more than could only two or four big guns. Furthermore, the United States, or Germany, could now build ships of the new type as fast as Great Britain could. England felt herself in a state of emergency.

Sims brought from England her methods of instruction for battle target practice. The "war game," so constantly practiced at our Naval War College, is also an English invention.

In all this naval development each power kept itself aware of what others were doing, tested out their inventions and ideas, and adopted many of them. But I may safely say that many of the elements dominating navies today are of American origin.

A philosopher might ask "Cui bono?" since our potential enemies have profited, sometimes more than we have, by all our inventions; and the chief net result has been to make war more terrible. But naval officers must do things that need doing, and have not the time to philosophize. It has repeatedly happened, as when the Wrights invented the airplane and Holland the successful submarine, that America has evolved the idea and foreign powers have been quicker to utilize it.

Competition between American and British inventors has been keen. Sprague once told me that when he patented his constant speed motor, an Englishman and a German were almost ready with much the same thing. The British may justly claim development of the destroyer and the battle cruiser, and of definitely fixing, through their yearly mobilizations and by the Battle of Jutland, the place and duty of each naval type in battle. It's fair to say that these two navies are today in the forefront of naval development.

I can conceive of no more splendid, no more efficient organization, than the U.S. Navy. Our Naval Academy provides the mold in which plastic youth is cast for naval purposes. Sea service brings contact with naval traditions, and naval life creates responsible knowledge of ships, maneuvers, guns, engines, men, and drills. The Naval War College provides higher education in naval history and in strategy and tactics. It is safe to say that all our officers of command rank know what Beatty did or did not do, what Admiral John Jellicoe did or did not do, what each should have done, in the great battle of Jutland on 31 May 1916. For twenty years the Naval War College has been studying the intimate details of this battle, which could justly have been called the (disappointing) Trafalgar of a century later.

After more than thirty-seven years of active naval service, followed by the study and reflection of twenty years of retirement, it's my earnest belief that our Navy today merits the confidence of every American. It is certain to do well what it is given to do.

3

HOW THE DAYS WERE SPENT

My purpose is not to write an essay about the Navy, but to present a moving picture of one naval career that must be typical of many others. Details differ, but the frame and the background are the same. Incidents in the life of a subaltern may have interest, even if they are trivial, and as the carefree life of a midshipman merges into that of a commanding officer, the note of tragedy—and my survival thereof—will be duly struck.

Our first practice cruise on the *Constellation* ended at Annapolis in August 1884. For ten weeks I had been living what seemed a rough life: in the daytime hauling ropes, making and furling sail, tying knots, drilling at our smoothbore guns; at night, spending some of the hours in a hammock below, and some in the breezes on the main deck above, manning gear for squalls, or for changes in wind, as necessary. It was a time of extreme and unceasing discomfort.

On our return, late in August, the upper classmen went on leave; but we plebes were transferred back to the old station ship *Santee*. With plenty of fresh water and a little more room, what a paradise! We scrubbed, bathed, and put on clean clothes. The call to dinner sounded, and we rushed out for inspection before marching to the mess hall, half a mile away.

When we got there, what a sight met our famished eyes! Once more on the table, clean white linen. Also on the tables, beautiful steaming ears of corn, smoking hot porterhouse steaks, fresh green peas, soft bread, and (believe it or not) great mounds of ice cream with huge slices of cake. And that delicious liquid in the glass pitchers! It may have been called "milk," but it was double distilled champagne, a gift from Heaven. No feast ever brought more happiness. Someone at the Naval Academy understood that the "hard life" occasionally had to be alleviated a little.

After our return to the *Santee*, a new naval cadet, who had just been admitted, came to me with some questions. We spent the afternoon together. He was entirely unknowing about the Navy, and had much to ask. I helped him swing his hammock, and he turned in early, not feeling well. I think I was the only member of the class with whom he talked.

I shall never forget that sweet-faced youth, whose name was Frederick Schwatka Strang. The next morning he was dead. During the night his heart stopped like an unwound clock.

Strang's gravestone may still be seen in the Naval Academy Cemetery, not far from the new Naval Institute Headquarters. The monument lists him as a "Naval Cadet," gives an incorrect date of death, and states that his gravestone was "erected by his classmates." Surprisingly, the *Register of Alumni*, published by the United States Naval Academy Alumni Association, Inc., does not carry his name, although it has always routinely listed deceased midshipmen as well as non-graduates for other reasons. Perhaps Strang had been "aboard" for such a short time that he had not yet been sworn in, and in those days there may have been other regulations governing eligibility for burial.

A few days later there were wild newspaper accounts of the hazing to death of Naval Cadet Strang. He had been "nailed in a spiked barrel and rolled downhill"; he had been "pitched over the sea wall" and "thrown from a second-story window." Whatever the means, the excited media accounts all coincided in concluding that he had been "brutally done to death," thereby illustrating the temper of the times on this particular subject. An inquiry that followed established the truth, that he had not been hazed in any way. He had not even been bumped out of his hammock at reveille by the time-honored method of someone suddenly standing up under it if the occupant wasn't stirring soon enough. His untimely death was purely an unusual medical occurrence, little understood in those days.

Strang's demise had a great effect upon me. I resolved never to haze, and I never did. Just a year later, having become a third classman, I was accused, with my classmate Ralph Bailey, of hazing a plebe named Gray. As an investigation showed, I had asked Gray, as a favor, to carry a parcel to my room. Bailey had given him a peremptory order to make up his bed. I was acquitted; Bailey was found guilty and dismissed. Naval Academy hazing has been defined as "assuming unauthorized authority over a lower classman," and Bailey was technically guilty. Severe criticism of hazing at Annapolis in 1882 had resulted in a law forbidding it. Since I might easily have given an order instead of making a request, this narrow escape strengthened my resolution never to haze. And I may add, in passing, that aside from unofficial pressure to perform a few playful antics, I myself was never hazed.

The days and nights of my four years at Annapolis were full of work. The competition was intense. Since the vacancies were so few, only about the ten highest of each class were eligible for commissions. Accordingly, we all studied with tremendous purpose and energy. The passing mark in each study was $62\frac{1}{2}$ percent, "2.5" in the Academy system, in which a perfect mark was "4.0." "Easy," I thought. But I found it harder to get this 2.5 mark at Annapolis than 90 percent (3.6) at any school I had known. Twice a year any cadet who had fallen short in one of the studies was forced to resign. Besides the deadly semiannual and annual examinations, there were monthly tests in which the ratio between time and questions seemed cruelly small.

Reveille was at six o'clock, but I used to get up for study at five. At night I often put blankets over my window to keep the light from showing after hours, and studied until midnight. By these earnest efforts I managed to scrape through. My class dwindled from ninety-six at the start to sixty-six at the end of the first year, and my rank was about number thirty. Only thirty-five were graduated after the four-year course; and of these I remained number thirty.

In those days there were two additional years at sea, as "passed midshipmen," on regular cruising ships. At our final graduation in 1890, twenty-nine of my class had survived, my number having risen to twenty-three.

At the Academy, our studies were chiefly mathematical. Beginning with advanced algebra, we hammered at mathematics during four long years, always at high speed and high pressure. However, though we raced, our instruction was nonetheless thorough. After two years our mathematics was applied to the design of steam and electric engines, bridges and hydraulic pumps, and to sciences like ordnance, navigation, and astronomy. We also studied world history, U.S. history, naval history, and international law. We spent much time studying the construction of modern guns and the mathematics of their design, with special attention to "interior and exterior ballistics" (how the bullet, or shell, behaves from the instant the gun is fired until it exits the muzzle, and how elevation above the horizontal, air temperature, wind conditions, and rotation of the projectile during flight affect its travel to the target). I vividly recall my troubles with Ganot's physics, and have never been able fully to understand the principles of "polarized light." Thearle's "Iron Shipbuilding" always seemed difficult. I clearly recall my desperation at the first lesson of some twenty pages. The first paragraph spoke of "an intercoastal, longitudinal, staple-shaped, angle-iron." This was Greek to me.

We also had chemistry. And we studied French, a source of momentous trouble. We used a textbook by someone named Robertson, from which we were required to memorize a short paragraph with which he began his book, and then to discuss it through a dozen pages. The opening sentences were: "Le jeune Alexis Delatour était un assez bon garçon qui n'avait qu'un seul défaut, la paresse; mais combien de fois n'a-t-on pas dit que ce défaut donne naissance à tous les autres? C'est une proverbe, vous savez." (Young Alexis Delatour was a nice enough lad who had but one fault, laziness; but how often has it not been said that this fault gives birth to all the others? It's a proverb, you know.)

How my soul loathed that miserable Alexis Delatour! Even after fifty-odd years, I still despise him.

The great thoroughness of our instruction was due, in part, to the smallness of the classes in which we recited our lessons, which averaged from six to ten members. It was all by textbooks, with no lectures or library work. With one hour for dinner, studies and recitations occupied the time from 8 A.M. to 3:30 P.M. Then drills from 4 P.M. to 6 P.M. Study hours after supper from 7:30 to 9:30 P.M., and finally taps at 10 P.M. The only considerable periods of freedom were Saturday afternoons and evenings, and Sunday afternoons. Sunday forenoons were consumed by an elaborate inspection, followed by marching to chapel in formation.

The drills were of many kinds, including infantry, artillery, great guns, seamanship, and boating. They went on to encompass sail drill on a square-rigger, steam and electric drills, and work in blacksmith, boiler, carpenter, and machine shops. In general, this training covered military, engineering, and naval fields. Sometimes, on a Saturday forenoon in spring, the whole cadet body went out on a sailing ship for strenuous sail drill, or for ear-splitting practice with great guns. I do not recall that (in those days) we often hit the target; but we had an exciting time burning powder, dodging guns as they recoiled, and standing on tiptoe, fingers in ears, when the big 8-inch pivot guns were fired. The concussion from these caused a sharp pain in the eardrums; and we sometimes returned from a morning on the bay pretty thoroughly deafened.

Though our lives were taken up with studies, recitations, and drills. So much interest crowded the day that I never had a sense of missing anything. Life of course had its ups and downs, but it was never dull. Often our brief periods of relaxation were spent discussing incidents of recitations and drills. There was constant excited talk about the greatly feared semi-annual exams—we had no specific name for the finals at the end of the year, for they were no different from the "semi-ans"—and of those who seemed in danger of bilging. To "bilge," in academy slang, was to fail academically and be forced to resign, but to "bilge someone" was to get a higher grade than he does. To "bone" was to study. My talented classmate Hartrath wrote a song of which the chorus ran:

> Exams they are a-coming
> Upon the same old plan;
> We'll bone like Hell as usual,
> And bilge the semi-an.

The discipline seemed strict. Each morning a list of reports was read out. These were usually for such offenses as "hair not brushed," "room not swept," "bed not properly made," "late at formation." Such reports were called "spots," or in later years "paps." To "hit the pap-sheet" meant to have been "spotted" in some dereliction and placed on official report.

During my time, a Lieutenant Todd reported for duty as discipline officer. Todd characterized the cadets as slouchy and careless in carriage. He accordingly formed an "awkward squad" of all who were not properly "braced up." It included more than half the battalion. The saying was "Todd'll get you if you don't look out!" I was one of the hundred or so Todd got. After supper, instead of having forty minutes' leisure before study hours, we had to fall in and march to the armory, where the famous fencing master, Corbesier (who spoke broken English), gave us setting up exercises for half an hour. We were often escorted to the armory by a derisive mob of those not chosen, all singing, to the tune of a well-known hymn, words written by the irrepressible Hartrath:

> *Like a mighty army,*
>   *Moves the Awkward Squad,*
> *Forward to the Armory,*
>   *All sent there by Todd.*
> *"Fall in!" cries Corbesier,*
>   *"Company, attensh!"*
> *Fingers on your trousers,*
>   *Carry back your hands!*
> *Onward, naval heroes,*
>   *Marching as to war,*
> *With your spots and zeroes,*
>   *You'll soon march no more.*

Soon after I became a third classman, Naval Cadet Wiley, then in the second class, the class senior to mine, was reported for hazing. The circumstances, as I recall them were these: Wiley was sitting in the grounds near the State House in Annapolis, on a bench just under the statue of Chief Justice Roger B. Taney. Near him was a "candidate," a youth not yet admitted to the Academy. Having duly ascertained this fact, Wiley gave him some emphatic orders. The emphasis was natural. During forty years of naval service, Wiley, thorough gentleman that he is, has never been known to speak without it. This was the extent of the damage to the candidate.

The latter, one Louis Lebadier Driggs, incautiously mentioned the matter later, and word of it reached the ears of Captain Francis M. Ramsay, superintendent of the Naval Academy. He at once preferred charges of hazing against Wiley, who was tried by general court-martial, convicted, and dismissed. This sentence made Wiley ineligible for any further appointment in the Navy, and he left the Academy, much to the regret of us all.

Nearly a year later, to our delight and amazement, Wiley reappeared. An order was published explaining this substantially as follows: Naval Cadet Henry A. Wiley had been wrongly dismissed for hazing one Louis Lebadier Driggs. But the attorney general of the United States held that the law defined hazing as "unlawful assumption of authority over another *in the government service*." Because Mr. Driggs was not yet in the government service at the time the incident took place, Naval Cadet Wiley might have been guilty of speaking forcefully to a citizen, but he had not been guilty of hazing as defined by law, and his conviction was erroneous.

By the same order, Wiley, who had lost too much time to keep up with his old class, was turned back into mine.

The net result of all this was the saving to the Navy of a fleet commander it otherwise would have lost, for there were so few appointments from Wiley's original class that he could not have gotten one. Wiley was finally graduated next to me at the completion of the full six-year course. As there were only twelve vacancies even for our class of twenty-nine, neither of us should have normally been commissioned. But Wiley was bent upon becoming a commissioned officer, and, almost on the last day, succeeded in a singular way (as explained in a later chapter) in securing vacancies not only for himself, but also for the other sixteen of us.

Anyone interested in a fictional description of Wiley's travail may read Father's *Midshipman Ralph Osborn at Annapolis* where the whole story is rehearsed, except that the fictional Osborn was returned to the Academy much more quickly than the real Wiley, and therefore lost no time in his own (never identified) class.

But in telling about Wiley I have gotten ahead of my story of Naval Academy life. Two drills deserve special mention: dancing, the first year, and fencing throughout the course.

In dancing, because of the absence of sweet young girls, we each took a chair for a partner. I recall the mad whirling those chairs received. During the first lesson I banged against Cadet Marble of my class with such force as to knock him down. He was wildly indignant and wanted revenge. But my partner was agile; and for a week, in spite of Marble's repeated assaults, he was badly battered. Not unnaturally, this caused resentment, and led to fist fights.

Believe it or not, the same sort of dancing instruction, with wooden chairs for partners instead of winsome girls, was still in vogue in 1935, when I entered the Naval Academy!

Marble, who stood second in the class, was a son of the famous Manton Marble, once owner of the *New York World*. We gave him a nickname, "Lord Marble," that stuck to him.

Two years later, during a week's fencing drill, Corbesier placed us opposite each other for an assault. Marble was particularly graceful in the grand salute, and in fancy fencing, but I had learned that his swordplay was all show. When it came to a determined assault, he could neither parry, prick, nor hit. I had some confidence in my own ability to hit pretty hard.

Marble was a cadet officer. As such, he had sometimes treated me in a way (perhaps justified) that fanned my smoldering resentment into real anger. Now I saw a chance to get even, and was determined to punish him.

One Monday, when we began our assault with wooden swords, I picked a spot on his left thigh, about ten inches above the knee, and gave him a painful whack. I repeated this several times, always striking him in the same place. My showy opponent was helpless. He simply could not touch me, while I hit him at will. He became furious, but that did not help him.

I repeated this Tuesday and Wednesday. Thursday he was limping badly, told Corbesier he would not fence with me again, and expressed his angry feelings at my way of handling a sword. But Corbesier told him to take the assault with me, and that he would show Marble how to parry and hit back.

"On guard!" he shouted. "Commencez, messieurs!"

Knowing that this would be my last opportunity, I resolved to give Marble something he would always remember. In a moment, with all the strength I could summon, I struck him on the same spot, which by this time must have been terribly sore. With a yell, Marble threw down his sword.

"Aha!" cried Corbesier, "Monsieur Beach does *très bien*. Monsieur Marble, *regardez-moi!* I show you! Monsieur Beach, *en garde!* Ha!"

I faced Corbesier, who had achieved fame in France as a master of fencing.

"Ha! *Prenez garde, vous!*" cried Corbesier, sharply slapping the floor with his fencing slipper.

The class gathered round, all anxious to see the bout between Corbesier and Beach. Here was my chance for fame. If I could touch Corbesier even once, I would do what no other cadet had ever done. Being a bit conceited, I thought I might do this. I had been fencing for three years, ranked second in fencing, and was certainly better than Marble, who ranked first.

Watching my chance, I disengaged and struck out, and things then happened fast. My sword, jerked from my hand so swiftly and strongly that my right arm was sprained, was thrown almost the length of the armory. I felt a terrific blow with a bludgeon upon my left thigh. My left leg was knocked from under me, and down I went on my head!

Loud and repeated were the roars of laughter. Marble was almost hysterical with joy. He had been amply revenged. I got no sympathy; and for days received ribald pseudo inquiries as to the cause of my limp. But one good thing resulted. From then on, no unfriendly word passed between Marble and me.

If we had to work hard, the hours of relaxation were joyous. On Saturdays there were football and baseball games. Saturday evenings there were "hops" in the armory, with beautiful girls instead of chairs for partners. On Sundays we often dined with the families of officers assigned to the Academy. Plebes, of course, were expected to stay away from the dances (sometimes called "tea fights"), but we all knew next year would be different.

We had prayers after breakfast each morning, besides chapel service on Sundays. I have one recollection from the sermons of the first two years and one from the prayers of the last two. Our first chaplain, then elderly, was from some inland town, and had made one cruise. That cruise had been in Peruvian waters.

For some reason, this had impressed him tremendously. At some point, in every sermon for two years, he would remark, in a sing-song voice, "When— I—was—down—on—the—coast—of—Peru . . ."

Always, when breaking ranks after marching back from chapel, cadets would race through the grounds mimicking him as loudly as they could, singsong tune and all: "*When—I—was—down—on—the—coast—of—Peerooo.*"

The next two years we had a different chaplain who preached scholarly, instructive sermons. But I remember only the last words of his morning prayers: "Therefore I say unto you, do away with all filthiness and the super-fluity of naughtiness; and receive with meekness the engrafted word."

4

A MIDSHIPMAN AT SEA

One beautiful June morning, four years almost to the day since I had first reported to that place, the thirty-five surviving members of the Annapolis class of 1888, veterans of innumerable hard-fought battles with trigonometry, calculus, conic sections, least squares, ballistics, and other entrenched foes, and determined enemies of that miserable Alexis Delatour, marched to the Naval Academy chapel. They were headed by the band, playing an air heard only on such occasions: "Ain't I Glad to Get Out of the Wilderness!" Behind them came the rest of the battalion, commanded by a tall, grave, noble-looking youth, Naval Cadet Richmond Pearson Hobson.

Immeasurable joy was in our hearts. Gentle breezes murmured through the trees. Fathers and mothers were there, along with lovely young girls in gay colors and visiting officers in brilliant regalia. It was the great day of the year.

At the end of the ceremonies, thirty-five cadets in worn uniforms emerged from the crowd, first in a walk, then in a mad dash for their quarters. But, five minutes later, who were in the offing? Thirty-five magnificent new officers in brilliant new uniforms!

And who could forget the beautiful graduating ball! Though number three of my class, Naval Cadet Curtis D. Wilbur had resigned voluntarily. Yet he was splendidly there, standing six feet three in an officer's full dress uniform. But Naval Cadet Charles Frederic Hughes, also six feet three, was missing. As Hughes never went to balls, he had insisted upon Wilbur's wearing his uniform. Although this was doubtless strictly against naval regulations, and noted by many present, there is nowhere any indication that anyone objected. Certainly, Wilbur was not "spotted," or "put on the pap."

Thirty-five years later, the greatest fleet of warships ever gathered under the Stars and Stripes dropped anchor in San Francisco Bay. Soon a launch from shore sped to the flagship; and, as it came alongside, a gentleman six feet three inches tall stepped lightly from the cockpit. Awaiting him, at the head of the ladder, was a naval officer, also six feet three inches tall.

"Hello, Magic!" said Hughes, the commander in chief of the U.S. Fleet, as he welcomed the chief justice of the supreme court of California.

"Hello, Freddie!" Wilbur replied.

While they were talking of old days in the admiral's cabin, Hughes jumped up, ran to his sleeping room, and returned with a faded pair of white kid gloves.

"By the way, Magic," he said, "these are your gloves. You left them in the pocket of my uniform."

Later, when Wilbur was secretary of the Navy, the Navy General Board recommended that Hughes be appointed chief of naval operations. As such, he filled the highest office ever reached by American admirals.

In 1888, shortly after graduation from Annapolis, I reported aboard the USS *Richmond,* at the time undergoing routine overhaul at the New York Navy Yard. The *Richmond* had been a great ship during the Civil War; and at one time was Farragut's flagship. In 1888 she was still one of our chief warships, even if we were ashamed to admit it. The saying then was that the duty of our warships was "to show the flag" in foreign ports. No one could have been foolish enough to say that their duty was to fight. The *Richmond*'s feeble, smooth-bore guns would have made no impression on the modern steel ships of other navies; her rotting wooden sides could not have stopped even a 1-pounder shell.

But such reflections did not bother me. Other troubles were more immediate. Where and how could I sleep? Where could I stow my clothes? The "steerage," where ensigns, cadets, junior engineers, and junior doctors were quartered, consisted of two small rooms with five berths in all. When I reported, these berths were already assigned. At night, mattresses were spread on the dining table, under the table, and on the deck between the table and berths. The space above the table and the berths was filled with hammocks slung for the cadets. However, something can always be squeezed into a well-packed trunk, and this, in a manner of speaking, we accomplished, albeit with some discomfort due to crowding. There was an added and worse discomfort. We were forced to sleep, if at all, with pajamas tied tightly about our ankles and sleeve ends about our wrists, and with the further protection of gloves, socks, and head guards. The bedbug is a mighty beast.

But as our ship was to be flagship of the China squadron, I was willing to stand incidental discomforts. The China Station was a favorite. Our captain, Robert Boyd, was away, and we were later to discover, seriously ill. The ship was under the command of the executive officer, Lieutenant Commander Timothy Lyons, a veteran of the Civil War.

During the post–Civil War period, as Admiral Dewey brings out in his auto-biography, discipline involved great severity. The enlisted man of those days was magnificent as a fighter and seaman, but tough and hard to control. (In 1888, citizenship was not yet the requirement it is at present; a man of any nationality might enlist if a good seaman and physically sound.) In 1861, when Dewey went aboard the *Mississippi* as executive officer, he found over a hundred men in chains between the guns and rioters in possession of part of the lower decks. (Dewey's autobiography does not mention this, however.)

Lyons had been brought up in those conditions. He was severe with officers and with men. He spoke, I thought, with fearful roughness; he denounced modern Naval Academy training; he wanted sailormen, not scientists, to stand watch on a sailing ship. As a matter of fact, the ship's doctor told me that Lyons was in constant pain from aggravated dyspepsia.

The one thing he ever did to please my shipmates was, in a passionate out-burst, to forbid my playing my beloved flute anywhere, at any time, aboard ship. Even when a thing was well done, Lyons found violent fault. For instance, our boatswain, William Anderson, with whom I made two long cruises, was the most skillful seaman I have ever known, and a fine fellow at that. One day Lyons directed him to "come up all dock fastenings" (carefully to slacken them so that the ship could be moved by hauling on some and slacking others) and haul the ship ahead to receive some stores. Lyons went ashore, and Anderson made the change as directed.

The next morning Lyons came aboard and fired a volley of denunciations at the boatswain. He concluded, "I'm going to breakfast now; when I come on deck I want to see the ship properly moored."

"Aye, aye, sir!" replied Anderson.

Being officer of the deck, I walked about with the boatswain as he made preparations and stationed men. Hawsers and securing chains were led out and manned. There may have been nearly one hundred deck seamen involved. At the after starboard bitts was Boatswain's Mate Crawford, an old sailor man.

"Crawford," said Anderson, "I'm going to give orders to slack, haul, veer, come-to. You repeat my orders with all the lungs you've got. But, damn you, Crawford, if you budge that chain an inch, I'll scald you alive. Understand? No matter what I say, leave it just as it is."

"I understand, Mr. Anderson," grinned back Crawford.

Similar orders were given to the other boatswain's mates in charge at each station. Anderson took position near the open skylight under which Lyons was breakfasting.

Only once in my life have I heard anything to equal the strength and volume of the reverberating roars that issued from Anderson's mouth. That "once" occurred when Clara Butt, singing "The Lost Chord," drowned out the great organ of the Symphony Hall, Boston. But the cacophony this day on deck rivaled the best Clara Butt could do, with the organ and a frantic director thrown in. First there was shrill piping, with answering echoes from all over the ship. Then an explosion of vocal sounds. Anderson gave a hundred orders in five or ten minutes. "Single up all lines! Slack away aft! Easy, easy! Haul-to for'rd! Hold her aft! Slack your springs! Haul in all breast lines! Slack aft—roundly, lads, roundly! Haul in handsomely for'rd! Check her aft! Haul taut everything! Haul well taut—hold all lines!" And then, after a moment's short pause, "Belay all! Pipe down!"

Each of these orders, coming like shells from a quick-fire gun, was answered with throaty shouts from his assistants. With it all there was a great rumbling of chain; but actually the ship budged not an inch. Timothy Lyons, trying to eat his eggs peacefully, got full benefit of the uproar through the open skylight. Soon after "Belay!" he came on deck, took a swift look about, and remarked, "She's all right now, Mr. Anderson. That's where you should have put her in the first place."

Soon after this episode, Lyons was put on the "sick list" and detached. I have often thought that, disagreeable as he seemed, he was an earnest, sincere, and able officer. His illness, however, prevented him from demonstrating that to me, or to anyone in the ship those last few weeks. Perhaps Anderson and Crawford, and some of the other chief petty officers, understood the problem better than we late-comers aboard did.

Lieutenant Commander Louis Kingsley took his place; he was a kindly, considerate gentleman, and a fine officer. The cabin was like the peace and quiet after a hurricane. He even gave me permission to play the flute, his one order that my messmates criticized.

I well remember Dad's big, black, wooden flute. It had a beautiful sound, I thought, and I wished he would play it more often.

Because our ship was fitting out for the China Station, we had no drills. A horde of yard workmen were caulking the seams of the deck and the sides, and replacing the rotten planking: an almost hopeless job, for the ship was all rotten. I had four hours on duty, and eight off, as a sort of glorified watchman. But my hopes were kept alive by thoughts of China.

Our regular captain was detached, and we heard that Captain Allen V. Reed had been ordered to command the *Richmond*. One day, not long after this, I was chatting with my classmate, Jimmie Reid, who had the day watches from 4 to 8 P.M. A short and somewhat stout elderly gentleman came walking along the dock to which we were moored.

I can see him now, as he stopped and faced the ship. His black hat, a relic of war days, might have been Abraham Lincoln's. He wore the long, black, double-breasted broadcloth coat of a statesman. His trousers, baggy at the top, fit closely around his legs, six inches above the ankles. The blue socks showing below, and his low, broad, and shapeless shoes, were suspiciously like those served out to enlisted men.

"A retired country parson," guessed Jimmie Reid. "I'll throw him out if he tries to come aboard."

The old man did try, with some success. Reid met him at the gangway.

"You can't come aboard!" he shouted peremptorily. "Visiting hours end at
5 p.m!"

Regarding my classmate severely, the old gentleman said, "I have come to
take command of this ship. I am Captain Reed. Please send for the executive
officer!"

Poor Jimmie Reid. Every morning, during his remaining weeks aboard, ribald shipmates asked about "Papa's" health. Every morning he explained that
his name was spelled "R-e-i-d," not "R-e-e-d."

And now came the winter of our discontent, made glorious by nothing at
all. The commander in chief of the China squadron, Admiral Carpenter, had
cabled the Navy Department, "Any captain for my flagship except Allen V.
Reed." The admiral was punished for this telegram by losing his flagship. The
Richmond's designation for the China Station was canceled, and she was
ordered to the South Atlantic. We never did discover whether a newer and
better ship took her place.

We were to sail for our new station by way of the west coast of Africa.
The story of this cruise (explaining our discontent) involves that of John
Wesley something or other, one of my messmates. John Wesley was an engineer officer who had graduated from the Naval Academy in 1879. During
the intervening years he had devoted himself with immense energy to John
Barleycorn. Such, at least, was the very plausible report. As there was no
steam on the ship during overhaul, he had no duties to perform. But his sin-
gularly appealing nature brought him protection. By private arrangement,
he was allowed no clothes; and for a week after I came on board he never
got out of his pajamas. His friends were trying to sober him up, and finally
succeeded.

But he never stayed sober long. He had a capacity for alcohol that I would
not have deemed possible. On one occasion within five minutes he drank
three full quarts of rum that I happened to own. Once (returning from shore
leave after our arrival in Montevideo) we took from his person thirty-seven
quart bottles of brandy, some in his trouser legs, suspended by cords from his
neck.

But, as I said, shortly before the cruise began, John Wesley had sobered up.
"I'm done with John Barleycorn forever," he convincingly announced. He
spent his time playing the guitar and singing. His voice was the most appealing I have ever listened to. His songs, combined with his wonderful voice,

brought tears to hardened eyes. Never were there such mournful, heartbreaking songs. Straight from the morgue they were. Even now, after many years, I can hear him singing:

> All the dreams of my life are broken through
>   Both what is done and undone, I rue;
> There's nothing steadfast, there's nothing true,
>   Save your love for me, and my love for you,
> My dearest little heart.

or,

> A maiden stands 'neath the rose bush fair,
>   The buds swell out in the soft May air,
> She presses her hand to her throbbing breast,
>   With love's first wonderful rapture blest,
> And the years roll by.

> Naked and lone stands the rose bush fair,
>   Whirled are the leaves in the wintry air,
> Withered and dead they have fallen to ground,
>   And silently cover a new-made mound,
> And the years roll by.

We young officers sat at John Wesley's feet as if at a fount of knowledge, and felt we were lucky to have such wisdom with us. He advised us to lay in a supply of sea stores before this long cruise. Other officers' messes did this, and even the men's, to a lesser extent. We considered it a privilege to put up fifty dollars each, and to have John Wesley apply his knowledge, and the several hundred we had subscribed, to the purchase of good food for our long cruise.

Just before we sailed, John Wesley was brought aboard, unconscious. He had been cruising in stormy seas with rough companions. Rags had replaced his decent civilian clothes. He did not have a cent on him; he had not spent a penny for sea stores; and our hope of food was in what we might draw from the paymaster. This officer had plenty of "salt horse" and salt pork, and was well supplied with potatoes, onions, coffee, hard bread, sugar, flour, pickles (by the barrel), and that was about all. And we received no sympathy and no help, only jeers when, from time to time, we asked other messes to help us out. If it is a "long, long walk from Schenectady to Troy," it's a long, long sail from New York to Montevideo by way of Africa.

Captain Reed was strict, but a good man and an able officer, in spite of his odd civilian apparel. He carried out naval regulations to the minutest detail; some regulations, dating back to 1812, were utterly unsuited to 1888. For instance, they required that cadets or midshipmen copy each entry in each day's log. This was the most tiresome and unprofitable job imaginable; columns had to be ruled, and the various figures, symbols, and notes transcribed. This consumed two hours a day. Standing forecastle watch, four hours on and eight off, with the required day's work in navigation each day, and with drills and other duties, we found it hard to make the time for this wretched, mechanical, log copying. On arrival at Montevideo I forwarded through the captain, at his suggestion, a protest to the Navy Department against this regulation. In due time the answer came that the regulation had been adopted when midshipmen entered at the age of ten or eleven; that the object had been to teach them to read, write, and spell, and to use or understand naval terms; that it was folly to impose this routine on graduates of the Naval Academy; and that this regulation was now canceled.

As Captain Reed handed me the Navy Department letter to read, he commented, "Let them cancel any they don't expect me to enforce." This was his way about everything. Sometimes it took extra time, but we always knew where we stood with him.

I recall little of that long cruise except that every meal was a torment. We had fair weather all the way, except for three weeks of breezeless days late in our graduating year (1888) spent directly on the equator, when, as mentioned earlier, he would not let us start the engines. Watch standing and drills were uninteresting. It was John Wesley's happy disposition (in spite of his mournful songs) that prevented complete listlessness. He was the only comfort we had. And he returned to us, by installments, the money given him for sea stores.

On Sundays, regulations required us to assemble at 9:30 A.M. in full dress. The full dress of those days was patterned after the civilian evening full dress, with its broad expanse of stiff white shirt front. One broiling Sunday on the equator, Surgeon Dick Ashbridge asked that the uniform regulations be dispensed with because, having had no opportunity to have laundry work done for months, he had no shirts to wear.

"Do the best you can, Doctor; we must carry out the regulations," directed the captain.

And on Sunday, Ashbridge caused great hilarity. He appeared with full dress coat, blazing epaulets, golden striped sleeves and trousers, and a flaming red undershirt. The next Sunday he had the blazing gold uniform with cocked hat and sword, but in place of a shirt, or even an undershirt, was a tremendously hairy naked chest and stomach.

This was too much even for Captain Reed. He relented to the extent of letting us wear our dirty white blouses buttoned up to the chin.

At last, after sailing for months, we anchored off Montevideo, about five miles out. A number of us got shore leave. I, for one, was wild to eat ice cream and cake. I wandered about the waterfront, trying to find someone who could speak English, as I did not know a word of Spanish. I addressed various people, but always got an answer that sounded like "Not in ten days." ("*No intende,*" meaning, I discovered later, "I do not understand.") I grew desperate at the thought of waiting ten days. Finally I saw a sign, "London and River Plate Bank," and through a window I saw a fine looking Anglo-Saxon. I rushed up the steps into a large room filled with clerks, and threw open a door that I knew would lead me to my Anglo-Saxon. I didn't even notice that it was marked, "President's Private Office. No Admittance" (in Spanish).

"What do you want here?" asked the bank president in forbidding tones.

"I need a plate of ice cream and I need it bad," I replied.

"Young man, you've made a mistake. This is not an ice cream parlor. It's a financial institution."

I hurriedly explained who I was and why I was in agonized need of decent food after our terrible cruise. Thereupon he sent a messenger with me to "El Telegrafo," where I spent an hour or two gorging myself with ice cream and cake.

The last boat for the *Richmond* was to leave shore at midnight. I was there long before that, but the boat did not come at midnight, nor did it ever come. At one o'clock a launch from a Russian warship came in, and an officer in it kindly put me aboard the *Richmond.* When I stepped aboard, Captain Reed met me at the gangway. In severe tones he asked, "Mr. Beach, where is the whaleboat? It left the ship at ten o'clock!"

After questioning me, roughly at first, he had our four-oared dinghy lowered, and ordered me to go in and "bring back the whaleboat and its six men." At half past one I started on the long pull to the shore. About three miles from the ship, we noticed some rocks in the moonlight, and there was the whaleboat, bottom up, impaled on an especially sharp-pointed rock. It was some time before we freed and floated the boat, which we then towed to an American warship, the *Alliance*, about half a mile farther in. There I was received by Lieutenant E. B. Barry, who had instructed me at Annapolis, and who let me tie up the boat at a boom.

Then I went ashore and found my way to a police station. A man there understood English. When I explained my needs, he took six policemen and started out with me. They knew just where to go. We found our six men in horrible surroundings and with horrible companions, all of them terribly drunk. The policemen carried them bodily to the wharf and put them into the little dinghy. I shoved off for the *Alliance*.

Near the *Alliance*, one of the drunken men jumped overboard. While we were trying to get to him, another started to jump. I grabbed a boat hook and hit this one on the head with the long handle, shouting to my oarsmen to knock down any other of our "guests" who stirred while we rescued our drunk thrashing around in the water. Finally getting him back aboard and the damaged whaleboat again in tow, we started on a long hard pull to the *Richmond*, three and a half miles away.

And then a pampero struck us. I know of no other storm that is so sudden and violent. The wind blew with terrific force. The situation would have been critical with only five in the small dinghy. But with six drunken men besides, it seemed almost hopeless. The boat repeatedly filled and was bailed out each time by the six passengers, now scared into near-sobriety. Luckily the wind was from aft, and the whaleboat, with its gunwales above water, broke the waves for our little boat. Otherwise, we certainly should have sunk. About a quarter of a mile from the *Richmond*, I saw lights moving about, and judged that Captain Reed was sending boats for us. He had lowered two steam launches, as well as cutters and whaleboats.

But these all missed us. Finally, with a thankful heart, I secured the dinghy to the Jacob's ladder trailing astern, and was quickly on deck with my ten men. It was now 4:30 A.M. Captain Reed met me.

"Mr. Beach, you have done well. I thank you. You may tell me what happened tomorrow. Now go below and turn in."

That was a lot from Captain Reed.

5

AN ENSIGN

At Montevideo Rear Admiral Gillis, commanding the South Atlantic Squadron, took the *Richmond* for his flagship. Flag quarters were, of course, always the best maintained on board any Navy ship, and although our ship was old and thoroughly rotten, her flag quarters were well maintained. We also had small offices on board for the few business and command details of an admiral's tour, and regular quarters for his small staff. For "the flag," accommodations were adequate and tidy. The flag stewards kept linen and silver clean and served good meals, particularly for occasional guests in port, in a professionally top class manner. But for the rest of us, life on board was dull, and, in addition, a constant battle with predatory nature. The ship, too rotten to keep clean, was a happy haven for rats and bugs. Resting secure by day, they sallied forth hungrily at night.

Surrounded as we were by other navies' modern warships, built of steel, with good engines and high-powered guns, we could not drill with enthusiasm at our old smooth bores. Our wooden Civil War sloop-of-war, with a decrepit engineering plant, was a laughingstock for all who observed her.

On our cruise, however, we visited Rio de Janeiro, Bahia, and other cities, including Buenos Aires, where I was very happy.

With his feet upon the fender,
    In a voice both low and tender,
From the clouds about his head,
    This is what the Captain said:
"Ah, I was a young man then!
    But it was very long ago."

Father never did say why he was "very happy" in Buenos Aires, but he was, indeed, a very young man, and it was long ago. There must have been something, or someone, connected with that fabulous city that greatly pleased him—well enough to have been remembered throughout the intervening years. No one will ever know, but I imagine there may have been a lovely senorita with whom the lonely American "passed midshipman" spent some pleasant hours. If true, I suspect he never saw her again; but she would have been pleased to learn, many years later, that her memory was still green in at least one small place in the U.S. Navy.

Admiral Gillis and our captain were not friendly. Years before, Captain Reed had commanded the *Minnesota,* and the admiral had inspected the vessel. His report was highly unfavorable. One of his criticisms was that the captain's bathtub had been converted into a potato bin.

Soon there was friction in the *Richmond.* Admiral Gillis was magnificent and magnetic. Captain Reed was so squat, so careless in dress, so strict in carrying out the regulations, that one had to know him intimately to appreciate his fine, true character.

Gillis was contemptuous in his treatment of Reed, and did not mind showing his contempt in the presence of junior officers. Once I heard him say on the quarterdeck, "Captain Reed, your special full dress waistcoat is of old design and not in conformity with present uniform regulations. I order you to provide yourself with proper uniform immediately!"

The admiral's antipathy toward Reed constantly augmented and affected their relations. As later events proved, he accepted all sorts of whisperings about the captain without trying to verify them. I had been detailed with extra duty as "captain's clerk," therefore saw much of the acrimonious correspondence that passed between them, and had the additional duty of preparing certain reports for our captain.

One day Captain Reed sent for me and said, "Mr. Beach, three months ago, without my knowing it, Admiral Gillis sent the letter I have in my hand to the Navy Department. The department has referred it to me for any statement I may care to make. In this letter the admiral makes thirty-three different charges against me, pronounces me unfit for command, and recommends my trial by general court-martial. I do not intend to discuss this at present, but wish you to file, with my official correspondence, this short letter I have written in response. It is a copy of one I have forwarded to the department through the admiral."

Captain Reed's letter informed the Navy Department that he had received the charges; that he had been kept in utter ignorance of them; and that by naval custom and in all fairness, he should have had a copy of them when they were made. He ended by requesting protection from the "unlawful acts of the admiral."

Before night, in consequence of this last paragraph, Admiral Gillis had placed the captain under arrest, relieved him of his duties, and ordered the executive officer to assume command.

This was an utterly cruel act. I can state from personal experience that it is distressing for an officer lost in a great city, under arrest, to await trial by general court-martial. But for a captain to be suddenly jerked from his pedestal and kept for months awaiting trial, under constant observation, in the narrow limits of the ship he had commanded—and this in foreign waters—was far worse. When the admiral's action became known, there was a burst of indignation among the officers of the ship. We forgot the captain's peculiarities and remembered only his character, intelligence, ability, and devotion. There was great lamentation, for we all admired our splendid admiral, and deeply regretted his actions toward Captain Reed.

Finally the *Richmond* was ordered home, and a court of flag officers was assembled at Fortress Monroe. After exhaustive investigation, they found the admiral's charges unfounded. He was scathingly censured, relieved from duty, and never again employed on active service. Captain Reed was restored to command of the *Richmond*.

It was now 1890. At this time, after nearly two years of separation, two years of cruising as "passed midshipmen" to all the corners of the earth, the U.S. Naval Academy class of 1888 was assembled at Annapolis for final examination. We enjoyed the reunion with a wild happiness known only to youth. Once more I clasped hands with my beloved roommate of three years, "Gabe" Lejeune, with Henry Wiley, and with many others. Lejeune, who had always learned so easily, came out first or second in the class. We learned that there were only a very few vacancies for our class, and that those of us who stood low had small chance of being commissioned. Others were hopeless, but not Wiley.

"Of course I'm going to be commissioned," he told me. "I haven't yet begun to fight for it!"

Lejeune had always intended to be a U.S. Marine officer, supposing that his high standing would as a matter of course give him his choice. Graduates were usually assigned to the Construction Corps, the Supply Corps, or to one of the combatant branches of the Navy: the Line, the Engineer Corps, or the Marine Corps.

To his consternation, Lejeune found that the Academic Board had recommended he be commissioned as an assistant engineer (which I, by contrast, had in fact applied for). He bitterly regretted having stood first in engineering. We left Annapolis by train together, bound for Washington, with an appointment to see Commodore Ramsay, our former Naval Academy superintendent, who was now chief of the Bureau of Navigation, and thereby in charge of all Navy personnel matters.

Many years later, during World War II, the name of this important bureau was changed to Bureau of Naval Personnel, the name it bears today.

Awed by this great man, Lejeune was nervous. He explained that his life's ambition, since his student days at the Military Academy in Baton Rouge, had been to become an officer of the U.S. Marine Corps. This ambition had dominated him at Annapolis, as elsewhere—and now he was recommended for the Engineer Corps! He begged Commodore Ramsay, with whom the final decision lay, to let him go where his heart was.

"No," said the commodore. "The Academy recommends you for engineering, and, knowing you well, I concur. Unless the colonel commandant of the

Marine Corps specifically asks for you, I will assign you to the Engineer Corps. Good morning!"

We left. Lejeune was completely dejected. "We'll go to see the colonel commandant," he said, "but I haven't much hope."

At Marine Corps Headquarters, we found the commandant, a Colonel Remy. Lejeune explained the situation, and begged the colonel commandant specifically to ask for him by name. But Remy was cold to this proposal. "I'm not interested," he said. "I'll not ask for any of you. The Marine Corps will take whoever is sent them."

Lejeune was now desperate. "Let's go to see the commodore again!" he said. We immediately did this.

"I'll not change my decision, Mr. Lejeune," decreed Ramsay. "You'll be assigned to the Engineer Corps unless the colonel commandant specially asks for you. That's all. Good morning again!"

"But commodore," persisted Lejeune, "may I ask you one question?"

"Yes—what is it?"

"Why will you not recommend me for the Marine Corps?"

"Because, Mr. Lejeune, I am well aware of your splendid, promising mentality. Frankly, you have altogether too much brains to be lost in the Marine Corps!"

Ramsay had barely finished speaking before Lejeune grabbed my arm and pulled me out of the office. He started on a run, dragging me with him.

"What's up, Gabe?" I gasped. "Where are we going?"

"Straight to the Marine Corps," he replied. "This settles the whole thing!"

This puzzled me, because I thought it was definitely settled the other way. He rushed me into the general office of the Marine Corps Headquarters. There was Colonel Remy, with eight or ten officers of his staff.

"Colonel Remy," shouted Lejeune, "Commodore Ramsay says that the reason he will not recommend me to be a second lieutenant is that I have altogether too much brains for the Marine Corps!"

Lejeune won, then and there. The Marine Corps went into action, and Lejeune reached his first goal. Since then, he has reached other goals. Years later, General Wotherspoon, president of the Army War College, said of the then Major Lejeune, that if he had to select a general for an army of 150,000, he would choose Lejeune. No one was surprised when, during the Great War (World War I), Lejeune was sent to France as a major general to command the

Second Division under General Pershing; nor when, after his distinguished war service, he became major general commandant of the Marine Corps.

But if Lejeune had arrived, my outlook was gloomy. It did not seem possible that, before 1 July 1890, there could be enough vacancies in the Navy to include me. And now Wiley got into action.

"Beach," said he, "I believe we will get our commissions too. I have listed here a lot of dead wood in the Navy. If the department won't, or can't, order them to duty, they should be retired to make room for us. Bassett and Kane are waiting. Let's all go to the commodore's office."

So we started at once, desperate young men, back to the same place, Wiley with a roll of foolscap. Just as we were entering Ramsay's office, Wiley suddenly stopped.

"Beach," he said, "Ramsay has always hated me since I was restored to the Academy over his protest. *You* must make the talk to the commodore! You'll know just what to say, and you'll find the names of officers who should be retired listed on this paper." He thrust the roll into my hand and pushed me in.

This was quite unexpected, and I was unprepared. I began to talk to the commodore in a halting way, hesitating and stammering.

"Yes, yes! Get to the point, Mr. Beach!" broke in Ramsay, impatiently.

Then I told him about the list.

"I'm interested," said the commodore.

I unrolled my list, which I had never seen, embarrassed and speechless.

"Come, come, Mr. Beach! What's the matter? Read your list!"

I began, fearful and faltering. "Commander . . . ," I read, "wife murderer. Navy Department has given him no duty for over twenty years!" It would be hard to express my feelings when reading these dreadful words.

Commodore Ramsay regarded me seriously. "That was not proved," he said. "The commander insisted it was suicide, but it's true that he hasn't been employed for some years. What's the next case?"

Gathering a little courage, I read, "Commander . . . , so inefficient that the department has given him no duty for twenty years."

"Quite correct," commented Ramsay. "The trouble is we can only get such officers when they come up for promotion, and there is no promotion these days. But I'll see if something cannot be done in such cases."

I looked at him, amazed. It actually seemed that Wiley's paper might accomplish something.

"Go ahead!" ordered Ramsay. "I'm very much interested!"

"Lieutenant . . . , inefficient. It is notorious that he cannot do the simplest problem in dead reckoning. A fraud. He recently was in Madagascar and published a book on that country that brought him distinction. When charged with the fact, he was forced to admit that the book was wholly the work of a French priest. It is believed that it is only regard for his distinguished father, Admiral . . . , that has made possible his retention in the Navy."

"I'm afraid that's all so," said Ramsay regretfully. "It's a pity this young officer doesn't inherit his father's ability and character. Proceed with your paper."

"Ensign . . . , a deserter. Last seen with a group of chorus girls in tow, heading westward from Kansas City."

"That's absolutely true. I'll see to it that he's declared a deserter today!"

There were many other names in the paper. Ramsay took it from me, and dismissed us, saying, "I will give this matter earnest consideration."

And he did. More than seventeen vacancies resulted, and—coincidentally—for the first time in seventeen years, every member of a graduating Naval Academy class was commissioned. I was appointed "assistant engineer," with the rank of ensign, and ordered to the brand-new, powerful, cruiser *Philadelphia!*

I cannot possibly describe my exultation at these orders. In the summer, shortly after these fateful interviews, I reported aboard the *Philadelphia* at Cramp's shipyard in this splendid ship's namesake city. Here, in the engine room, were triple expansion engines developing ten thousand horsepower; with wonderful air pumps, circulating pumps, condensers, Marshall valve gear: a magnificent assemblage of modern machinery. The boilers actually carried 160 pounds per square inch of steam pressure. I plunged into my work with joy. Machinery was to be tested; brasses fitted; valve rods packed with metallic packing; leaky condenser tubes, with soft packing; leaky steam joints set up; boilers cleared of grease. A thousand parts needed overhauling after the wracking strain of the forced draft speed trials just completed. After my third day on board, I proudly wrote the "remarks" in the steam log. These were to be copied into the "smooth log" by a yeoman, Virginius B. Sturtevant.

I have never forgotten Sturtevant. When he brought the smooth log to be signed, I found that under the blank space for my signature he had abbreviated my title to "Ass Engineer." At luncheon I spoke of this with indignation; but my messmates loudly insisted that the evidence showed Virginius B. Sturtevant's keen discernment!

One of our engineer officers was Robert S. Griffin, not large in stature, but splendid in intellect and overflowing with kindness. Later, for many years, he was a famous engineer in chief of the Navy.

But there soon came a check to my happiness. Our chief engineer was Robert Potts, an aged man. His previous work had been with slow-moving simple engines and boilers carrying only ten pounds pressure. Suddenly, when over sixty years of age, he was thrown into a hell of high pressures and high velocities. He was under a terrific strain, and became wild. Everything worried him; nothing was right; he howled, yelled, and wept all day, and Assistant Engineer Beach got it all.

One day, at the New York Navy Yard, we received some zinc plates to put into the boilers to prevent pitting. It transpired that no holes had been bored in the plates to aid in hanging them from the tubes. Nothing would have been simpler than to bore these holes on board. But Potts burst into violent rage, and took me to interview Assistant Engineer Rommell, who had charge of the yard stores from which these plates were drawn. He assailed Rommell with wild, hysterical anger. Rommell was chewing tobacco. He listened quietly for awhile, chewing on. Finally, in kindly tones, he said: "Mr. Potts, calm yourself. Calm yourself, sir!"

Then he squirted a mouthful of tobacco juice on one of Pott's patent leather shoes, and another mouthful on the other, and repeated, "Calm yourself, calm yourself, Mr. Potts!"

Potts rushed back to the ship, a veritable madman. That night he addressed a letter to the secretary of the Navy, B. F. Tracey, asking that Assistant Engineer Beach be detached, since he was "inexperienced as an engineer and therefore not fitted to direct the handling of the *Philadelphia*'s high-powered engines." I was in despair.

A few days later a stocky, bearded gentleman came on board. The captain, Fred Rogers, recognized him as Secretary Tracey.

"Captain," said the secretary, "I wish to see Chief Engineer Potts."

Chief Engineer Potts came bustling up.

"Mr. Potts," began the secretary, "I recently sent a young engineer officer here to get his first engineering experience under your direction, just as you once got your first experience. You do not seem to appreciate all of your responsibilities here; so I have detached you, and have detailed Chief Engineer Ezra J. Whittaker in your place. He will know what to do with Mr. Beach."

The next day Mr. Potts asked me to come to his room, and talked earnestly to me. He said he now realized that he had not done his duty by me, and that his letter to the Navy Department should never have been sent. He also realized that he had been unkind, and, perhaps, abusive. He asked me to forgive him.

I was astonished. Suddenly I felt that Mr. Potts was not a brute, but was at heart a good man. His actions were simply the result of an overwrought mental condition. For years after, as new, powerful cruisers were commissioned, time and again the newspapers ran the headline: "Another Chief Engineer Breaks Down Under the Strain." Invariably, these were old men thrust into conditions for which they had been neither emotionally prepared nor properly trained. I have never heard that one of our present chief engineers, some charged with engines of thirty thousand horsepower or more, has crumpled under the strain of his duties. A chap who can survive modern battleship conditions, and the severe, not to say extremely difficult, service on destroyers or submarines, will not break under any pressure.

Chief Engineer Whittaker was also an ancient officer, about the same vintage as Potts, and he wore, in addition, a long white beard. But it was soon evident that he was not bothered by strains. He was an engine designer, a mathematician, and a thoroughly experienced engineer. He was also a professor of engineering, with a sole pupil, whose name was Beach. He gave me long lessons in Cotterill's "Steam Engine as a Heat Engine," Wilson's "Boilers," and Seaton's "Engine Design." He heard me recite, and gave clear explanations. In port, when I was cleaning up after a hard day with the engines or boilers, I was sure to see the washroom door open gently and a long white beard poke through. Then three calls, through the beard:

"B—E—E—E—Each!

"B—E—E—E—Each!

"B—E—E—E—Each!"

Each call began with a deep resonant bass, and rapidly ascended to a high falsetto at the end, like a siren.

And when I would answer, "All right, sir!" I was told "Cotterill" or "Wilson" or "Seaton." All this amused my messmates more than it did me.

I had only one reprimand from Ezra J. Whittaker, but it was a severe one. The history of this again takes me ahead of my story. The old "line and staff" war was raging in those days, deck officers against engineer officers. Whittaker, a chief engineer, had to bear the brunt of it for his assistants. We appreciated this. Once I had a chance to shield him, did so, and got the reprimand.

We were in the harbor of St. Thomas, in the West Indies. I was in charge of the engineer's storeroom, to which the yeoman also had a key. St. Thomas was then famous for its bay rum. I bought a case and hid it in the storeroom, in a place where no one would be likely to find it. While placing it, I noticed another case, marked "E. J. Whittaker," in plain view on a shelf.

Next morning at 5:30 A.M. (0530 in naval parlance), I found half a dozen firemen stretched out drunk, a dozen empty bay rum bottles, and an empty case with Whittaker's name on it. I promptly reported the matter to the executive officer, Lieutenant Commander E.H.C. Leutze, and added: "I had bought a case of bay rum and stored it in the engineer's storeroom. During the night these men evidently broke into the storeroom, found a case of bay rum on a shelf, and drank it in the boiler room."

The thought in my mind was that the owner of that bay rum would be severely hammered. I also realized that I should have stowed Whittaker's case near my own where it would not have been seen. And I remembered his many acts of kindness.

"Tell Mr. Whittaker to report to me immediately!" ordered Leutze.

When Whittaker arrived, Leutze ordered him in vigorous terms to reprimand me for my carelessness. When we reached the storeroom, Whittaker did this with much heat.

Waiting until he had finished, I said, quietly, "Chief, I also had a box of bay rum in the storeroom. The bay rum stolen was yours. Here is the empty case with your name on it. They didn't find my case, but yours. My case is over there."

Whittaker's eyes and voice showed feeling. "Beach, you tried to save me from trouble, and generously took reproof you thought coming to me. For this I thank you. But you made two mistakes. In the first place, I'd done nothing to be jumped for. I had ordered the yeoman to stow my case in the wardroom storeroom, which was my privilege. He should never have put it in the engineer's storeroom. In the second place, your report, though technically correct, was misleading. I ought to report the exact facts, but that might be hard on you. Now take your own case out of here. It can't stay here."

For a few minutes I had felt pleased with myself. Now I felt cheap. After some fifty years, I still have grateful remembrances of Ezra J. Whittaker.

But (again) turning back to my story. Rear Admiral Bancroft Gherardi hoisted his flag in the *Philadelphia,* and soon afterwards we were steaming for Port-au-Prince, the capital of Haiti, the black republic.

Some months before this, Gherardi—"Jerry," as we called him in his absence—had interfered in a Haitian revolution. He was aboard the *Galena,* at Cap Haitien. Outside was a steamer whose name, I believe, was the *Black Republic,* laden with weapons and ammunition for the revolutionists under General Louis Mondestin Flarvil Hyppolite. But the existing government, under President François D. Legitime, had two warships that prevented the *Black Republic* from entering the harbor. Gherardi broke up the blockade, and let the *Black Republic* into Cap Haitien. Hyppolite got much needed supplies, marched south, and in Haitian fashion, elected himself president of the country.

For some time the United States had wanted to acquire St. Nicholas Mole, a fine, spacious, protected harbor on the north coast of Haiti, for a naval station. Later it was openly alleged that our government had made a secret agreement with Hyppolite to this effect. I do not know, but cannot suppose that Gherardi had helped Hyppolite without instructions.

In any case, late in 1890 Gherardi, with his North Atlantic Squadron, steamed into the harbor of Port-au-Prince, capital of Haiti, with a proposed treaty by which Haiti was to cede St. Nicholas Mole to the United States. And five months later Admiral Gherardi steamed out of the harbor of Port-au-Prince with the same treaty, which President Hyppolite had emphatically disapproved.

The American minister to Haiti at this time was one of America's outstanding black citizens, Frederick A. Douglass. Our admiral had paid an official call on him, and the same day had received a return call from the aged [diplomat]. This former slave, whose burning eloquence had been very effective in Civil War days, was still splendid in appearance. He was said to be the half-brother of the great-grandfather of one of our cadets, who in the days that followed had many solicitous inquiries about "Uncle Freddie."

6

ENTERTAINING A SENATOR'S SON

Within days, "Uncle Fred" arranged for an exchange of official calls between Haiti's President Hyppolite and Admiral Gherardi. Hyppolite was greeted with twenty-one guns, receiving the same honors that would have greeted Victoria, Queen of England, Scotland, and Ireland, Empress of India, and, by the Grace of God, Defender of the Faith.

The *Philadelphia*'s brass shone like burnished gold, her steel guns glittered, her white sides gleamed in the tropical sun, her decks were as spotless as sand and stone and water could make them. On the ship's rail, from bow to stern, stood four hundred sailors in clean, white, mustering suits, their hands at the salute. Forty officers, toeing a seam, waited in their special full dress to do the president honor. This costume, I may say, was cordially hated, partly, I'm sure, because of the $240 that some of us still owed for it. Additionally, such a heavy, gold-braided, brass-buttoned, belt-girdled blue uniform, with epaulettes and cocked hat, redolent with the smell of camphor, was the last word in discomfort in the scorching Haitian sun.

As the "President de la Republique d'Haiti" came aboard, the guard of Marines, sixty magnificent sea soldiers, slammed into: "Pre-*sent* HAHMS!"

and two buglers rang out four strident flourishes each: "*Ta—a—a—ta, ta, ta—a—a—a,*" with a lingering wail at the end. Exactly at the death of that lingering wail, the *Philadelphia's* bandsmen fired a round of volleys from their brass weapons, from which the sharps and flats of "Hail to the Chief!" ricocheted in all directions.

President Hyppolite was accompanied by his secretary of state for foreign relations, Monsieur Firmin, a solemn, small, elderly gentleman, dressed in a solemn high hat, a solemn, long, black frock coat, and solemn trousers. And when, at the end of five long months, we sailed away with the peremptory refusal of the Haitian government to cede St. Nicholas Mole, or any part of Haiti, to any other government, we had a solemn admiral aboard.

On this first official visit, Hyppolite was accompanied by his personal staff of twenty-nine strikingly uniformed military aides. Each wore a light blue long coat, flaming red trousers, military cap, and sword, all blazing with gold braid. Knee boots, with spurs, completed the outfit. The president himself was dressed with simple magnificence, in a heavy black-blue jacket with gold trimmings, white linen trousers, a military cap, and patent leather hip boots. The admiral, the president, the secretary of state for foreign affairs, and Lieutenant H. McL. P. Huse, now disappeared into the admiral's cabin, leaving on the quarterdeck, among other things, forty of those hot, ridiculous, special full-dress uniforms, enclosing a sticky substance that chemical analysis would have shown to be "naval officer."

After a glass of champagne, the admiral's guests reappeared. The buglers "ta-ta'd" again, the band opened fire, the Marines presented "*hahms,*" and twenty-one guns crashed a farewell. It was all over.

The admiral was in a hurry; but Haiti is never in a hurry, except to install a new president. There was certainly no haste to meet the admiral's wishes. After some delay, hoping to stir up good feeling, the admiral gave a reception to the president, his family, and his friends. He came. So did the solemn, short, long-coated Firmin. So did the twenty-nine military aides, as splendid as ever, and about twenty young women.

To me, these people seemed very well dressed. All, of course, were blacks. But that did not prevent them from having attractive clothing of French style and French make. True, the president's salary was not large; but I heard that in making money, Croker of Tammany Hall had nothing on Hyppolite of Haiti.

We wanted to help the admiral, but did not enjoy dancing in that swelter-ing afternoon, with pitch melting from the deck seams. Sometimes one slipped; sometimes one stuck. But even this reception could not hurry Hyppolite. Appointments were made, and invariably broken. At most unfortunate times Hyppolite would be called into the interior. Once all negotiations had to stop because his daughter was to be married. Once there was a threatened rebellion. Then Firmin suddenly discovered that Admiral Gherardi's commission was signed by the secretary of the Navy instead of by the president—and the sov-ereign state of Haiti could not treat with a mere department of our government. For weeks we had to await a properly authenticated commission for our admi-ral. This was brought to Port-au-Prince by Rear Admiral John G. Walker, com-mander of the much talked of "White Squadron."

The White Squadron consisted of our first four steel warships, finally authorized by a congress tired of being embarrassed by a nonfunc-tional, decrepit, wooden navy. These ships, painted white for at least partial defense against the tropical heat of the Caribbean Sea, were the cruisers *Atlanta, Boston,* and *Chicago,* plus the tiny "despatch boat" *Dolphin,* an afterthought when the need for speedy communi-cation became clear.

Since Admiral Walker brought his entire squadron, almost the whole American Navy was now anchored at Port-au-Prince. And now I personally witnessed a more beautiful piece of hazing than any ever perpetrated at the Naval Academy. These were the days of "iron men and wooden ships"; and Walker was the most ferrous naval officer in a generation. Mighty in stature and in build was he. He wore long side whiskers. I recall that once, when he spoke sharply to me, those whiskers seemed to wave a threat. "Look out! Look out!" they kept saying.

For the twelve years before Ramsay became chief of the Bureau of Navigation, Walker had occupied that position. And as such he had the entire Navy: ships, shore stations, personnel, in the hollow of his hand. I believe the Navy esteemed him for his forceful personality combined with wisdom and high character. But the truth is, wherever he was, he dominated everyone around him.

Admiral Walker's flagship was the *Chicago:* five thousand tons of grandeur, I felt, as she came dashing in. Twenty-eight years later I had command of a thirty thousand ton battleship; but never did she seem so great and glorious as the *Chicago* in 1891.

Soon—but not soon enough—the famous Admiral Walker reached *Philadelphia*'s quarterdeck. Since Walker's real rank, in our superannuated Navy of the time, was "commodore," he was only an acting rear admiral, and, as such, junior to Gherardi and under his orders as SOPA, the "senior officer present afloat" (of our Navy).

"Admiral Walker, I have been expecting you for some time to report to me," was Gherardi's greeting. Perhaps this was only a poor choice of words.

The powerful John G. Walker regarded him as if with scorn. "I have not come here to report to you, sir," was the reply in ringing tones, "but to hand you this commission, signed by President Harrison, empowering you to treat with Haiti. I bid you good day, sir!" Without further words, Admiral Walker, turning on his heels, strode across the deck and down the accommodation ladder into his barge.

Gherardi's face showed blank amazement. And hot anger filled the hearts of his staff officers, Lieutenants W. P. Potter and Conway H. Arnold. Their chief, our beloved "Jerry," had been contemptuously and publicly affronted!

Hence the hazing by which two lieutenants stood Admiral Walker on his head, tied his long whiskers into bow knots, wrought him into a fury, and spoiled his afternoon nap. They conferred with Admiral Gherardi, and soon signal flags were fluttering at the *Philadelphia*'s yardarm, spelling out an order: "Junior squadron commander report immediately on board the flagship of the senior squadron commander."

I heard later that this was a shock to everyone aboard the *Chicago*, as it had not occurred to them that the great John G. Walker was junior to anyone on earth. The smoke from the *Chicago*'s smokestack clearly spelled, "Damn!"

By the time he reached our quarterdeck, his side whiskers were flapping up and down. Some said it was the afternoon breeze, but everyone aboard the *Philadelphia* knew it was rage. Gherardi met him. "Admiral Walker," he said, "I note that you are sending boats from your flagship to the shore. I will send you my printed order which regulates sending boats and communicating with the shore. You will please scrutinize this and recommend any changes that may suit your convenience."

Admiral Walker looked at Admiral Gherardi. His whiskers suddenly sent out silent messages. But he merely took the order, touched his cocked hat, and returned to his own ship.

As we heard later, he promptly threw off his heavy uniform and quieted his whiskers. At last he was enjoying a needed nap when he was awakened to receive another signal: "Report immediately to the flagship of the senior squadron commander."

Here, as previously, he was greeted with all the courtesies due his rank. The buglers, Marine guard, side boys, and band, every one of them, did their prescribed parts. Admiral Gherardi, the captain, and others were at the gangway to meet the junior commander.

As he spoke Gherardi looked pointedly at the *Chicago*, where hundreds of hammocks were being aired. Walker had given an order to "air bedding," which on this particular day was not in accordance with Gherardi's squadron routine. Walker's glance followed Gherardi's. The *Chicago* was clearly out of order. Then both admirals grinned at each other.

"Your squadron orders shall be carried out, sir," said Walker. "Have you any other orders for me?"

"Not at present, sir."

"Have I permission to return to my flagship?"

"Yes, unless you will give me the pleasure of first visiting me personally in my cabin."

Walker accepted the invitation with very good grace. Two hours later, two old boys, beaming with mutual friendship, came arm in arm from Gherardi's cabin. They addressed each other as "Jerry" and "John." Thereafter good will and kindliness reigned.

When we steamed away without the treaty, little could I have dreamed that twenty-four years later, acting under the orders of a later admiral, I would present another treaty to a later president of Haiti. As will be seen, that treaty was duly executed, and from 1915 to 1934 it regulated the relations between Haiti and the United States.

We now made a regular cruise through the West Indies, visiting many of those beautiful islands. The liberation of slaves in all the islands, beginning just a century before, had, in effect, for the time being ruined them. To the liberated slave, work and slavery were synonymous. Why sweat in the sun that a white man might revel in luxuries?

So the freedman swung his hammock in the shade. When hungry he stretched down and dug up a yam with his great toe, or reached up and plucked a banana, then dozed off again. Avocados, coconuts, oranges, and sweet apples abounded. The juice of the slender reddish sugarcane was nectar. From it he made a white, fiery rum. Fish were abundant if he could spare time from his hammock. And old coffee sacks provided what clothing the grown ups (of course not the children) might need. This lack of ambition in the former slave, with the great fall of price in the world's markets for sugar, drove the once flourishing white population from the islands. No longer did Alexander Hamiltons or Josephines de la Pageries leave the West Indies to build nations or become empresses. Most of the once populous cities were in ruins, the once thriving plantations choked with weeds. In every port there were still some whites, but merely agents (except the Germans) and residents only for a time.

But today this condition is rapidly changing. Fruit and sugar plantations have been reestablished. Luxuries and fineries are for sale, schools are everywhere, steamers come and go often, tourists trot about, and the descendants of the slaves are beginning to work hard. The time is surely approaching when the West Indies will again become famous for their beauty, their fertility, and their splendid climate, perhaps a little warm for us northerners, but wonderful for those who live there.

———————

I fear Dad was too optimistic. He expected things to improve as a matter of course from whatever their present condition might be, and did not consider that they might get worse instead of better. Writing in 1935, or thereabouts, his memories of Haiti were colored by the improvements made during what the liberal press called the American "occupation" (a word not used by U.S. officialdom). Having had a hand in setting up the Haitian government and its altruistic infrastructure in 1915, he should be forgiven for not foreseeing the problems resulting from our premature departure after only nineteen years. We should have continued our benevolent assistance for a century. The debacle of the "Papa Doc" and "Baby Doc" regimes would undo everything accomplished during the "best times" of Haitian history.

———————

A year later, late in 1891, we were steaming south, at high speed. Relations with Chile had become strained. Civil war had been raging there. Jose Balmaceda, the president, had arrogated himself dictatorial powers and dissolved a congress that displeased him. The congressional party, in turn, had enrolled an army with which to attack Balmaceda.

To supply their army with arms, the Chilean congressional party had bought a ship, *Itata*, loaded it with contraband of war, and dispatched it from our Pacific coast to Iquique, a Chilean port under their control. Acting under the advice of Mr. Egan, our minister, our country favored the president. Our government sent the cruiser *Charleston* after the *Itata* to prevent the landing of this war cargo. The *Baltimore* was then anchored off Valparaiso, and after the *Charleston* had caught the *Itata*, the *Baltimore*'s captain, W. S. Schley, sent several hundred men ashore on liberty. The Chileans, sympathizing with their congress, were furious with the Americans and mobbed the U.S. sailors. Boatswain's Mate Riggin and Coal Passer Turnbull were killed. Our government, outraged at this, sent all available warships to Chile.

When the *Philadelphia* reached Montevideo, we learned that the president's army had been slaughtered; that Balmaceda had shot the top of his head off; and that the Chilean government, after expressing regret for the killing of our men, had paid indemnities of twenty-five thousand dollars each to their families. The *Philadelphia* returned to the United States.

The *Philadelphia* was always active with drills, but seemed to me to steam about purposelessly. Instead of following a carefully arranged program, as would be the case today, we were able to attend flower shows and carnivals from Maine to Florida. We seldom cruised in squadron formation. "Line and staff" fights were regular occurrences, keeping us constantly interested, with tempers at white heat. Often the officer of the deck and the engineer officer on watch would disagree, precipitating yet more fights.

The officer of the deck, irrespective of rank, is supposed to represent the captain, and is clothed with the captain's authority in giving orders. Once, in the *Philadelphia*, Assistant Engineer Danforth was stationed for a test of the engine's main steam pipe, with orders from the chief engineer, my friend Ezra Whittaker, not to leave that station until the latter relieved him. But soon he got an order to report immediately on the quarterdeck, to the officer of the deck, Lieutenant John C. Fremont.

"Tell him I can't come now," Danforth replied. "I'm busy with a steam test, and have orders from the chief engineer not to leave until it's over."

The messenger soon returned with peremptory orders for Danforth to report on deck immediately. "Tell the officer of the deck I won't go up now unless the chief engineer tells me to do so," said Danforth.

As a result, Danforth was tried by court-martial, convicted of disobedience of orders, and suspended from duty for a year. In my judgment, both these officers were at fault. Fremont was too quick to send peremptory orders. After receiving Danforth's first message, he might well have sent his second order to Whittaker. Better a little consideration than a burst steam pipe (with probably loss of life) or the court-martial of a brother officer. Danforth was at fault in letting Fremont know, in provoking language, that he intended to disobey the order. These line and staff fights no longer occur in our Navy, but were frequent and hot thirty years ago.

Later, I had an experience very similar to Danforth's, and a comparison of the incidents is instructive. But I will tell of this in its place.

Congress had provided for a naval celebration, in 1892, of the four hundredth anniversary of the discovery of America, but so many delays occurred that it could not take place until 1893. A great armada of many flags was to steam from Fortress Monroe to New York.

More than fifty-three warships anchored at Hampton Roads, ready for the parade. Almost every naval power was represented. America had three flagships: Gherardi, our senior admiral, was aboard the *Philadelphia;* Benham had the *San Francisco;* and our friend with the side whiskers, Walker, had the *Chicago.*

The day before we sailed, three U.S. senators and three congressmen came aboard with their baggage. The same number, I heard, embarked on the other two flagships to represent Congress.

At this time I was acting as treasurer of the junior officers' mess; and as such I kept accounts and bought food. Before I took this unpopular job, our mess affairs had been mismanaged; and to our indignation we learned that we were four hundred dollars in debt. The mess wanted to pay this off out of the usual mess bill of thirty dollars, but without living differently! I was in the position of the chief engineer who was ordered to burn only so much coal per hour, but make more steam. Ensign L. A. Bostwick, a tall, red-bearded young officer, issued a decree: "Our food's going to cost twelve dollars a month. The rest goes to reduce our debt. And if anyone kicks at the grub Beach supplies, there's going to be trouble!"

It is unlikely that, in the history of the Navy, such food had ever been served to an officer's mess. There were deep mutterings at first; but Bostwick met these with such overwhelming fierceness that they faded away.

A tall, bearded vice admiral recently commanding the battleship fleet may remember this incident.

Admiral Bostwick, of the Naval Academy class of 1890, died in Washington, D.C., in 1940.

Just before the armada sailed, Admiral Gherardi sent for me. An elderly gentleman was with him, and a young man apparently in his early twenties. "Mr. Beach," said the admiral, "I wish to present you to Senator Victor MacPherson of New Jersey. And also Mr. Victor MacPherson, son of Senator Victor MacPherson. Senator MacPherson will be my guest on the trip to New York, and I shall permit the young gentlemen of your mess to have *Mister* Victor MacPherson." There was just the barest emphasis on our younger visitor's title, or lack of one. "Take Mr. Victor MacPherson below and introduce him to his messmates."

I expressed to the admiral the unqualified joy we would feel in having Mr. Victor MacPherson in our mess for the trip, and added: "But, Admiral, our quarters are small and terribly crowded. There are but ten berths there, and we have nineteen officers. Also, for reasons I needn't go into, our food at present is awful stuff that could not be eaten by Mr. Victor MacPherson, the son of the senator."

"Tut, tut," replied the Admiral. "I know you'll take good care of him, and I'll drop in at your quarters at eight tonight and see how he is fixed."

My messmates joyfully joined in my plans for taking proper care of Mr. Victor MacPherson, the son of Senator MacPherson of New Jersey. When the admiral arrived, he had to duck, as all overhead space was filled with hammocks. Two hammock mattresses were spread over the mess table, one mattress was under it, and a fourth was in the bathtub. The admiral looked around.

"Dear me," he remarked in worried tones, "where is Mr. Victor MacPherson to sleep?"

"Right here under the mess table, Admiral," I replied. "It's a splendid place, perfectly safe."

"That won't do at all," he answered indignantly. "Have you no other place?"

"Yes, indeed, sir; but I'm afraid he wouldn't be so comfortable. Pay Clerk Norris sleeps in the bathtub. Mr. Victor MacPherson may have that if he prefers."

The commander in chief of this mighty armada gave a snort of disgust and left, taking our guest with him. When Mr. MacPherson returned, he asked if any of us would join him in a game of poker. We would, and we did. The "steerage" was the one place in the ship where poker, if not legalized, was winked at. In four days, Mr. MacPherson was just ninety-three dollars poorer than before he became our guest.

These days young officers no longer play poker on shipboard. Not once, on the five ships I have commanded, did I ever see or hear of any gaming.

I fear Dad was a bit optimistic here, too. Most captains don't see it, but gambling still happens.

Later the admiral sent word that Mr. Victor MacPherson would sleep in his cabin, but would have his meals with us. He did, except that in the four days he was with us he was seasick, and only once attempted to eat. We had "lobscouse" that day, a splendid old sailorman's dish. Mr. Victor Mac-Pherson took a look at the mess in the dish before him, and promptly faded away; but that one mess of "salt horse" cost the U.S. government exactly forty dollars.

The trip to New York was slow. When we finally anchored, Mr. Victor MacPherson, son of Senator Victor MacPherson of New Jersey, hastened away. I have not heard of him since.

Some days later the pay clerk, looking at some papers, remarked, "Admiral Gherardi is losing money. He's only charging the government seven dollars a day for each of his official guests. The other two admirals are charging ten dollars."

"Thanks," I said. "Make out new requisitions for Admiral Gherardi at ten dollars a day for each congressman. Tell him he's losing money at seven. And give me a blank requisition."

I went with the pay clerk to the admiral. Probably ten dollars was not too much, considering the empty bottles marked "Mumm's Extra Dry," "Chateau Yquem," and "Chambertin," relics of the admiral's regular nightly dinner parties for his guests. He signed the requisitions prepared by the pay clerk. Then I handed him the one I had just made out. He stared at it.

"What do you mean by this?" he asked, looking a little puzzled.

On the requisition I had written: "Mess bill for Mr. Victor MacPherson, son of Senator MacPherson of New Jersey, quartered upon Junior Officers' Mess by order of Rear Admiral Bancroft Gherardi, Senior Squadron Commander." and "4 days at $10.00 per day . . . $40.00."

"What do you mean by this?" he repeated.

"I think that's right, sir," I replied. "I believe you have established the rate at ten dollars a day. And you remember, Admiral, you recently hoisted the signal, 'Follow the motions of the senior squadron commander,' which I am doing."

The good old fellow grinned and signed the paper. We had a meeting of the mess. I was declared to be a wonderful financier. We voted that the ninety-three dollars made at poker, and the forty dollars for a plate of lobscouse, should be spent for decent food, which was accordingly done. Such, let us freely say, were the ethics and the justice of our happy-go-lucky days in the steerage of a cruiser of the U.S. Navy.

And now, after three years, my time in the *Philadelphia* was ending. After the tumult and shouting of the Columbian celebration had died, and the foreign captains and admirals had departed, the *Philadelphia* was sent to the Brooklyn Navy Yard to be fitted up for a cruise in the Pacific. The officers and the crew were replaced. I was given leave.

But a final *Philadelphia* incident remains to be told. Soon after her commissioning, inclining tests had caused great alarm. Owing to faulty design, the ship had virtually no metacentric height. Her center of gravity and her center of buoyancy practically coincided. This meant that if the *Philadelphia* rolled deeply enough, she might, like the ill-fated British warship *Captain*, simply keep on rolling and capsize. To correct this, her heavy masts were replaced by light ones, heavy weights were lowered wherever possible, and a great quantity of pig iron was secured along the center of her double bottom. Getting weight low was the great consideration.

A month after my detachment I was in the Navy yard, and naturally went aboard my old ship. The officer of the deck (whose name is now known to most Americans and to many others) was a tall ensign with a heavy brown beard. I had evidently seen him somewhere, but did not know his name. He greeted me pleasantly.

"I think I've seen you," he said. "I'm Sims."

"I'm Beach," I replied. "I've just finished three years on this ship."

It was like Sims, then and ever since, to get immediately to the point of whatever was bothering him. He wasted little time now. He quickly said, "Beach, if you were assistant engineer here for three years, you know the ship. A very serious problem has arisen. We are all new here, and we are stumped. Perhaps you can help us out.

"We came here for repairs. The coal bunkers were swept clean. According to the ship's specifications, they will stow eleven hundred tons of coal. We have just finished coaling; eleven hundred tons of coal were weighed into barges and brought alongside. We tallied every bag of coal dumped aboard; and we checked the tally by taking the draft of the ship and of the barges before and after coaling.

"Our tally shows that only 860 tons have been taken aboard; the increase of the ship's draft indicates 860 tons; the decrease of the barges' draft shows 860 tons. And about 240 tons remain on the barges. And yet the bunkers are full! Every bunker has been inspected, but they can't be full by the 240 tons that are still on those barges. What's the answer? Can you tell me?"

"Yes, I sure can," I replied. "Lower bunkers 28, 29, 30, and 31 are empty."

At this instant an elderly officer hurriedly came up. "Mr. Sims," he began, "I report that I have again personally inspected every bunker, and every bunker is chock full of coal."

"Chief Engineer McNary, this is Assistant Engineer Beach. He served three years in our ship. Chief, Beach says lower bunkers 28, 29, 30, and 31 are empty."

It was a hot day, and the worried chief was under a heavy strain. Sims' remark exasperated him. He took it as questioning his veracity.

"I tell you I've just come from those bunkers!" he shouted. "They're full! Every one of them!"

"Beach," asked Sims, "why do you think those bunkers are empty?"

"I don't care for his reasons," McNary said, too angry to listen.

But Sims convinced McNary that this mystery was too serious to warrant ignoring any clue, especially in view of my previous experience on board. We three went together to bunker 28 in the after fire room.

"Now, I'll show you," said McNary disdainfully, and he ordered a fireman to open the bunker door. Coal ran out from the bunker.

"What did I tell you?" he exclaimed.

"You're wrong, Beach," said Sims.

"Have someone dig out the coal from the doorway," I suggested.

This was done. Soon the coal stopped running out; a moment later we were all three in the bunker. Except for about a ton of coal that had been against the door, it was quite empty.

"How did you know this, Beach?" asked Sims.

"This bunker is filled by dumping through that coal scuttle overhead," I replied. "While it is being filled, men inside must trim it; and the scuttle is the only way they can get out. Two years ago, a man named Dailey was working inside. The coal came faster than he could handle it. The bunker was apparently full, and the people above, not knowing he was there, closed it up. Hours later, at muster, we noted his absence, and finally found him here, almost dead. After that, our firemen were afraid of these bunkers, and we had to keep watching them. They evidently passed the word along. Your men heaped coal against the fire room door, shut the scuttle, and filled just the upper bunker."

The same had happened in the other three bunkers. This was my last experience aboard the *Philadelphia*. I never saw the ship again, but have often thought of her being top heavy. Had she struck bad weather with her upper coal bunkers full and her lower ones empty, she would have been in her most unstable condition, and had she rolled over, it might well have been without warning. There would probably have been no time, and no way, to get out a message of distress. One of the true mysteries of the sea might have ensued.

7

~⁓

LIFE ABOARD THE NEW YORK
AND THE ERICSSON

During 1894 and part of 1895, I served on the armored cruiser *New York*, then the pride of the Navy. She was brand new and of nine thousand tons displacement, twice that of the *Philadelphia*.

I gloried in her. Her engine room was a palace; her boilers and machinery, works of art. The uniform of a Haitian general shone with no more brilliancy than her profusion of burnished brass. Our chief engineer's force went about their work with an enthusiasm that never abated. No young engineer was ever surrounded with happier conditions.

At Navy yards crowds came aboard to see the crack ship of the U.S. Navy. One day, at New York, an old farmer from near Darien, Connecticut, appeared in the engine room with his wife and granddaughter. They were eagerly curious to see everything, and found the ship full of wonders. They said this was their first long journey; Darien was the only big city they had ever before seen. They were nice people; their diction and appearance confirmed that were not very worldly. So I happily took them about the engine room, eloquently describing the machinery, and into the boiler rooms. A machinist named Stevenson accompanied me.

In the engine room we paused, and I answered innumerable questions. We happened to be standing directly under a blower engine used to blow cooler outside air into the hot engine room, but it was not running at the moment.

"I've read," said the old lady, "that you Navy boys can raise a wind at any time by whistling. Is that really so?"

Realizing that she wanted me to answer "Yes," I did not want to disappoint her, but naval officers are taught to be truthful, even if hurts. This was an unexpected problem. I took a minute to figure out the best reply. Finally I said, "With these wonderful engines we don't need sails any longer; so we don't have to whistle for a breeze."

The old lady's eyes were full of pleading. Long ago, someone had told her this, and she wanted so very much to discover he hadn't lied to her. At that instant Stevenson gave me a quick nudge and jumped up a ladder to a grating overhead, calling back to me: "Go ahead, whistle!"

I went ahead. I must have cut an absurd figure, whistling into those eager eyes.

And then, of a sudden, a hurricane descended upon us. The old man's hat went flying, as did my cap. The old lady's bonnet was blown off her head, and her skirts were lifted as high as those of a modern flapper.

Then the hurricane suddenly stopped. The old lady, who was screaming, but satisfied, could testify of her personal knowledge that at least some sailors can raise a wind by whistling.

It was a great pleasure to show the ship to such appreciative visitors. Next I took them on deck and showed them an 8-inch gun turret and its guns. They were spellbound. I explained how the gun was built up. First a massive, extremely strong tube was forged, then great steel hoops, expanded by being heated red hot, were allowed to cool over it, thus shrinking themselves into place with tremendous compressive force. I told how our mighty guns could fire a shell weighing 250 pounds half a mile, in just one second, and sink an enemy warship.

Then the granddaughter, a cute girl of fifteen or sixteen, made her first and only remark. She said, "Isn't it just too awfully sweet for anything?" I could think of no appropriate answer to this.

Our captain was Robley D. Evans, well known as "Fighting Bob Evans," who had been severely injured during the Civil War when Union forces attacked the Confederate Fort Fisher, and had a permanent limp as a consequence. Because Navy regulations specified that injuries incurred in battle could not force retirement if an individual could otherwise perform all required duties, he had limped through thirty years of naval service. I have sailed with many captains, but no other had the knack of securing the respect and liking of officers and men as did Evans. He said but little. I never saw him make the slightest effort for personal popularity. But when he stumped about with his Fort Fisher leg, men wanted to cheer.

His eyes, his rather stern face, his great limp at every step, all these together seemed to express a forceful good will. I loved to see him come into our engine room. His occasional criticism, his frequent commendation, inspired men with the desire to obtain and keep his good will. Some psychological force streamed from his personality. Its effect was to make the ship efficient throughout, and cause contentment on board. Such a combination, not at all rare, becomes known as a "happy ship."

We had one, and only one, line and staff fight on board. In this latest fracas, I was one of the principals, a junior lieutenant of the line was the other. As I was hoisting aboard some engineering stores, he, as officer of the deck, gave me an order that I resented. He then became offensively peremptory, and I offensively defiant. Accordingly, I was reported to Captain Evans for disobeying the order of the officer of the deck, and for insolence. Danforth's actions and reactions, previously mentioned and similar to mine, had resulted in his suspension from duty for a year. Later that day Evans sent for us.

"Make your report!" said he to the lieutenant, who did so in clear, forceful tones.

"What is your statement?" he asked me.

I made my statement, also in clear, forceful tones. Evans then said to the lieutenant, "You think you were right, but at best you were only technically correct. You thought you had a good opportunity to put another officer in the wrong, and you made the most of that opportunity.

"And you, Mr. Beach, by your offensive manner and words, made it certain that a line and staff row would result, and that you would stand out in the limelight as a defender of the rights of engineer officers.

"None of this was necessary. I have about decided to severely reprimand you both for creating dissension on board ship, and to have you detached from this ship. I'll tolerate no quarrels between my officers. But before doing this, I suggest that you step into my after cabin and discuss matters."

In the after cabin the lieutenant said, "Beach, I think we'd better shake hands. What do you say?"

"You bet we'd better," I answered. "I won't give up this ship or Captain Evans if I can help it. I'm at fault. I apologize."

"And I'm just as much at fault and I apologize," returned the lieutenant.

A moment later we stood before Captain Evans. "Captain," said the lieutenant, "Beach and I agree we were both wrong. We have apologized to each other; we have shaken hands, and we ask your pardon. We have resolved ourselves into a committee to stop any line and staff fight whenever brewing. We hope you won't have us ordered from your ship, sir."

"We'll forget all about it," was the reply. And there was never another line and staff fight during that cruise.

Just before we sailed on a West Indian cruise, Admiral Richard Worsam Meade, a nephew of the famous general who had fought at Gettysburg, joined us as flag officer. There was a long quarterdeck abaft the *New York*'s after turret, directly above the section of the ship where our wardroom and staterooms were located. It had been customary for the officers, when we were at anchor in the tropics, to place chairs after dinner on the port side of this deck, near the rail. There we enjoyed talking in the cool evening until time to turn in. But Admiral Meade issued an order forbidding any officer to remain on either side of the quarterdeck except on duty. This was a real deprivation.

Meade was aloof in manner, and stately in appearance. It was rumored that he and Captain Evans were not on friendly terms and never spoke except on official matters. With one exception, I never heard the admiral's voice the entire time the *New York* was his flagship.

On the one occasion when I heard the admiral speak, we were steaming in squadron with the *Cincinnati*. The admiral ordered an exercise in squadron evolutions. In such a case, orders to perform certain maneuvers are given by hoisting signal flags. On seeing such a signal, each ship either hoists the answering pennant or repeats the signal, both flag movements signifying the order has been received and understood. Nothing further is done until the admiral orders his signal hauled down, which is the "signal of execution," and the ships then perform the maneuver. In those days, flagships of the highest class, of which the *New York* was foremost in her time, had two bridges, a navigating bridge and a "flag bridge." All ships had a navigating bridge; it was forward, usually around the foremast. From here the ship was steered and her engines controlled, and here the officer of the deck stood his watch when the ship was under way. Theoretically, the admiral in charge should treat all his ships with equal attention, and not become too involved in the details of command of his flagship. Thus, vessels built to be fleet flagships had a second bridge for the admiral's use. He was expected to send signals to his own flagship as though she was another ship entirely, maybe hundreds of yards away.

Usually, the flag bridge would be located in the after part of the flagship, almost always around the aftermost mast, which would be fitted with flag-hoisting paraphernalia just as was the navigating bridge from which the captain conned his ship in obedience to the admiral's signals. Things are very different now, naturally enough, with radio telephones everywhere available, but in those days a flag hoist, instantly read by all the ships in visual range, could well be the quickest way to maneuver a squadron. Most particularly, if the admiral and captain wished to keep their personal distance from each other, commands would be hoisted by signal flags on the flag, or after, bridge, and answered by all the ships in the squadron, including the flagship, from their forward bridge, the captain's navigating bridge.

On this day the admiral hoisted a signal. Captain Evans answered, as did the captain of the *Cincinnati*. But nothing happened. The signal and the answers continued to flutter. Evans, limping back and forth on the forward bridge, kept casting an eye up and aft, but did nothing. Meade, on the after bridge, seemed nervous, looking repeatedly from the *Cincinnati* to the *New York*'s navigating bridge.

Finally, he shouted in loud and angry tones through a megaphone (he was, of course, less than a hundred yards distant): "Captain Evans, sir! When do you intend to obey my signal?"

Instantly, in clear, bell-like tones, came the reply from Evans: "When you haul it down, sir!"

This answer caused us unalloyed joy. It would be hard for an outsider to appreciate the interest we all took in this little episode. We had not forgiven the admiral for spoiling our pleasure on deck, and this rather public humiliation was far from displeasing to us.

In thinking of the ships, and of the ship life of thirty years ago, I am struck by the differences between then and now.

Then there were few ships of the modern type: the old *Texas*, rated as a second-class battleship, as was the *Maine*; the *New York*, classed as an "armored" cruiser; several "protected" cruisers, approximate in type to the *Philadelphia*; a few gunboats, from the *Yorktown* of seventeen hundred tons to the *Petrel* of nine hundred tons; and some monitors, old relics of the Civil War that theoretically still went about "showing the flag" and having target practice with smooth-bore guns. In fact they seldom went anywhere, nor (sensibly) did they often shoot their ancient guns. A squadron might consist of the biggest battleship and the smallest gunboat, with such diversity of size types, and such small numbers of ships, that anything like present-day methods of drill was out of the question. As late as 1903 the *Columbia*, a steam cruiser, then about the fastest ship in the Navy, and the *Monongahela*, an old-fashioned sailing ship, were in the same squadron.

In the 1890s, the movements of ships followed haphazard needs rather than thought-out plans. Ships went about, usually alone, some cruising in the West Indies, others between American ports. Nevertheless, their service was of immeasurable value. Some American officers and enlisted men were serving in modern steel cruisers equipped with triple-expansion engines, high-pressure boilers, and modern guns. Mighty enthusiasm pervaded every such ship. Both officers and men were possessed with a desire to develop the highest possible efficiency. Every duty was a joy.

The interest of American civilians in their new Navy was developing. Whenever a ship reached port, she was visited by thousands. Newspapers ran daily columns describing naval life, weapons, and engines. The prompt result was a big appropriation for us to build ships equal to Great Britain's best. Officers on shore duty were inventing, experimenting, investigating, studying; those afloat subjected everything to the severest tests. Soon after the *New York*'s completion in 1891 came the three *Oregon*-class battleships carrying 18-inch armor and 13-inch guns. Our Navy had really started toward the goal it has since reached.

When Lieutenant Sims was naval attaché in Paris, in the 1890s, he made it a point to visit every foreign warship to enter a French seaport. From this excellent post of prestige and observation, he indefatigably wrote voluminous reports on British, French, and Russian warships, weapons, and drills. These so impressed our Navy Department that copies were sent to all ships and shore stations, and Sims became the best known officer in the Navy. He then came home and proposed a change in our methods of target practice. We were still following the methods of 1812: a buoy was planted and ships steaming by fired at it. No one expected to hit the buoy, but observers in anchored boats plotted the fall of shot, and drew diagrams showing where the shot might have hit a real ship had there been one anchored in place of the buoy.

Sims' idea was to shoot at a large canvas target marked into squares, and he coined the slogan that "the only shots that count are those that hit the target." At first he was a terrible disturber of the peace. The Bureau of Ordnance turned down his recommendations. The Bureau of Navigation scorned them. But a gentleman of some authority, Mr. T. Roosevelt, who as assistant secretary of the Navy had been reading Sims' extraordinary letters since before our war with Spain, appointed him to be "director of target practice" and gave him the new battleship Indiana to play with. Sims instituted a modern system of drilling gun crews, his object being actually to hit the target instead of drawing pictures of what might have happened. Promising men were trained as gun pointers. Every day they went through the motions of aiming at a miniature target encased in a tough iron box, mechanically moving it to simulate the ship's roll in various weather conditions, and firing a miniature gun mounted on one of the ship's big ones. The sights of the big guns were used to aim it. It was cranked up and down and side to side as though it were actually to be discharged, and its own regular trigger was pulled to shoot; but only 22-caliber "parlor rifle" bullets were in fact fired—at the small target in the iron box. And the gun pointer could see where he hit, if at all. Meanwhile, the real gun was being loaded with dummy shells and handled as if actually in action or at a real target practice.

The Indiana was in competition with other battleships, but after the first practice under Sims' direction, there was never a question as to the value of what he had done. In the first short range target practice, every shot fired by the Indiana hit the target! The old system was completely discarded, and the one developed by Sims and his supporters was installed on every fighting ship in our Navy. The results were amazing.

Bradley Fiske's telescopic sight, and Sims' method of training, had converted the gun that seldom made hits into an instrument of near precision. There followed a revolution in naval ship life. Officers lived with their guns in action and in thought. On battleships, almost nothing was discussed but "hits per gun per minute."

When I was in the *New York,* we had not yet reached this stage; but our beautiful, powerful ship was the pride of every officer and enlisted man aboard. And this pride animated us in our duties. After nearly two years' service aboard this ship, however, I was detached, and ordered as engineer officer of the torpedo boat *Ericsson.* The *Cushing* was our first torpedo boat; the *Ericsson,* our second. This assignment caused me much content. Evidently some confidence was felt in me. (I had never forgotten the opinion of Robert Potts.)

Some three months later, when in New York City, I heard that the *New York* was at the Brooklyn Navy Yard. I thought to visit my old ship. My old captain, Evans, had been replaced by Captain Winfield S. Schley. A crowd was streaming on board. On the quarterdeck, in a stately pose, was a captain who, though I had never seen him, I recognized from pictures as Captain Schley. He was cordially welcoming visitors, and stopped me as I passed, offering his hand.

"I am Captain Schley," he said. "I command this great ship of war. In time of war I will sweep the seas of our country's enemies! With my high-powered 8-inch guns I will pierce heavy armor and destroy and sink my country's foes! With my powerful triple-expansion engines I will—"

"Yes, Captain," I interrupted, "I know all about your engines. I am Assistant Engineer Beach and served aboard your ship—" but Captain Schley had turned on his heel and left me. Evidently he had no interest at all in Assistant Engineer Beach.

The history of my service aboard the *Ericsson,* a "box of machinery" of a type not then fully evolved, intended to be a forerunner of the "torpedo boat" our Navy was then trying to develop, is one of rapidly succeeding breakdowns and explosions. The boat, still in the hands of the builders, was at New London, Connecticut, for her engine and speed trials. I was technically merely an observer for the Navy Department, although designated to be her engineer officer when she was commissioned.

On arriving in New London, I found a boarding place on Howard Street, in a house kept by a Mrs. Lepard. She was an earnest, hardworking woman, who gave her boarders good food and clean rooms.

However, like the never-to-be-forgotten Alexis Delatour, she had one fault. She was, from time to time, possessed of a delusion that seemed insane. At such times she had a notion that she could see only half a thing; and would so tell her boarders. These attacks came at irregular intervals. We would humor her a bit, sympathize with her, advise her to see an oculist, and change the subject.

One morning, after I had been with her for several months, as I was leaving to go to the *Ericsson*, she exclaimed, "Oh, Mr. Beach, I can only see half of you! Oh! Oh! My eyes are getting worse all the time! You have such a big moustache, but I can only see half of it!"

"Which half, Mrs. Lepard?" I asked, twirling the ends.

"Oh, the right half. That's all I can see!"

I mumbled my sympathy, and left. On my return, Mrs. Lepard was in the living room with some of her other boarders, and I heard her telling them that she could see only half of each of them.

While washing up for dinner, and thinking of this strange notion she had, I yielded to a sudden impulse, cut off the left half of my heavy moustache, and shaved my lip clean where it had been. I then went to the dining room where Mrs. Lepard was serving soup.

"Mr. Beach! Mr. Beach! Is there anything the matter with your moustache?" she cried.

"I hope not," I replied, twirling the right end between the fingers of one hand, and an imaginary left end between those of the other.

Poor Mrs. Lepard shrieked and ran out of the room amidst roars of laughter, while I went back and took off the rest of my moustache. After that she never again referred to her failing, but I sensed a lack of confidence in me.

But I must return to the *Ericsson*. We were in New London for the preliminary contractor's speed trials. The requirements were severe; and as events proved, the engines were not strong enough to meet the demands on them. We went out for speed runs thirteen times; each time some part of the machinery gave way, and the boat limped back to the Morgan Iron Works for repairs. Sometimes the pumps gave way; again, the forced draft blower engines broke down, and so on.

On the morning of 23 July 1895, we started our fourteenth speed run. We had hopes, despite previous breakdowns, that this run would be successful. I took my usual station at the forward end of the engine room, near the recording instruments and gauges, from which I recorded steam pressures, revolutions of the engines, and other data.

We worked up to speed gradually, and soon had everything to our complete satisfaction. After noting data for two hours, and finding everything in order,

I went up on deck for a breath of cool air. I walked aft between the rapidly moving vertical engines, passed the eight men who had been between me and the engine room hatch, and went up on deck. Just as I was emerging through the hatch, there was a sharp noise, and immediately the upper deck was enveloped in steam. A branch from the main steam pipe had burst.

The three men nearest my station were scalded to death. The next five were so badly scalded that they had to spend months in a hospital.

We were fifteen miles from New London; it was a hot day; the boat was disabled and helpless, and the scalded men were in agony. After several hours, a small launch passed near us. We shouted what had happened, and asked to have a tug sent to tow us in. The launch crew gave out news of the disaster, and a lighthouse tender towed us to the Morgan Iron Works. Our berth was at the end of a long curved tongue of land. By road it was a mile and a half to my boarding place. I should say *our* boarding place, for Lucie Quin and I were married just before I reported to New London. Back of our boarding house room was a private porch right over the water, only a quarter of a mile across water from the *Ericsson*'s berth. Here, in the afternoons, my young wife would sit, waiting for the *Ericsson* to come in. As the boat glided in we would wave to each other, and I would soon mount my bicycle and speed home, shedding, as I raced, all thoughts of piston rods, crank shafts, and hot brasses, and thinking only of the loving welcome that awaited me.

So when the *Ericsson* reached her berth, there was beloved Lucie, happily waiting for me. I waved to her, more vigorously than usual. As she recognized me and waved back, the doorbell rang, and a visitor was announced; this casual acquaintance was bound on an errand she must have imagined was of supreme importance.

"Oh, Mrs. Beach!" she cried. "Two hours ago there was an explosion on the *Ericsson*, and your husband was killed. Oh, I'm so sorry!"

Father should have told a little more of his personal life at this point. This is his first mention of Lucie. What in the world was her reaction to the mustache business? Did she sympathize with Mrs. Lepard? It's easy enough to imagine how Lucie and Father might have handled the woman who thought she was bearing terrible news, but what was their reaction to Dad's narrow escape? Had he delayed only a few moments longer leaving the little torpedo boat's engine room, he would never have been able to write this book, and I would never have been born.

But to get back to the *Ericsson*. After repairs were made, we were again at our trials, but requirements had been reduced, and these were successfully passed. We now steamed to the Brooklyn Navy Yard for a "fitting out."

The *Ericsson* was put into dry dock, along with the yacht *Minnie*, which was used for naval purposes. After the dry dock gate was in place the dock was pumped out, repairs begun, and the ship's bottom painted.

One morning, while we were still in the dock, I was standing by Lieutenant Usher, who was to command the *Ericsson*, but who had not yet taken charge. He had no authority over the yard workmen, all of whom were civilians in naval employ.

He suddenly exclaimed, "Beach, look at that dry dock gate! The men there are hoisting out the ballast! Come quick!"

Dry docks, built to contain rather large things, like ships, also need big gates at their entrances. The only time the dry dock gates need to be open, however, is for entrance or egress of a ship, that is, when the dock is full of water. It was customary to use floating gates for ease in handling. After a ship was put into the dock, the gate was floated into position and sunk there, usually simply by being flooded with water. Our dry dock gate, however, was an old model that was sunk by being loaded with rock. Once the gate was in position, the water in the dock was pumped out. To remove the gate it was, of course, first necessary to re-flood the dry dock, and then remove whatever ballast had been used to sink the gate in its place on the dry dock sill.

"Don't you know," protested Usher to the yard foreman, "that if you hoist out this ballast the gate is supposed to float? It will probably pop up and the whole Atlantic Ocean will rush into the dock. Everything inside will be smashed!"

But the man did not answer. Perhaps he could not understand the language. Impervious to Usher's protests, he continued hoisting out rocks. Usher dashed over to see the commandant, but could not find him. He rushed to see other officers, but could find no one who would assume authority to stop this job of removing ballast.

Never was a man more earnestly aroused than Usher. He knew his intended command would be destroyed before his eyes; yet despite his imperative demands and warnings, the foreman continued stolidly hoisting out rocks.

The tide was coming in. It would be high water at 3:20 P.M. At exactly 3:20 P.M. the greatly lightened dry dock gate made a desperate leap heavenward, and as Usher had predicted, the Atlantic Ocean rushed in. Instantly the *Ericsson* made more speed than on her trial trip. She first sank the yacht, her dry dock mate, then rammed the end of the dock itself. The dock would not give, but the *Ericsson*'s bow did, and the whole forward part of our little torpedo boat was crushed inward. The force of the rushing water was so great that big ships a thousand feet away had their mooring lines snapped like threads.

It was Saturday afternoon and the crew of the yacht *Minnie* had left, leaving two sailormen to keep watch. And there she lay sunk! Great regret was expressed at the sudden loss of these two young lives.

But the fact was that two worried young men, who should have been lying stiff and cold inside the *Minnie*, were awaiting their fate in a saloon outside the walls, having slipped away to get a few drinks. I mention this as evidence that even saloons have been known sometimes to save lives.

Thanks to a misunderstanding, and to the conscientious obedience of what could only have been an unusually dense civilian employee, the *Ericsson* was laid up for rebuilding. There was no engineering to be done on board, not for a long time, at any rate, and I was ordered to the monitor *Puritan*.

8

A LIEUTENANT

I reported for duty aboard the USS *Puritan* when she went into commission in 1896, and almost immediately was ordered to Philadelphia to be examined for promotion. Though I had studied hard in preparation for this, I was still anxious. Chief Engineers S. L. P. "Starboard Low Pressure" Ayres and John Scott were my examiners. In the five days I was there I wrote reams in answer to the questions, and felt I was doing well. But finally, toward the end, I was given the following question: Explain the difference between the crushing and the compressive strengths of metals; and state how you would take advantage of knowledge of this difference in choosing metals for particular purposes.

I was appalled. I had never heard such a matter discussed. I knew absolutely nothing about it. And I have never increased my knowledge one iota on this subject. But this was not the time to throw in the sponge. Promotion exams were serious business. I began to write; and thoughts popped into my head. My plan was to write metal, metal, metal; to say as many undisputed things as possible, as solemnly as did Holmes' "Katydid." I have been told that I have a good memory. However that may be, I was able to work in, as bearing on strength of metals (crushing, compressive, or other), page after page, practically verbatim, of Cotterill's "Steam Engine as a Heat Engine," Wilson's "Boilers," and Seaton's "Engine Design," carefully avoiding any credit to those celebrated teachers. And once I got my gait, I wrote furiously. I started at 9 A.M.; at 5 P.M. Chief Engineer Scott, a fine old Civil War relic, came to me and said, "Beach, aren't you about finished with your answer to that question?"

"No, indeed, sir," I replied. "I've really only begun. This is one of the most important subjects in the whole realm of engineering. What would you do, sir, if you had to design everything for a vast engineering project, and lacked a thorough knowledge of the difference between the crushing and compressive strengths of metals? How could you make any practical use of your knowledge of such matters as moments of inertia, radii of gyration, reciprocal diagrams of strains and stresses? What good would your knowledge of quaternions be? Chief, when you consider the importance to an engineer of knowledge of this big subject, upon which, in the last analysis, all engineering decisions depend, you must see that I can have hardly started."

"My God, Beach, is it as bad as all that?" asked the chief engineer, appalled. "Look here, let me have your papers. I'll read them tonight, and I imagine you have said enough to show you know all about this subject."

"No, sir. I'm far from finished; and if I hand you my papers, you may think my knowledge incomplete. I can't take that chance, sir."

But he was adamant, and insisted on receiving my day's output. Next morning he told me it was the most comprehensive answer he had ever read; that he had marked it "100," and that "100" was all I could get. I need not complete my answer. He would not even read it.

Then Ayres came to me and said, "Beach, you will now have your last question. It will be to translate a short chapter from Victor Hugo's *Les Misérables*. Here's the book."

Never was there written more difficult French. It was about the poor French woman, Fantine, who had her beautiful hair cut off, and her beautiful teeth pulled, one by one, to buy food for her little girl, Cosette. But I despaired of being able to translate it. I went to Mr. Ayres and said, "Chief, is this my last question?"

"Yes, Beach."

"How do my marks run?"

"Oh, you've already passed. If you should get only a zero on this question you would pass easily and have lots to spare."

"Then give me a zero, chief. I'd get no more if I spent a week trying to translate that chapter."

The fine old gentleman took another book from the shelf.

"Write down what I dictate," he said.

He started to read from an English translation of the chapter of *Les Misérables* previously given me. When he had finished, he gravely read my dictation and marked it "100."

Then I said, "Chief, you and Mr. Scott are certainly mighty kind. But please tell me what is the real purpose of your board of examination?"

"The purpose," replied Ayres, "is to promote worthy and deserving young officers."

Some time later, aboard the *Puritan*, I received an impressive document signed "Grover Cleveland," in which he said that, reposing special confidence and trust in my patriotism, valor, and a few other things, he had appointed me a passed assistant engineer in the Navy, with the relative rank of lieutenant, junior grade. "What a formidable title!" I thought. "It's as long as a main-top bowline!"

The *Puritan* was nearly, but not quite, finished. She had been begun in 1868, though her construction had never been continuous. She was the biggest and heaviest of all our monitors. Four others had been laid down at the same time; but modern monitors were yet to be built.

The *Puritan*, of about eight thousand tons, was the most unwieldy craft that ever put to sea. She carried four 13-inch guns, and had ancient engines and boilers. Her propeller shafts, which were sixteen inches in diameter, were enormously heavy; solid instead of tubular, and of great length. Her engines moved, but oh, so slowly! The most terrific speed she ever reached was eight miles an hour, about seven knots. This involved the consumption of eighty tons of coal a day. We used ten tons a day even at anchor, and she could stow only three hundred tons altogether.

For her, the indefinitely lengthy cruising days of sail were long gone. The *Puritan* could make only short trips, never longer than a few days, and even then there was always worry as to whether we should have enough coal to make port. While the deck officers were working constantly with her 13-inch guns, which were modern, my time was spent chiefly in stowing coal and in cleaning up afterwards.

She had a great, broad, clear deck only a foot above the waterline. Sometimes, late in the day, when at anchor, we would ride our bicycles on this deck around both turrets. A newspaper reporter, famished for news, wrote this up. Later, we were in a gale off Hatteras. A passenger ship, seeing our low deck awash, reported that we were sinking; and the New York paper came out with a half page picture showing the *Puritan* battling mountainous waves, with officers dashing about the decks on bicycles! A cruiser was dispatched to our rescue, and was indignant when our captain, Purnell F. Harrington, refused a tow.

With *Puritan*'s tiny freeboard, a storm would have inundated her main deck with savage waves.

Captain Harrington was a grand skipper. I never knew him to do or say an unkind thing. He was consideration itself. And yet, in a way, he was a terrifying individual. When his black, searching eyes bored through me, I always had a vague sense of guilt. Our executive officer was James Russell Selfridge, a kindly and courteous gentleman, and the chief engineer was George Cowie, as forceful a character as ever lived. I loved them all, and feared them, too; but the big, important thing, which we all knew and yet did not recognize, was that in the *Puritan*, with a cruising range of only about 675 miles, we were all wasting our time.

After considerable wandering from port to port, running as far south as Charleston, we put into the New York Navy Yard for repairs. When these were finished, we raised steam on the boilers to test the engines. Just before we were ready to open boiler stop valves, I inspected each boiler. And something I saw in the furnace of the after starboard boiler caused me to shout at the top of my lungs: "Out of the fire room, all of you! A boiler is bursting! Out you go! Get out! Get out of here!"

What I had seen was that this furnace was red hot at the top, and that the "crown sheets" were slowly moving downward in a shape like that of a big hornet nest. I knew they would give in a moment, and they did. But we had opened the safety valves and the boiler stop valves, so that the steam pressure was low, and no harm was done except to the boiler.

Some days later a board of engineering survey composed of three high-ranking chief engineers was called to determine the cause of this accident, and the responsibility. The chief engineers were McConnell, Wharton, and Allen, all three ancient relics of the Civil War. Candor forces me to confess that I am now older than any one of these three was then, but a photograph in the archives of my brain shows that these three men were ancient.

Their brains were not old, however, and by the time they had finished, they had examined everything examinable. The next stage would be their carefully worded report, which would then be filed permanently in some out-of-the-way pigeonhole. So far as the *Puritan* with her ancient machinery was concerned, that was the only thing that could be done. She couldn't—shouldn't—be rebuilt. As a warship she was an impotent monster, and the best thing that could be done with her was to decommission her as soon as possible. In a few years this was done.

But events far away, in our nation's capital, provided a big diversion from our concerns of that particular moment. Early one morning, while the engineering survey board was considering how far it could go in its report, I entered the fire room with a morning paper.

"Here's news, chiefs all!" I began. "Have you read that the Navy Department will probably recommend that the line and engineer corps be amalgamated, and that hereafter officers of these corps will be called upon to perform both duties?"

Then there was another explosion. I was assailed by three red-hot, mad, chief engineers, of the high rank of captain, all shouting at me at once.

"This is the most infamous thing ever proposed in the history of our country!" roared McConnell.

"Incompetent line officers will cause boilers to burst, with wholesale death and destruction!" cried old man Wharton.

"They know nothing of engineering! Any Navy ship that isn't sunk will be a lame duck, with worthless machinery," yelled Allen.

I waited for a calm moment in the storm, and when their rage had subsided a little, I broke in, "But Chiefs, there is an interesting paragraph toward the end. Just listen!"

I read that all chief engineers with good Civil War records would, when retired, be promoted to the next higher grade, those now ranking as captain to be retired as rear admirals. There was a sudden profound calm. I was asked to read that paragraph again. It was copied on the backs of old envelopes. Then these three old fellows went into corners and behind boilers and performed some calculations. When they returned, trying to control their facial muscles so as to neither laugh nor weep, I said to myself, "Lucky that these old boys haven't got split lips!"

They talked a little, in subdued tones. Perhaps it would be well not to be too hasty. Perhaps the line officers, with their splendid scientific and mathematical training, might, by hard work, become reasonably good engineer officers. Then they hurried ashore, perhaps to tell dear ones of the nefarious law that would make them rear admirals.

And now, in mid-1897, with the *Puritan* business and my promotion at last settled, a peculiar set of conditions aboard the USS *Baltimore* in faraway Honolulu caused me to be suddenly detached from the *Puritan* at Brooklyn, hurried by train to San Francisco, and rushed to Honolulu for duty in the *Baltimore*. The peculiar conditions were such that, in the particular case involved, it was impossible for the *Baltimore*'s captain to carry out both Navy regulations and a special order of the Navy Department.

In the "wardroom country" of the *Baltimore* was a most unpopular stateroom, known as "Darkest Africa," because it had no porthole, and therefore never saw daylight. Besides, part of the room was used as the entrance to a coal bunker. There were coal scuttles in both deck and ceiling. Despite a canvas tube rigged between them, whenever coal was taken aboard the tiny space was permeated with coal dust, which impregnated the drawers, the wardrobe, the bunk, and every nook and corner of the room. And the *Baltimore* had to coal often, although nowhere nearly as often as the *Puritan*.

Assignment of staterooms of course went by seniority, and the junior officer on board always had to take this horrible room. Seldom in the history of shipbuilding has there been such an assemblage of discomforts as Darkest Africa afforded.

In the *Baltimore* there were three officers: First Lieutenant Williams of the Marines, Passed Assistant Engineer Winchell, and Passed Assistant Surgeon Haesler of the Naval Medical Corps. Each of these, strangely enough, was by Navy regulations senior to one, and junior to one, of the other two.

This came about through the fact that while Marine officers took rank with Navy officers of the same grade according to dates of commission in the grade, engineer officers took rank with medical officers according to date of entrance into naval service. In consequence of these conflicting rules, each of these officers was senior to one of the other two, and junior to the other.

Captain Nehemiah Mayo Dyer, generally known as "Hot Foot," was in a devil of a fix. He earnestly desired to carry out the regulations, but this was impossible. Williams was thirteen years younger than either Winchell or Haesler. Hot Foot therefore ordered Williams into Darkest Africa. But Williams politely refused to obey orders. That is, he addressed a letter to Captain Dyer, quoted the Navy Department order assigning the room to the *junior* officer, proved by reference to the regulations that he was senior to Winchell, and protested that the captain could not lawfully order him to this detested room. Then Dyer sent for Haesler and ordered him to move into the room. Haesler proved that his commission antedated Williams', and begged to be excused. Then Dyer, his temper warming up—he was not called Hot Foot for nothing—peremptorily ordered Winchell to inhabit the room. Winchell, in turn, started to quote Navy regulations, but did not get far. A hurricane that suddenly raged on the *Baltimore*'s quarterdeck blew Winchell, with all his personal effects, into Darkest Africa.

Winchell now, by letter, reported his captain to the Navy Department for violating the regulations and disobeying the department's specific orders. Regulations required this letter be sent via the captain, and Dyer's endorsement on it, also required, was to explain matters. This he did, and then requested that one of the three officers be detached and that another of the same corps, unquestionably junior to the other two, be sent to relieve him. This is how and why I came to inhabit Darkest Africa.

As the *Baltimore* was similar to the *Philadelphia* in almost all respects (except that *Philadelphia*'s design, perhaps thoughtfully, had no Darkest Africa), I was at once at home in my job. The chief engineer was John D. Ford, a capable engineer and a scholarly gentleman. There were two other engineers, Price and Hutch I. Cone, fine fellows. Both rose to distinction. Cone, while still a young officer of the rank of lieutenant commander, was appointed engineer in chief of the Navy and made a rear admiral.

As previously mentioned, Hot Foot Dyer, though a man of the highest character, was addicted to amazing outbreaks of temper. Indeed, there has always been much temper mixed up with naval duty. An inefficient officer is sure to be reproved in high, scornful tones. Officers work, as a team, for the efficiency and good name of their ships; and sloppy, careless, stupid work arouses intense personal indignation. A captain may not "reprimand" publicly; but he may "admonish" as publicly and as severely as the occasion requires.

Many times I have heard officers severely admonished—and have gently admonished some myself—but the most violent of these rebukes, compared with those administered by Dyer, were as a light breeze to a howling gale.

Dyer had spent his early youth and manhood as a seaman, mate, and master, in whaling ships. That meant a hard, rough life, with a tough crew to be controlled, and the fist and belaying pin in daily use. With the outbreak of the Civil War he stepped from a whaling ship to a man-of-war, and was commissioned as a volunteer lieutenant. He greatly distinguished himself. Though the crews of our warships were tough in those days, no sailor man was ever as tough as Dyer, nor had as hard a fist. Once, early in his naval career, a sailor was insolent to him. Dyer jumped at him and knocked him overboard. Then he dived into a heavy sea and saved the man's life.

Like England and Horatio Nelson, Dyer expected every man to do his duty. On Dyer's ship every man knew he would "catch Hell" if he did not. I had heard of him for years, and expected to find a rough specimen of manhood. Instead, I met a courteous, polished, cultured gentleman. Officers and men held him in high regard. He was unintentionally over-violent in his denunciations of inefficiency; to him a thing done 10 percent poorly was 100 percent unsatisfactory. Intentionally he was just, kind, and considerate. One could not serve with him without realizing that, in personal character, he was high-minded, pure, and good, all of these to the limit.

I vividly recall an occasion when Dyer, another officer, and I were having a personal conversation. This officer made a remark concerning women. Dyer suddenly exploded with concentrated fury. He jumped up from his chair. "You scoundrel!" he shouted. "You scoundrel! You disgrace the uniform you wear! It's a crime for you to be a married man! Get out of my sight!" Dyer drove that man off the ship.

We cruised quietly about the Hawaiian Islands. But we were thrown into a state of intense excitement when news reached us that the *Maine* had been sunk in Havana harbor on 15 February 1898, for this almost certainly meant war! In two weeks the *Mohican* came in with ammunition for Commodore Dewey's squadron at Hong Kong. And soon, with extra ammunition crammed into every available space, we were on our way across the Pacific.

At Hong Kong, Commodore Dewey came aboard. I was impressed by his quick, decided way of speaking. He wasn't paying much attention to passed assistant engineers of the rank of lieutenant junior grade, but that did not keep me from listening. We were coaling ship, and my job of indicating where coal was to be dumped gave me a chance to follow Dewey and Dyer in the commodore's inspection of our ship. Dewey's comments and questions were like shots from a machine gun, and Dyer's replies corresponded. These splendid officers had no time for personalities or general news of the world. With them it was all "ship," 100 percent of the time.

Soon came word of the declaration of war, and Dewey's squadron started for Manila. It was a small and feeble squadron composed of cruisers and gunboats upon which now rested a tremendous responsibility. We were at war, and we were going to attack Spanish forces in the Philippines! The flagship *Olympia* was followed—in order of size—by the cruisers *Baltimore*, *Raleigh*, and *Boston*, and the gunboats *Concord* and *Petrel*.

The American consul to Manila, a Mr. Williams, had left that city for Hong Kong, where he conferred with Dewey, and was now returning as a passenger in the *Baltimore*. He and I were probably the least busy officers aboard, my concerns being the routine engineering I had been doing for years, while just about everyone else was working over his guns to get them into the most perfect possible condition for combat. Williams and I, being also near the same age, found ourselves together a lot during that short cruise. I asked him innumerable eager questions about Spanish defenses: forts, ships, and torpedoes. His knowledge was only general; he had never paid much attention to these subjects, but I learned enough to become convinced that although the Spaniards had eleven warships to our six, they were smaller, with smaller guns. Though there were several formidable forts armed with heavy modern Krupp and Armstrong guns, they could probably not hurt us, since the Spaniards had had little, if any, target practice or useful gun drill. Mr. Williams had heard that the entrances to Manila Bay were mined and that the Spaniards had torpedoes. But from what he told me, I doubted then, and still doubt, their ability to adjust mines or torpedoes to make them dangerous. I likewise became convinced that the engines and boilers of their ships were in lamentably bad shape.

On the evening of our departure for Manila, a number of the *Baltimore*'s officers met informally and discussed the coming battle. In view of the many guns of the Spanish ships and the powerful armament of the forts, some felt that our chances of success were small. Several thought that we might lose as many as three ships; others said two. The general opinion was that we would be victorious, albeit at some cost. However, analyzing what Williams had passed on to me, I felt I had better information than anyone else, and then and there expressed my conviction that we would win the oncoming battle hands down and escape, not only without losing a ship, but also without losing a man.

No one believed me, and events proved, indeed, that I was wrong. On the revenue cutter *McCulloch*, which, convoying two colliers full of coal, followed Commodore Dewey at a distance of three miles, was an officer, it was said, who drank a bottle of Old Rye during the battle and dropped dead. What the whole Spanish squadron, backed by forts, was unable to do, John Barleycorn accomplished with neatness and dispatch. This unfortunate soul was our only casualty of the Battle of Manila Bay.

9

DAVILA'S MESSAGE
TO THE FILIPINOS

Two different occasions proved to me that Captain Dyer had a natural unconscious eloquence. He had the ability, without planning or intention other than his need to speak out on some important issue, to catch the hearts of his listeners. The aroused violence of this man's passion swept everything before it. His voice was a trumpet call, creating at the right time and place a surge of feeling that could become a tremendous flood. Truth and emotion poured from him in a torrent, seizing, in crescendo fashion, our very beings. At the end we were completely his, not by force of naval regulations, but by the power of his soul, which had entered and possessed ours.

The first of these occasions took place the day before we entered Manila Bay. Before our captain stood hundreds of men, his officers and crew, in an attitude of expectant intensity. Steaming ahead of us was the *Olympia*, flying the broad pennant of Commodore Dewey. We were second in line. Astern were the *Raleigh*, the *Boston*, the *Concord*, and the *Petrel*. Once more was Dyer to do battle for his country, and with him were comrades of that great war of thirty-five years before: Dewey, Charles Gridley, Benjamin Lamberton, Coghlan, Wilders—and others, years younger, who were to fight in a far

greater war fifteen years later. All of us were inspired by his true, splendid, personality.

We were steaming in a smooth sea. Far out of sight behind us lay China;
ahead, not too far away now, lay the Philippine Islands. It was an impressive
moment. There stood our captain, his very person radiating force, power, and
confidence. From a little hook on his white blouse, he lifted with his left hand
a pair of eyeglasses. As he was putting them on, he raised his head, and with
it his left arm akimbo, he then slowly moved his head from left to right, and
back again, his left elbow following his head in its movements, in which there
was an unconscious grace. An intense stillness pervaded, except for the splash-
ing of seas against the bows of our ship, and the subdued thunking of her
engines. He had caught the attention of every man on deck. We were soon
to go into battle, and our captain was about to speak to us.

"Men of the *Baltimore*," he said, "you are about to listen to the most shameful set of lies, the most abominable falsehoods, the most horrible statements,
ever made against Americans. You are denounced as thieves, scoundrels, mur-
derers, violators of women, destroyers of religion. Listen! This is what the
Spanish governor general of the Philippine Islands has published. And this
means me, and you, and you! and you! *and you!*"

An electric shock seemed to go through me. Every man standing before him
on that deck of the cruiser *Baltimore* knew the "you!" was specifically for him.

Then Dyer read as follows:

Spaniards! Between Spain and the United States of North America hostilities
have broken out. The moment has arrived to prove to the world that we possess
the spirit to conquer those who, pretending to be loyal friends, take advantage of
our misfortunes and abuse our hospitality, using means which civilized nations
count unworthy and disreputable.

The North American people, constituted of all the social excrescencies, have
exhausted our patience and provoked war with their perfidious machinations;
with their acts of treachery; with their outrages against the law of nations and
international conventions.

The struggle will be short and decisive. The God of Victories will give us one
as brilliant and complete as the justice of our cause demands. Spain, which counts
upon the sympathies of all the nations, will emerge triumphantly from this new

test, humiliating and blasting the adventurers from those states that, without cohesion and without a history, offer to humanity only infamous traditions, and the ungrateful spectacle of Chambers in which appear united insolence and defamation, cowardice and cynicism.

A squadron manned by foreigners, possessing neither instruction nor discipline, is preparing to come to this archipelago with the ruffianly intention of robbing us of all that means life, honor, and liberty. Pretending to be inspired by a courage of which they are incapable, the North American seamen undertake, as an enterprise capable of realization, to take possession of your riches as if they were unacquainted with the rights of property, and to kidnap those persons whom they consider useful to man their ships or to be exploited in agricultural or industrial labor.

Vain design! Ridiculous boastings!

Your indomitable bravery will suffice to frustrate the attempt to carry them into realization. You will not allow the faith you profess to be made a mock of; impious hands to be placed on the temple of the true God; the images you adore to be thrown down by unbelief. The aggressors shall not profane the tombs of your fathers; they shall not gratify their lustful passions at the cost of your wives' and daughters' honor, or appropriate the property your industry has accumulated as a provision for your old age. No, they shall not perpetrate any of the crimes inspired by their wickedness and covetousness, because your valor and patriotism will suffice to punish and abase the people, that, claiming to be civilized and cultivated, have exterminated the natives of North America, instead of bringing to them the life of civilization and progress.

Filipinos, prepare for the struggle! And, united under the glorious Spanish Flag, which is ever covered with laurels, let us fight with the conviction that victory will crown our efforts; and to the calls of irreverence let us offer, with the devotion of the Christian and the patriot, the cry of "Viva España!"

Your General, Basilio Agustin Davila. Manila, 23 April 1898.

As Captain Dyer read, he became possessed of a mad fury that constantly augmented. His wonderful voice rolled over the deck and reached and roused every heart. With the last words he had become a mass of passion. He lost control of himself, threw the paper on the deck, jumped on it, threw his hat at it, cursed it, then broke into a most beautiful, though violent, statement about the soul of America, past and present.

A wild cry went up from the hearts and souls of the Americans before him. He had stirred us as a body in a way I had never before seen men stirred. The cry became a mighty roar. Then up went Dyer's arm; there was perfect silence.

"March divisions to their quarters! Pipe down!" he ordered.

IO

THE BATTLE OF IRWIN'S BOOTS

I propose to write of the Battle of Manila Bay as I saw it. Histories of battles are sometimes too much the same, with comparisons of the opposing forces; discussions of their objects, methods, strategy, tactics; and a summary of results.

But I shall write of my personal experiences, however unimportant. All I saw of the Battle of Manila Bay was a pair of boots, directly over my head. I looked upward at these boots innumerable times during the hours of crashing reverberations (from our own guns) that poured down upon me through the engine room hatch.

I don't know that battles are ever named by law. People simply adopt names they choose themselves that seem to fit best—but once a fairly good name has been used a few times, it becomes a convenience for everyone. Availing myself of this privilege, referring merely to my own experiences, and doubting that anyone else will want to use it, I shall call this "The Battle of Irwin's Boots."

Ensign Irwin later became the father of Mrs. Charles A. Lockwood, who in her turn became wife to the much admired "Uncle Charlie," commander of our submarine forces in the Pacific (ComSubPac) during World War II. It is doubtful, however, that she or her husband ever heard of the impact her father's boots had on the *Baltimore*'s engines and boilers, or, for that matter, on the young engineering officer whose duty station happened to be immediately below the grating on which Irwin strode as he commanded his gun battery.

As the roar of each gun resounded, I naturally looked up from the engine room where I was stationed. Each time, through the hatch I saw the soles of the boots worn by Ensign Noble E. Irwin, who, standing on the grating, was directing the fire of his 6-inch guns. That was the battle as I saw it.

During the preceding months, we had been frequently drilled at "Clear ship for action." A thousand things had to be done in this drill. All past naval battles had brought out the fact that much damage is caused by wood splinters. Jagged pieces of wood flying about with high velocity could ruin machinery, maim, or even kill personnel. In 1898 there was still a great amount of wood used in all naval ships of all navies. Part of each drill was to tag all sorts of splinter-making objects: all wooden stools, implements, equipment, that could be spared in battle, with a card marked "Overboard." On Saturday afternoon, 30 April 1898, the boatswain's shrill pipes were heard all over the ship. Then ringing calls: "All—hands—clear—ship—for—action!"

This time it was real business. We were to heave overboard all the articles we had been merely tagging before. The first thing to go over was the chaplain's pulpit. This was followed by ladders, chests, mess tables, benches, and all such other things. The sides of our staterooms had been made removable, and overboard they went; and with them, chairs and furniture (at least, this did away with the confines of Darkest Africa; I was now entirely in the open, in a corner with coal scuttles above and below). The other five ships were doing the same. Soon this debris, spreading out over the waters as our squadron progressed, presented a strange spectacle.

I had the dog watches, from 4 to 8 P.M., on this afternoon of 30 April. Towards five o'clock a young officer came to the engine room to see me. He had but recently been appointed from civil life, and was not of the combatant branch. He was so gentle, timid, retiring, so utterly unused to the peremptory, stern, exacting methods of shipboard life, that he was utterly out of place

on a warship. We who had become inured by years of training were not star-
tled at the sudden calls, day and night, for gun, collision, or fire drills, or to
repel imaginary torpedo attacks; we rushed full speed to our stations. But this
young officer never knew where to go, and was in a permanent state of star-
tled worry.

Before we arrived at Hong Kong, he already avoided everybody except me.
I was his confidant. He wanted very much to do his duty, but hated the
thought of going into battle. In his psyche he had somehow formed the utterly
wrong notion that the other officers on board believed him to be a coward,
and were whispering about him behind his back. Nothing that I could say to
him could remove this conviction.

He came to me on the day before the battle. He was evidently distraught,
not to say excited. "Oh, Mr. Beach!" he cried. "The captain has given me the
most dangerous position on the ship! I am to follow Dr. Wise wherever he may
be in the battle tomorrow. I will be in all the smoke and fire! It isn't right.
I'm not a doctor; I've had no training in medicine. I may even be ordered to
kill men. I can't do that! This is all horrible to me!"

"Where do you want to go?" I asked him.

"I asked Captain Dyer to let me go into the double bottoms, where I
wouldn't see any of the horrors. But the captain cursed me for being a
damnable coward. I thought he was going to kill me! He's an awful man! I
don't believe I'm a coward, but I'm just sick at heart to think that I'm to be
in the midst of slaughter and perhaps helping to slaughter some other poor
men. Oh, Mr. Beach, tell me what to do!"

"I'll tell you. Just stay with me as much as you can. We'll talk of all sorts
of other things. And when the fight begins, go to Dr. Wise, touch your cap—
like this—and say you report to him for duty."

He did his duty well the next day. Though he was not scratched himself,
a 5-inch shell struck a nearby box of 1-pounder cartridges, and the air about
him was filled with flying fragments; later a 6-pounder shell exploded near
him. He noticed none of this; he was intent upon his duties to wounded men,
of whom the *Baltimore* had about a half dozen. During the four hours of battle,
his conduct won good opinions. But his nervous system was badly hurt. He was
utterly unfitted for such scenes as he saw, and even more for those he imagined. For weeks after the battle he never spoke to a soul except me. Having
done his duty manfully, he was unspeakably sad. Everybody realized that the

dear young fellow had a nature so gentle and so tuned to the beautiful, quiet, kindly things of life, that the crash of battle, the roar of guns, the destruction of ships, the slaughter of his brother men, had shocked his innermost being.

At nights he poured out his grief to me. This daily increased. After some weeks he was transferred to a transport leaving for San Francisco. At least, we felt, we were sending him home, to a place where the old familiar atmosphere would help him recover his normal equilibrium. This was a mistake. He should have been put under psychiatric restraint, or at least under a supervisory watch of some sort. Could I have continued my ministrations, even they might have averted the tragedy that ensued. At daybreak on the morning after his transport reached Nagasaki, the quartermaster on watch observed the young man standing at the outboard end of a boat boom rigged out from the ship's side, holding on with one hand to the "topping lift."

"What are you doing there, sir?" called out the quartermaster. "Is there something wrong out there?"

"Tell my dear wife good-bye! Give her my love!" was the answer.

He jumped, and the waters closed over him. He had received a mortal wound in his first and only battle, but not the sort of injury any of us had any idea of how to handle.

I will now go back to a somewhat consecutive narrative of the Battle of Irwin's Boots.

The entrance to Manila Bay is divided into two parts by the large island of Corregidor. The northern and more narrow channel is called Boca Chica, the southern, wider passage, Boca Grande.

Corregidor and the coast opposite were both fortified with heavy modern guns. Commodore Dewey chose to enter by the wider entrance. This was wiser than we knew because, as we learned later, the modern guns on Corregidor bore only across Boca Chica. For reasons unknown to any of us (maybe Consul Williams had explained all this to our commodore) the Spanish expected an attacking fleet to use only the more narrow channel.

Shortly after one o'clock, on Sunday morning, 1 May, we were entering Boca Grande. It was very dark. We were steaming slowly, for it was only twenty miles to the naval arsenal at Cavite, where Dewey correctly expected to find the Spanish fleet.

Ahead of us, the *Olympia* was merely a dim shape in the darkness. She carried no lights except one astern, so screened as to be visible only from dead aft. To port was the big black island of Corregidor; to starboard, an islet, El Fraile. Aboard the *Baltimore*, everyone except those on watch in the engine and fire rooms was on deck. Intense stillness and intense expectancy prevailed. The gun crews were at their guns. Everything was ready.

Suddenly a rocket blazed up from Corregidor. We took this to be a warning of our approach. Then El Fraile fired several shots—we must have been discovered—but on we crept. At four o'clock I went to my battle station in the starboard engine room. Here I was on the platform where I was to handle the reversing levers of the starboard engine in accordance with signals from the bridge, or from other predesignated stations on deck. Here also were voice pipes to the bridge and to the fire rooms. The chief engineer's station was also in the starboard engine room, and I was to pass any communication to him from the captain on the bridge.

All were now at their battle stations. The minutes dragged; but at 5:42 A.M. an 8-inch gun jarred the ship mightily with a great roar, and this was followed by a succession of other roars chasing each other down the engine room hatch. I looked up—and there were the soles of Irwin's boots.

Our gunfire was rapid. Non-naval people have asked me how it could have been that during the whole fight I never once heard the report of any gun that was not on my own ship. But so it was. Our own guns were the closest of any and there may also have been some psychological reason, but the sounds of our own gunfire preempted our attention. They may also have deafened us somewhat.

There was little for me to do. There were, indeed, frequent signals to change speed, stop, and go ahead slowly; but our department was crowded with men of all watches, and with sixty others in excess. Steaming slowly as we were, one watch alone would have had an easy time of it.

I was, of course, intensely interested; but it did not occur to me then, nor has it since, that I was in danger of getting hurt. My fine old chief engineer, John D. Ford, was sitting on a brass rail, smoking a cigar, a pleasant smile on his face.

"Chief," I asked, "you were in battle during the Civil War, weren't you?"

"Yes, many times, Beach. With Farragut, in the Mississippi River and at Mobile Bay, and other places."

Bang! roared an 8-inch gun.

"Chief, would you consider this a battle?"

He laughed. "Yes, this is a battle."

"But do you think it will be ranked as an important battle?"

Just then five guns roared almost at once, and the chief also roared. He was greatly amused by my questions.

I had read much of naval battles, and had supposed that each was marked by feverish excitement. But in this great battle that changed the course of Philippine history, and our own, too, men were lazily smoking and chewing tobacco, and, before long, "swapping yarns."

At this time it is a fact that in the *Raleigh*, just astern of us, there was a dance in progress on the gun deck. Lieutenant Hugh Rodman, who years later was Admiral Rodman, or Sir Hugh Rodman, knight commander of the Bath, was commanding a 5-inch gun division. But with the ship at battle stations, he had far more men than he could use. Thinking it best to keep them all employed, he found someone who could play a fiddle and organized a Virginia Reel. While on the upper deck bombs were bursting, on the gun deck it was: "Balance yer partners!"

"Chassez to yo' right!"

"Doe's ee doe!"

"Gran' right an' left."

Some time after the firing began I had a call from the forward fire room. Here Assistant Engineer Hutch I. Cone (later engineer in chief of the Navy) was caged in with the boilers and the fire room force of which he had charge. Armored gratings were overhead, and heavy doors, usually left open, were closed, barred and bolted, the purpose being to reduce the possibility of damage from enemy shells exploding nearby. The speaking tube alongside my station was the only means of communication from the fire room to the outside world.

"Beach," called Cone, "for God's sake send me some news! I've got to let my men know what's happening on deck!"

And as Cone's voice faded out, I could hear a furnace door slammed shut, and a stern Irish voice calling out, "Take that, will ye, ye damned dirthy Dago!" [*sic*].

Now, I had not yet received news of any kind. No bulletin of passing events reached the engine room of the *Baltimore* that torrid Sunday morning. I only knew that a succession of roars was crashing down the hatch. But this was no time to make excuses. Cone needed something to interest his firemen. Circumstances demanded that I furnish them with something. Anything, in fact.

"Hurry up! Give me some news!" shouted Cone. "What's happening up there?"

"The *Olympia* just landed a broadside on the Spanish flagship, and has smashed her side!" I shouted back into the voice pipe.

Then, with my ear to the tube, I heard Cone repeat the message, and caught the frenzied hurrahs of his men. They were fighting the Spaniards with shovels for weapons and coal for ammunition. Half an hour later Cone demanded more news. I returned word that the *Baltimore*, attacked by two torpedo boats, had sunk them both. From time to time I gave out further information; and altogether, that morning, I think I sank more ships than Spain ever possessed.

After about two hours' fighting, Commodore Dewey drew off five or six miles. His captains were called to the flagship, and the ships' crews were ordered to breakfast: probably the most reviled order ever received in the heat of battle. We did not want food, we wanted to sink all the Spanish ships in Manila Bay. Food of any sort was a distant bottom among our priorities of the moment. We didn't know then, as we learned later, that the commodore was checking into an erroneous report that nearly all the 5-inch ammunition of the *Olympia* had been expended, and possibly of his other ships too.

However, we were soon at it again; and I resumed my battle function of inspecting Irwin's boots. It is safe to say that in no other naval battle has a pair of boots been so carefully scanned.

After the battle I had a chance to go on deck and look about. The masts and upper works of eleven Spanish ships were sticking out of the water. That evening I thought to write home about the battle I had just been through, but found it hard to tell anything at all about it. All I knew that evening is narrated above. Later, conversations with many officers and men, and with Spanish officers, gave me a satisfactory and detailed knowledge of the action.

Two or three days later a miniature Spanish gunboat steamed proudly toward our fleet, with all colors flying. This was the *Callao*, which had come from the southern islands. No information had reached young Captain Pou, her commander, that war had been declared between Spain and the United States. Poor Pou was amazed and dismayed at the one gun salute he received from Admiral Dewey, in the shape of a shell that raised a fountain of spray under the *Callao*'s bow.

Admiral Dewey was glad to report his capture to Secretary of the Navy John D. Long. As the secretary was interested in colleges, several ships recently acquired by the Navy had been given names like "Yale" and "Harvard." It was natural for him to cable to Dewey to suggest a collegiate name for his latest capture.

Dewey looked at the cable message. The *Callao* was about as big as a large steam launch. He cabled back to the secretary, "Recommend that the captured Spanish gunboat *Callao* be renamed The United States Ship *Massachusetts Institute of Technology*." It was the longest name Dewey could think of, but evidently it did not appeal to Secretary of the Navy Long, and the *Callao* retained her Spanish name.

The following days were busy and hot. We expected torpedo boat attacks at night, and had boats on patrol. But no torpedo boats came. We heard that the Spaniards were planning to send a fleet of powerful battleships through the Suez Canal to destroy us. And indeed such a fleet started, passed through the canal—and returned home because of the destruction of Admiral Pascual Cervera's squadron at the Battle of Santiago de Cuba, two months after our victory at Manila.

Emilio Aguinaldo, the chief of the Filipino revolt of 1896, arrived at Cavite on 19 May. With amazing dispatch he created a Filipino army, and in a few days was capturing Spanish forts.

The *Baltimore* and the *Raleigh* were sent to Mariveles, north of Manila, and received the surrender of the fort at that place. Then Captain Dyer was directed to meet the *Charleston*, which was convoying a fleet of army transports, filled with American soldiers, to Manila. This first expedition reached Manila Bay on 30 June.

By this time squadrons of British, French, German, and Japanese warships were anchored in Manila Bay. There was much gossip among American officers to the effect that the Germans were officially impolite, and that Commodore Dewey had very carefully informed Admiral Diedrichs of Germany that there were certain requirements of international law regarding communications with a blockaded port. The British were boisterously friendly to American officers. The Japanese were friendly in spirit. The French were courteous, and neutral in manner. Transports continued to arrive; soon many thousands of American soldiers were encamped south of Manila.

It was wearisome waiting, anchored off the city of Manila. But the evenings on deck were pleasant. Night after night we heard artillery fire and saw the flash of guns where the Filipinos were attacking Spanish forts on the shoreline.

Finally our interest was aroused by orders to prepare for an assault upon the city of Manila. These reached us on 12 August. It was to be a combined Army and Navy attack, the Army attacking from the south, the Navy from the Bay. On 12 August the German and French ships steamed toward Mariveles, while the British and Japanese remained at Cavite.

Early on 13 August 1898, Admiral Dewey's squadron hove up anchor. Each of our ships steamed past the British ship *Immortality,* from which we received enthusiastic cheers, led by that fine old beef-eater, Captain Edward Chichester. On shore we saw thousands of soldiers marching toward Manila. We steamed slowly. Some of our ships, close in, were firing ahead of the soldiers to clear the way for them.

Soon our engines were stopped, and word came to the chief engineer that they might not be used for some time. "Beach," Ford said to me, "this is a funny sort of battle. Here we are attacking Manila and within easy range of their 9-inch Krupp guns. Why aren't they shooting? And why are we not shooting at them? Run up on deck and find out what it's all about!"

I was burning with curiosity and impatience, and up I ran. Here was our squadron, close to the walled city of Manila, dangerously near those big, heavy-calibered Krupp cannon. But now that our guns had stopped shelling the shore, Manila Bay, in spite of the valiant defense of the Spaniards, was just about the quietest harbor in the world.

"Something queer," I thought.

On the *Olympia* a signal was flying. "What does that spell out?" I asked a quartermaster.

"It says," he answered, "'do not fire upon walled city unless walled city fires upon us.'"

"What's this?" I called out to a line officer acquaintance, "a hometown gathering of friends?"

"Why, don't you know?" he replied grinning. "This is the famous bombardment and capture of Manila."

Another signal was hoisted on the flagship. It read: "Examine southwest bastion carefully for white flag."

Soon a white flag was visible fluttering from the southwest bastion. The fierce bombardment, the brilliant assault by American troops, and the glorious, though unsuccessful, defense by Spanish troops, was over.

On my way back to the engine room I passed a hefty Negro [sic] fireman on one side of the port waist. He was sound asleep. I kicked his shins. "Get up, Higgins!" I said. "Have you no more respect for a battle than to sleep while it's going on?"

"I ain't got no respec' fo' this kind of battle, Mr. Beach!" replied Higgins, "an' I respec'fly reques' permission to go on with my sleep. This battle sure makes me sleepy!"

This was about all I knew of the battle, up to the time that a flag from the *Olympia* replaced the Spanish flag. I learned more later from a magazine article by Oscar King Davis, a reporter for the *New York Sun*.

The Spaniards had wished to surrender, but Spanish tradition would not allow this except when faced by an overwhelming hostile force. The Belgian consul to Manila, a Monsieur André, conducted negotiations between the Americans and the Spaniards, and this was the result.

But the Filipinos were unhappy. Except those already in the City of Manila, no Filipinos were permitted inside. It was current talk (and I believe correct) that the Filipino army had anticipated an orgy of looting. This, it was believed, had made the Spaniards eager to surrender the city to our commodore and General Wesley Merritt of the Army.

However that may be, Filipino soldiers became ugly in manner. A Filipino republic, headed by Emilio Aguinaldo, had been proclaimed. Under that intrepid and remarkably successful leader, the Filipinos defeated the Spaniards everywhere in the archipelago, except for Manila and Cavite, the two places clearly taken by American forces. Though thousands of American soldiers crowded Manila, our sentries stopped at the outskirts of the city, and there Filipino sentries began. Soon they became offensive in speech and manner. No longer did the American officer receive a salute when he passed a Filipino sentry. He was more likely to hear the words, "Yankee Pig!" It became necessary to give our people stringent orders of restraint to prevent pitched battles in the streets of Manila.

Meanwhile the Filipino troops continued their successes. One Spanish fort after another succumbed to their smashing attacks, or, it must be admitted, to starvation or the imminent prospect of the same. By December 1898, except for Manila, the arsenal at Cavite (seven miles away), and the Spanish fort at Baler (about two hundred miles northeast of Manila), the Filipinos were in complete military control of all parts of the Archipelago, with its hundred thousand square miles and a population of over seven million. Intrepid Filipino troops had secured this, with little help from us.

Then came the peace conference at Paris, in December 1898, by which Spain ceded the Philippines to the United States, and we handed Spain twenty million gleaming dollars for what no one in America has ever clearly understood. Was it for Manila and Cavite? Or was it for the vast area of the islands never touched by American forces and formally surrendered by Spanish officers to the Republica Filipina? It is true that these successes were largely in consequence of conditions brought about by American military operations. But nonetheless the bald fact is that Spain ceded to the United States sovereignty over territory she had already surrendered, in great part, to the inspired army of the Philippine Republic.

Perhaps the Filipinos were amazed when they heard of this treaty. They must have thought that, by the rules of war, what they had captured belonged to them as conquerors. One thing, however, they did not fail to grasp: they did not belong to the union. They were "scab" workmen.

And so they declared war against the United States. A more hopelessly gallant, ignorant, pitiful war was never waged by any people. Of course they were conquered. Their strongholds were taken by American troops. Their armies were smashed. Their great leader, Aguinaldo, was captured.

But the real conquerors of the Filipino people were not soldiers, but some three thousand young American women: school teachers. They penetrated to every part of the islands, and they conquered the people by winning them over. A remarkable result of their work is that the average Filipino of today speaks Tagalog, Ilocan, or Visayan; and in addition, not Spanish, but English.

My opinion of the Filipino people, formed by fighting in company with them and against them, by living among them, by having many friends among them, is that they are entitled to admiration and respect. They have developed great leaders, some eminent in the sciences and in the professions. After talking with Filipinos of any class, one is sure to be impressed, on the whole, with their intelligence, their earnestness, their patriotism, and their high aspirations. Admiral Dewey was quoted as saying, in a congressional investigation, that the Filipinos were fully as capable of self government as the Cubans. Having also traveled some, I would add to that comparison a number of folk besides the Cubans.

In my autobiography (*Salt and Steel: Reflections of a Submariner,* Annapolis: Naval Institute Press, 1999) and one or two other places, I've described Father's friendship with Emilio Aguinaldo, which stemmed from a chance encounter with his wife. Years after both had retired from public life, they exchanged occasional correspondence. I remember seeing at least one letter, and possibly more, from the Filipino leader. In his various writings, Father made considerable effort to tell the story of the Filipino insurrection fairly and accurately. One of his books, the novel *Midshipman Ralph Osborn at Sea,* published in 1910, was essentially devoted to a sympathetic examination of the hopeless war waged against us by that would-be independent country. The Philippines could not understand how Spain could "cede" them to the United States immediately after their successful revolution. They declared war on us, and we overwhelmed them with superior force— but it took three years. In this book, the chivalry Father showed Mrs. Aguinaldo when he accidentally "captured" her (described in *Salt and Steel*) is fictionalized to the point that his hero saves her from drowning, instead of merely redirecting her party away from its inadvertent intrusion into our lines. But the incident did happen, though less dramatically than in Dad's novel, and it did earn Aguinaldo's gratitude.

It is also true that Father was once captured by Filipino forces, as was Ralph Osborn. In the novel, Ralph found himself surprisingly protected by special order of the Filipino leader, who ultimately assisted him to "escape" and return to his ship. In true life, after his capture, Dad was immediately returned to our lines by direct order of the Filipino leader. In my small opinion, the actual incident was dramatic enough to have gone into the novel exactly as it happened. I never understood why Father felt it necessary to fictionalize it so much. Perhaps he believed a true occurrence should not be described in a novel by a participating officer of the Navy still on active duty. Perhaps there were other pressures on him, but, in any case, the foregoing are the true as well as the fictional facts.

II

A BEACH VIEW OF THE
FILIPINO INSURRECTION

But I must finish my Manila tale. Soon after our heroic assault that overwhelmed Manila's Spanish defenders, Hot Foot Dyer became so explosive that he was impossible. The intensity of his angry rages, paroxysms in fact, gradually increased.

We were not so much disturbed by what he said, so much as by his manner, his high voice, his overwhelming rage, the convulsive workings of his facial features. His denunciations became terrific. He seemed to be always about the decks, and always, with clenched fists, on a dead run. He was unbearable, and constantly grew worse. Every one of us, officers and enlisted men, was hit somehow, sometimes actually struck with his fists. And, one day, a new development occurred. After a violent admonition or order, he burst into uncontrollable sobbing. From then on, nearly every outbreak was followed by an outburst of wild weeping. On the second day of this, Dr. George Pickrell, now the *Baltimore*'s senior surgeon, made some report that was received with a Niagara of tears.

"Captain Dyer," said Pickrell, "you are a sick man. You should not be on duty, and I must inform you that you are now on the sick list. I shall call for a board of medical survey."

"Do you mean you are taking me away from the command of my ship, sir?"

"Yes, sir; you will go to bed immediately!"

And just this simply can the surgeon of a ship, if endowed with Pickrell's firmness, depose a captain or an admiral. But let him be careful how he uses his power! Admiral Dewey sent over Dr. Isaac W. Kite, unofficially, to request Pickrell not to ask for the survey.

"Go in and see Captain Dyer!" said Pickrell.

Kite was convinced; the board met; and it found that Dyer was suffering from a complete nervous and physical breakdown. It recommended that he be detached and sent home immediately.

By this time, all the officers and men of the *Baltimore* were on edge. Like those aboard the other ships, we had performed extremely arduous duty, day and night in extremely hot weather. We were minus all the convenient "strip ship" items we had left floating in the Pacific before the famous battle. I even missed the wooden bulkheads that formerly enclosed Darkest Africa. For months we had been suffering all the deprivations the unusual conditions entailed. Dyer's violence, capping the climax, daily getting worse, had aroused intense feelings of injury.

Therefore, when "Polly" Briggs, our executive officer, came to us and said the captain was detached, we were anything but sorry. We were too full of our own feelings to realize how ill Dyer was.

The next morning, when Briggs announced that the captain would leave in two hours, and that the officers and crew would be assembled to bid him an official farewell, we officers had a quiet talk. Our feeling of injury was so strong that we each and all agreed, the moment the captain emerged from his cabin, when by routine we would be standing in line at attention, each of us would raise his right hand to the salute and look straight ahead. Not one of us would lower his hand to shake hands when the captain passed. Briggs knew of this. He argued, expostulated, and finally swore at us. But we were adamant.

In a short time, all hands were called to quarters and marched aft. Officers reported their divisions, then fell into line on the quarterdeck. The boatswain reported, "All up and aft, sir!" and took his place in line.

Briggs sent for Boatswain's Mate, First Class, "Mickey" Locke.

"Locke," said he, "our captain is sick. He is leaving the ship. As he goes over the side, I'd like you to pipe 'three cheers' for him."

"I'm sorry, Mr. Briggs, sir," replied Locke, "but you'll have to excuse me, sir. I'm short of breath when it comes to piping for the captain, sir. I'd choke if I tried to pipe three cheers for him, sir. You must get some other boatswain's mate; but they'd all strangle trying to pipe cheers for the captain. And anyway, you'll not find a man in this ship's company that'll cheer for him, no matter what you say. You don't know how he has howled and yelled at us. No, sir. I couldn't pipe a single cheer for Captain Dyer!"

Briggs went to the cabin with tears in his eyes, and soon reappeared with Captain Dyer. Not one of us shook hands with him. But something else happened—and this was the second time I felt Dyer's ability to inspire men, whether he was sick or not.

There was never so still a minute as when he slowly walked out of his cabin. Near the end of the engine room hatch he stopped and looked about. To his right were the officers, each with his right hand at the salute; before him, the four hundred men of the crew. These were his own men whom he had led into battle. His left hand picked the glasses from the hook on his blouse; slowly his bent arm went up. He looked to the right; and then his eyes roved over the men before him. An oppressive stillness seemed everywhere. Some inexplicable feeling clutched me. My heart began to thump.

"Men of the *Baltimore*," he began, "just a few words of appreciation, and then I'll say good-bye. I am an old man now; I have fought a good fight; I have kept the faith. I have finished my course." These were halting, hesitating words.

And then he began to speak of the year we had been together; of storms weathered; of battles fought together. Soon his voice rang out clear and penetrating. Gone was the hesitation; again our lionhearted captain stood before us. Once more that noble heart was in complete control of itself. Down went our hands from the salute. Forgotten were the hurts we had received, as we yielded to a spontaneous, burning eloquence. The feeling that throbbed in the captain's words found its way straight into our hearts.

Suddenly he stopped. Then, in halting words, he said, "Men, I have not been well of late. I fear I have been harsh. My last word is to ask you to forgive me, and never to doubt my love for you."

With these last words he broke down completely. Tears gushed from his eyes as from a fountain; he sobbed convulsively.

Where now was Mickey Locke? On top of the engine room hatch frantically piping for cheers, with no one listening to him. Officers and men were shouting and weeping. Hundreds of men, reacting to a sudden, violent, deep emotion, were creating a wild uproar. Never before nor since, in my naval experience, have I seen such a display of feeling. We were completely his again. We'd have followed him anywhere, and now, knowing of his disability, we'd have supported him all the way.

Some time before this, the expected outbreak of the Filipinos had occurred. On the night of 4 February 1899, in the Santa Mesa district, about four miles from the walled city of Manila, a single shot was immediately followed by thousands of others.

The Filipinos were occupying a trench built and previously held by the Spaniards. Curving around Manila, it was seventeen miles long. In it the Filipinos fought with desperate bravery, but to no avail. The ships in the bay, including the monitors *Monterey* and *Monadnock* with 12-inch and 10-inch guns, hurled hundreds of big shells into the area occupied by the Filipino troops. The next morning that trench was a long, long grave.

The Navy's problem was now to prevent the smuggling in of arms and ammunition for the Filipino army, and to prevent export of hemp, except by license. The *Baltimore* was sent to Lingayen Gulf, where we did some tiresome blockading. From there we fired many shots, but, so far as I know, killed only one black crow. This was before Sims revolutionized gunnery practice in the Navy.

In *Midshipman Ralph Osborn at Sea,* Father devotes considerable space to a discussion of hemp. Today it is a source of marijuana, but in those days it was practically the only fiber for manufacture of marine cables, strong ropes, or lines of any kind. It grew in profusion in the Philippines, and had become a principal income producer. In what the United States called the "Philippine Insurrection," the natives' rebellion against the takeover of their country, hemp was listed as contraband.

On our return to Cavite late in 1898, I was detached from the *Baltimore* and sent as chief engineer to the Navy's yard there. My new commandant was Captain Leutze. I do not know German, but if Leutze means "efficiency," he was correctly named. Having repeatedly been subject to his orders before, I knew what to expect. Each morning I was in my office by 6:29; at 6:30 he invariably looked in to see if I was there. He usually had a vast amount of work in hand: extensive repairs on all of the ships, which kept me hopping; and the never-ending unloading of coal from four colliers into barges.

For the officers and enlisted men who worked intelligently and hard, Leutze was the kindest captain imaginable. But he had one fault that, to a sluggard, was unpardonable. He had a clear knowledge of every job under way, and knew, in minute detail, what daily progress was made. He was never bluffed; if dissatisfied, he left no room for doubt. When hurried repairs were being made on ships about to leave, I knew him too well to remind him that I had worked hard all day and would have to work hard all night.

My master mechanic, Gomez, was a skilled machinist and most efficient foreman. He maintained strict discipline by means of a club he carried, and with which, whenever he came across a bad job, he rapped the head of the Filipino workman responsible.

The master boilermaker was Chinese, with Chinese workmen who seemed slavishly anxious to please him. It was easy to understand this maestro, who could build boilers as well as repair them. When I would bring a job to him, he would say, after patient deliberation, either "Can do" or "No can do." And to change his decision was like moving the Rock of Gibraltar.

After some months at Cavite, I was ordered to the gunboat *Helena*. We cruised about, destroying small craft, hemp, and unlicensed hemp warehouses. Occasionally we found cause to fire some of our ship's guns, but usually the mere visible presence of our little warship was all that was needed. I was now a lieutenant junior grade, and the amalgamation of the line and engineering corps, that my old engineering board in the *Puritan* had denounced as nefarious and vicious, had made me eligible for line as well as engineering duties.

Along with other warships, we were looking for the *Alva*, a good sized vessel smuggling war supplies in to Aguinaldo, and running hemp out. Near us, at one time, was the former small Spanish gunboat, *Callao*, now commanded by Ensign Luke McNamee. Instead of the USS *Massachusetts Institute of Technology*, which Dewey had suggested, all American sailors called this miniature warship the "*Calamity Jane*," a name she sometimes deserved.

One night McNamee sighted a steamer plowing along. As a shot under her bow had no effect, McNamee put one into her stern. The ship stopped and anchored. Soon a British captain, boiling with wrath, came aboard the *Calamity Jane*. He had his license papers with him. Shaking his fist at McNamee, he threatened him with all manner of dire consequences. He proposed to find out what the British government and the British navy intended to do when a British ship, commanded by an officer of the British Naval Reserve, was fired into outrageously and without cause.

McNamee had a worried night. As he well knew, the British government does not make light of such occurrences. The next morning he donned his $240 dress uniform (which smelled terribly of camphor), and, equipped with gold fringed epaulets, cocked hat, sword, and stained white gloves, got into a boat and boarded the British steamer.

"Will you please tell your captain," said McNamee, "that the senior U.S. officer in this locality wishes to speak with him?"

The British captain came up quickly. "God Almighty!" he exclaimed, as he reached his visitor's side. "What the divil does this mean? In Hivin's name, what be ye up to now?"

"Sir," replied McNamee, "I am the senior United States officer in these waters. You are the senior British naval officer in the same. I have learned with great personal regret that the commanding officer of an American gunboat carelessly and with misguided zeal fired last night into the British ship under your command. I have come, sir, in my official capacity, to express to you, and to her Britannic Majesty, the regrets I am sure my government would feel should it learn of last night's action by an overzealous young officer."

"Good God!" ejaculated the British captain, "Do ye mane to tell me ye have appointed yerself invoy extraordinary and minister plenipotentiary av yer government in this region?"

"Yes, sir—but for this occasion only. And I sincerely hope you will accept the regret that my government would surely have, which, in its name, as senior officer here, I express to you; and that you will not consider it necessary to go further in the matter. Consider, sir: your government is engaged in war in South Africa. If it should be cabled to the world that an American warship had fired into you, this fact would kick up an immense rumpus; strained relations might follow; the overzealous young officer might be court-martialed and dismissed! All this just to make some British lord feel good, bad cess to him! Now, sir, would it not be far better for me, representing the U.S. government, to tender to you, representing Victoria, of the Kingdom of Great

Britain and Ireland, and of the British Dominions beyond the Seas, by the grace of God, Queen, the regret my government would surely have should it learn of what happened last night? I'm quite certain it would be far better for the overzealous young officer referred to."

The speaker grinned. A broad smile was now on the face of the British captain. "What's yer name?" he asked suddenly.

"McNamee."

"Ha! I knew it! I knew it!" cried the captain. "By my soul, ye're Mac-na-Mee—Mac, son of Mee! Mac, me bye, ye're from ould Ireland! I knew it!"

"My father was. I'm a grandson of old Ireland."

The British captain exploded with uncontrolled laughter. "'Tis the best I've iver heard in me life!" he shouted. "A grandson av ould Ireland shoots into a steamship av Queen Victoria. And now a ripresintative av the United States expresses the regret his country would have felt if it heard about it! He thinks she'd better not hear about it, because it would make bad feeling between the countries, and might cause trouble to this grandson av ould Ireland!

"Mac, me bye, as ripresintative av Queen Victoria, God bless her! I accept the regrets tendered by you fer yer government.

"And now, Mac, son of Mee, you and I are going into my cabin; and we'll drink confusion to the inemies av ould Ireland, and damnation for any man who'd make trouble for the son av Mee!"

I feel sure that now, after thirty years, it is safe to tell the story of how this young ensign, with signal success, entered the diplomatic field; and that a distinguished admiral, Mac, son of Mee, will not now be court-martialed for once, in misguided zeal, putting a shell into a British steamer.

12

THE OLD NAVY

Sailing in a Square Rigger

Except in the case of commanding officers, the cruise of a naval officer, by long custom, though not by regulation, is for three years. Then he is entitled to three months' leave (if he can get it), followed usually, though not always, by shore duty.

Thus it happened that in January 1900, I found myself in the United States once more. While busy deciding what shore duty I would like, I was suddenly ordered, two weeks later, to sea duty aboard my old ship, the USS *New York*. Such unexpected orders, often by telegraph, are a feature of naval duty not much relished by officers or by their wives, who often find their own plans utterly upset overnight.

This is only the second mention of Father's first wife, Lucie, whom he married in 1895. They were married twenty years and had no children. Lucie died of breast cancer in 1915. I was curious about her, and he freely answered my questions, so that I truly felt I knew her. As I wrote in *Salt and Steel*, she was a vital and understanding woman who helped him write his novels about Navy life, "followed the ship" whenever she could (in those days it was not uncommon for naval wives, if not encumbered with small or school-age children, to do this), lived alone for long months when his ship was on a cruise, and always welcomed him home with a loving embrace. Her maiden name was Quin, and it was no accident that Father's last book was called *Dan Quin of the Navy*, nor, for that matter, that both *Run Silent, Run Deep* and *Dust on the Sea* had in them a character—a yeoman, as was Dan Quin—named "Quin."

Lucie had an older sister, to whom she was devoted, who obviously reciprocated the feeling. Father once asked me, after I had entered the Naval Academy, to write to her. Her response to my letter was an invitation to visit her in her retirement home in New York state, where I found a warm and gracious little old lady, full of stories about Lucie. Evidently she thought of me as the son Lucie might have had, and passed on to me all the affection she still held for her long gone sister. Thinking to please me, she had rented a rowboat for me on a nearby lake, but lacked the confidence to embark in it herself. For part of that day I therefore rowed around in front of the resort, remaining in sight of the huge covered porch from which she watched. Finally I thankfully returned the boat to its mooring and followed her into the house for dinner. In return, I invited her to come see me graduate from Annapolis, but she declined on grounds of age, and died about a year later.

These particular orders were very pleasing to me. First, because I would go as a lieutenant of the line, and gain needed experience in deck and gun duties; second, the *New York* had a fine gift library, and on my previous cruise I had failed to read some of the several thousand volumes it contained. So I gladly rejoined this fine armored cruiser, which was still new, and was immediately detailed as a watch and turret officer, and as assistant navigator. On the afternoon of the day I reported I was told by Lieutenant Commander Murdock, the ship's executive officer, that next morning I was to command a battalion of

Marines and bluejackets ordered to march several miles to the military funeral of Captain C. P. Howell.

"Are you ready?" asked Murdock, no doubt fully aware of my previous "engineering only" experience.

"I certainly am," I replied.

I had put in eight years in engine and fire rooms, and by a blessedly nefarious law had just been transferred to deck duties. During the previous eight years I had been wandering about in a most unmilitary way with an oil squirt can in one hand and a bunch of waste in the other. Now I was ordered to perform the duties of the major of a battalion.

But I was determined to accept any such orders that might come. That night I spent long hours studying Fullam's "Revised Small Arms Instructions," which seemed easy and simple enough. Next day I took command of my force of several hundred men with perfect confidence. General Napoleon Bonaparte himself could not have given commands with more volume and decision. It was "Battalion! For-WARD—March!" "Fours RIGHT—March!" "Right shoul-DER—hahms!" "BATTALION—Halt!" "BATTALION, pre-SENT—hahms!"

I had an excellent, efficient aide, Naval Cadet Edgar B. Larimer. I did well with my first line assignment, but must confess that now and then I received a nudge from this faithful aide.

We marched to Chopin's "Funeral March." Next day a New York daily said the battalion had marched to an old, familiar air, "Somebody's Coming When the Dewdrops Fall." One cannot blame the reporter. Chopin probably heard this good old tune before writing the "Funeral March."

For some ten months my cruise on the *New York* was the happiest of my career. I was filled with an intense ambition to become efficient in my new duties. I had received the ground work at Annapolis, had performed sea duties of the line as a naval cadet in the *Richmond*, and had always, in my engineering work, been in close contact with deck officers. I did not feel strange in my new duties because, in the main, they were old duties. Moreover, I was aboard a ship I knew well.

My turret, containing two 8-inch guns, was a bundle of complicated mechanisms, but I was at home handling machinery, whether in a turret or in an engine room. The drilling of my turret crew, the hoisting up of ammunition, the loading of the guns, seemed the most natural thing in the world. We had drills all day long, mornings and afternoons. Morning drills were at gunnery, the afternoon drills went to sailing and rowing. I had never before had anything easier than a watch in three, which entailed four hours on and eight off, day and night. But aboard the *New York* we had five officers to stand watch, which meant four hours on and sixteen hours off. I thus had plenty of time for study, and never felt tired. From the standpoint of routine duties, nothing could have been more satisfactory than my situation in the *New York*.

With this was my pride in serving aboard a fine ship. And there were other conditions tending to make me happy. Our admiral was Norman H. Farquhar. To know him was to admire and to love him, to be proud of serving under his orders. From all his squadron officers he demanded devotion to duty; from each ship, high efficiency. At the same time he was very considerate of his subordinates. Unlike Admiral Meade, he was quite willing to allow off-duty officers to enjoy the port side of the quarterdeck after dinner.

Seconding him in every purpose was his aide, Lieutenant W. S. Benson, who later earned distinction as the senior admiral of the Navy in charge of naval operations during the World War.

World War refers to the first war, World War I, the Great War as it was sometimes called.

Our captain was A. S. Snow, who was always efficient, always kindly, always quiet. His purpose seemed to be to secure team action. The executive officer, as previously mentioned, was Murdock. He habitually attended drills, and later, in a conversational way, would discuss points that could be improved upon. The results were excellent. Our navigator was C. C. Rogers. I was with him hours every day, whenever I was not on watch or at drills. By the end of nine months I was quite certain I had brushed up all I had ever studied in navigation; and to that I had added much practical knowledge.

One of the officers was Ensign John Halligan Jr., number one graduate of the Naval Academy class of 1898, who became the engineer in chief of the Navy before his early death in 1934.

We had with us, by courtesy to Greece, a midshipman of that country named de la Gorgas. The latter was always a subject of amused interest. He would observe, with his sextant, the altitudes of the sun, moon, planets, and stars, then rush to his room to work out the ship's position. But no one ever saw his results. He spent hours daily taking notes that he said were for the navy department of his country. We would have enjoyed seeing these notes because everything he saw filled him with enthusiastic astonishment and admiration.

Every night our wardroom dinner, with twenty odd officers at the long table, seemed a banquet. The genial friendship and mutual interests that pervaded the *New York* seemed to reach their apex at the dinner table. The work of the day was done; but the details, full of interest, were recounted.

One night de la Gorgas suddenly called out, "Mr. Halligan, I see in your signature, after your name, always the letters 'Jr.' Where do you get those letters?"

"From my father."

"What! Did you inherit this title from your father?"

"Yes, indeed; and my father from his. He was also John Halligan, junior."

"Was your father a nobleman?"

"De la Gorgas, he was in every sense a noble man."

"We Greeks have been deceived!" shouted de la Gorgas. "We have been led to believe you had no inherited titles of nobility in America. I shall report this matter to my country." And with blazing eyes, de la Gorgas jumped up and rushed to his room. Evidently, this information was of immense importance.

Cruising south, we visited many of the West India islands. Soon enough, our fellow American citizens will surely realize that the most beautiful, delightful, fertile, tropical islands in the world are only a few hours by airplane from U.S. shores.

Every hour I spent on this fine ship was serene. I felt that I never wanted to leave her. But things happen quickly in the Navy.

We reached Newport, Rhode Island, in the fall of 1900. Near us, when we had anchored, lay a small and ugly sailing vessel used by the Navy Department for special service. I strolled over to the rail and remarked to the officer of the deck, "Knockie, I'm sorry for the fellows who have to serve on that miserable old tub."

He looked embarrassed. "I was about to send for you, Beach," he replied. "I'm sorry as Hell, but I've got to hand you these orders." And then and there he handed me an order from the Navy Department detaching me from the *New York* and directing me to report for duty aboard "that miserable old tub."

While writing this portion of his autobiography over thirty years after the events that took place on "that miserable old tub," Father chose not to identify the ship by name. Nor did he identify the captain, the executive officer, and nearly all the other officers and men. His reasoning may be guessed. The old adage says, "If you can't say anything good about someone or something, it's best to hold your tongue." There were so many things wrong with this ship that she must have been a terrible embarrassment to all U.S. Navy people who knew of her. Her captain must have been well known as an unscrupulous "sundowner" to have been given such a demeaning command, was doubtless bitter about that, and then proved his own total unfitness and mental instability by the way he handled his crew. At the time Father wrote this, both ship and sundowner captain were long gone from the Navy list. No good could come from identifying either, and some bad might come of it from some possibly deranged descendant.

There has been, I believe, a radical change in the attitude of naval captains toward their officers. Histories, sea tales like those of Frederick Maryatt, and court-martial records have given me that impression. In sailing ship days the captain was sometimes a despot.

For example, take the 1842 action of Captain Alexander Slidell MacKenzie in willfully hanging, without court-martial, and with little justification,

Midshipman Philip Spencer, Boatswain's Mate Cromwell, and Seaman Small, three victims of his distrust.

Or take the case of Commodore B—— after whom a destroyer has been named. In 1822 he was reported by Lieutenant Joel Abbot, on duty under him at the Boston Navy Yard, for as flagrant graft as Tammany Hall has ever been charged with. Abbot accused the commodore of using Navy yard workmen, naval material, and naval teams, to build houses outside the yard on his personal property. Abbot also accused him of drawing and pocketing the pay of more than two hundred workmen who had died or had been discharged, and of granting officers leave in exchange for money. Apparently these charges were well founded; at least, B——, while denying some of them, merely pleaded ignorance of the facts on others. Certainly his plea is amusing in the light of modern naval methods and standards. But it was quite good enough for the Board of Navy Commissioners, who duly and solemnly accepted it. Then they court-martialed poor Abbot on twenty-nine counts; chiefly, one suspects, for his temerity in exposing the peculations of the mighty.

In 1812, of his own accord, Commodore David (*Essex*) Porter conducted an amazing campaign of conquest of the Marquesas Islands, in the Pacific, and solemnly annexed them to the United States. Twelve years later the same doughty commodore, again without instructions, landed troops at Fajardo, Puerto Rico, seized forts, and captured the city—leading, naturally, to strained relations with Spain. In 1847, Commodore M. C. Perry prepared a plan for the capture, with his entire fleet, of certain forts and cities south of Vera Cruz. He sent a young captain to make a reconnaissance, and the young captain proceeded to take, with his one ship, all the forts and cities that were to have fallen to Perry's thirty-odd ships. For this act of *lèse majesté*, Perry had the young officer tried and dismissed from the naval service.

Captains could, and continually did, have sailors flogged with the cat o' nine tails. Not until 1851 was flogging in the Navy abolished by an Act of Congress.

In sailing ship days our officers were competent seamen, as, in a different sense, they are today. But in those days the only powers aboard ship were wind, muscle, and the determined wills of the officers. Now in addition to a captain's determined will, thirty thousand horsepower can be put into action by throwing a lever or pressing a button.

Sailing ships frequently acted singly, and were away for years at a time. And the captain, out of reach of telegraph, or of radio—and often of mail—was at least a potentate and sometimes a despot. Naval tradition has it that once, years before the Civil War, the sloop-of-war *St. Mary's* cruised two years in the South Pacific without mail of any kind.

The captain of the sailing ship to which I was now suddenly transferred was of the old school. He would, I think, have been more at home in the days of absolute naval monarchs than in the year 1900, when he was merely the agent of the Navy Department and almost constantly in touch with higher authority. In his fifties, he was vigorous mentally and physically. His personal character was high. In normal society, he was said to be witty, jovial, and friendly. This ship was his first command. His aim, I am sure, was the highest possible efficiency. But his rigid insistence on the methods and atmosphere of a bygone day put him out of joint with modern naval thought and conditions. I had never seen him before, nor, so far as I remember, had I heard him discussed.

In a few days we set sail for England. My spirits rose. It was grand again to shout through a speaking trumpet: "Reef topsails!" "Stand by to lay aloft topmen!" "Man the topsail clewlines and buntlines! Weather topsail braces!"—and all the other orders that the roar of machinery had almost driven from my mind.

The day we sailed the executive officer handed each of the five watch officers a program, made out by the captain, of drills, exercises, inspections, other divisional work, and navigation work with the sun during the day and with the moon, stars, and planets at night. "It'll keep you busy, Beach," said the executive officer with a grin.

"That's a fine program!" I replied. "Hello—we're going into old-time as well as ultra-modern work. We're to correct chronometers by lunar distances and to work out sights by the new Aquino and Marc St. Hilaire methods as well as by Sumner and Johnson. But with five officers standing watch we can swing it."

"Only four," corrected the executive officer. "The captain thinks a watch in five makes an officer soft."

Nonetheless, I was content; I was glad to have work and experience that I needed. But my contentment faded. During many day watches while I was handling sail, the captain stood by my side and constantly criticized me. Of course, criticism was deserved and even necessary, for no man can be away from sails for eight years without forgetting details; but his biting, scornful contempt killed my joy. The only salve to my self-respect was that all his other officers got the same treatment.

One day the executive had the speaking trumpet during an "all hands" sail drill. He was a master in the art of handling sail. Orders roared from his trumpet automatically, with no apparent thought on his part, and with the sure touch of a Paderewski at the piano. The captain, at his side, made a contemptuous criticism. The executive stopped short, regarded him with a peculiar expression, and said, offering him the trumpet, "I must request you to have me relieved, sir." He was not relieved; nor was he ever again, to my knowledge, criticized by the captain.

That night, at mess, another officer started to speak of the occurrence. The executive slammed his fist on the table. "I forbid criticism or discussion of any kind!" And never after that did I hear any open discussion of the captain in the wardroom.

Our chaplain, a devoted minister, was an elderly man near the age of retirement. His feelings were hurt each Sunday after services. The captain would send for him, criticize the sermon, and inform him as to what he wanted preached. Soon the surgeon and the paymaster were also worried by orders that, they believed, in some respects violated detailed instructions laid down in Navy regulations.

Early in the cruise, when the captain had us pretty well by the ears, the navigator came to me. "Beach," he said, "we haven't known each other before, but I will ask you to believe that my feelings are friendly. I have thought to suggest, since you and other officers seem to feel badly about the captain's methods, that you be extremely careful. First, remember your duty to the Navy and to your captain. However you feel, never do anything to cause gossip or undermine his authority. Never discuss him except privately, and under no circumstances in the hearing of a servant or an enlisted man. It is your bounden duty, as an officer of our Navy, to be loyal to our captain. Your rights and his authority are completely laid down in the regulations. It is up to us to accept his methods and obey his orders cheerfully unless they are clearly against regulations. We must accept his opinions. As captain he is responsible for everything on board. If you have a serious complaint, go to him with it. Don't talk about it."

I was profoundly impressed. I had reason to believe that the navigator gave the same advice to others. We came to know that he had the mind, heart, and soul of a Robert E. Lee. During the long, lonely months that followed, he was of daily help in keeping our interest in our duties. He more than compensated for a disagreeable, inconsiderate captain.

I soon had occasion to make a complaint. One morning I had the watch from four to eight o'clock. We were bowling along on the starboard tack under plain sail to topgallant sails. Eighty boys, young sailors, only very recently enlisted in the Navy, were, as was customary, sleeping in the lee gangway, where they were available if needed, or if the watch were to be called. These were little fellows, some not over age fifteen. At six o'clock I gave an order to haul taut the weather braces. The boatswain's mate of the watch, Kelly by name, piped the order, and then, shouting "Turn out! Turn out!" physically ran over these sleeping boys, trampling them with heavy boots.

This was cowardly and brutal on Kelly's part. He would never have dared to trample on sleeping *men* in this way. Some of the little chaps were crying piteously; many were bruised; at least two were kicked in the head with these heavy boots. I stopped Kelly as quickly as I could, and, in no mild language, told him the brute he was.

After my watch, I went to the ship's office and, on the report book, entered against Kelly the charge of "brutality." Just before drill the captain sent for me. "What is this report of 'brutality' against Kelly?"

I told him. He answered, "Apprentice boys are here to learn; they have had a good lesson; tomorrow morning they won't need it. Cancel that report."

I made no reply.

"Do you understand me, sir?"

"Yes, sir, I understand you."

"This is an order."

Later in the morning the executive officer said to me, "The captain tells me he has ordered you to cancel your report against Kelly. 'Mast' will be held in a few minutes. Do you wish to withdraw your report?"

"I do not. So far as I am concerned, that report sticks. But suppose he orders you to take my report off the book? What will you do?"

"He would never dare to give me such an order! Be at the mast at 11:30. I'll have Kelly there, and will read the report. You had better have as witnesses two of the boys who got hurt. Who do you want?"

"Snyder and Steger."

A few minutes later the captain held mast. The executive officer read my report. The captain looked at me. Young Snyder and Steger, striplings perhaps fifteen or sixteen years old, stood beside me, their bruised faces and bloodied uniforms conclusive testimony to the trauma they had undergone. (Ordinarily, "inspection uniform" was the order of the day for "Captain's Mast." At my request, they wore, instead, the uniforms in which they had been injured.) The captain barely glanced at them, asked them no questions at all, but could not but have seen them, and must accurately have guessed why they were dressed the way they were. Then he turned back to me and paused. His eyes bored into mine: "Do you make this report, sir?"

"Yes, sir; I make this report against Kelly."

No other words were said. After an oppressive silence, Kelly was given two hours extra duty. Then, as expected, it was my turn. "Mr. Beach," ordered the captain, "Come to my cabin at one o'clock."

13

CARRYING OUT REGULATIONS

Before one o'clock I had done much thinking, and had carefully read the parts of the Navy regulations covering the duties and responsibilities of commanding officers and subordinate officers. Behind me were the experiences of seventeen years' service and personal convictions resulting from them. With this was an intimate knowledge of the experiences of other officers in our ship, always matters of intense interest to the others on board.

I realized that I was in opposition to my captain. This was a serious matter to any officer, because his record, upon which his assignments to duty, his promotion, in short his entire future, depend, is determined to a large extent by the reports of his commanding officers. These are by no means perfunctory. Twice a year, and when officers are detached, the captain answers a long list of detailed questions regarding each officer under him. He states whether the officer knows and carries out his duties well, whether he is expeditious and effective in any special situations that arise, and whether he is properly subordinate and respectful to officers assigned over him. The captain reports on whether a subordinate uses liquor to excess, fails to pay his debts, or has been guilty of any conduct unbecoming an officer and a gentleman, and whether he is clean and neat. He reports on his subordinate's relations with other officers and his control of enlisted men, as well as on his efficiency in getting work done.

Most important, he answers the question, "Would you object to having this officer again under your command?" Should he answer "yes," or in any other category describe him as unsatisfactory in any way, a special and full report is required, with a copy to the officer concerned, who must immediately submit, via the chain of command, his response to the unfavorable allegations.

I therefore fully realized the gravity of the situation. And before one o'clock I had determined my course, and prepared for it as well as I could. The interview that followed burned into my mind. Years afterwards it influenced my own actions as a commanding officer.

At one o'clock I was in the captain's cabin, facing an irate man. "Lieutenant Beach," he said, "this morning I gave you an order that you deliberately disobeyed. You have defied me, sir! I will listen to any statement you may wish to make before taking further action."

There was really but one thing the captain could do. He technically should relieve me from all duties, place me under arrest, and recommend that I be tried by general court-martial for "disobedience of the lawful orders of my commanding officer." The captain may also suspend an officer from duty for a period not longer than ten days; but such a punishment would not fit the offense of deliberate disobedience of orders, nor, of course, would a "private reprimand." I could not let him punish me privately, as it were, and then submit low-grade reports of my "fitness," which would hurt, or even ruin, my further career in the Navy. From these there could be no recourse, unless he was foolish enough to make the reports downright "unsatisfactory" and thus give me an avenue to challenge them.

The captain's words came like bullets. This was no mere conversation. He was very angry with me; he would take my scalp if he could. "What have you to say, sir?" he cried.

"Sir," I said, "I do not defy you. I earnestly wish to deserve and receive your good opinion. But I must speak frankly. I cannot believe you will take any further action in this matter. I would like to believe that what you call an 'order' was really the expression of a wish. I refused to accede to your wish, and I believe my action was entirely correct."

"I told you to cancel your report against Kelly and told you it was an order. You cannot pretend it was not an order, sir."

"Then, sir, it was an improper order. It is distinctly stated in the laws for the government of the Navy and in the oath taken by officers that the orders to be obeyed must be proper orders. Navy regulations require me to report such acts as Kelly's. The trampling on those boys was abominable cruelty that might have resulted in permanent injury, or a fractured skull, and death. You saw their injured condition this morning. What would happen to me, if, because I obeyed your improper order, one of the boys assigned to this ship was killed next time? I simply do not believe you will report me for disobedience of orders, since you technically justified my action by awarding Kelly a punishment for the offense."

As far as reporting me was concerned, the captain was tied hand and foot, and he knew it. I could see the working of his face as he digested my carefully thought-out words. After a pause, he said with much feeling, "Mr. Beach, you displease me. You haven't the right attitude toward your captain. Because of this, I shall instruct you as to the relation that should exist between a captain and his officers. I have given my entire naval service to the study of command. This is the most important duty of an officer. The efficiency of a ship depends in every way upon efficiency in command. I want the highest possible efficiency. To assist me in producing it, the Navy Department assigns me officers for specified duties. To achieve it, my will must reign supreme. They must become automatons, surrendering to my will all their intelligence and skill. I am here to define and interpret naval regulations for you. I take all responsibility. You are merely an intelligent machine. You will consider these as instructions to guide you. That's all, sir."

I opened my mouth to speak, but the captain stopped me. "I desire to hear nothing further from you, sir," he said.

I saluted, turned, and left his cabin, still very worried. But I found that word of my confrontation with the captain had spread through our entire crew. No one knew what had gone on in the captain's cabin, but Kelly was well known as a brutal maverick, and the sick bay that treated some of his victims had no reason to keep secrets. The captain must have realized that he could not afford to have the affair become better known.

In narrating these incidents, my aim is to contrast the spirit of sailing ship days with that of today. As far as this ship was concerned, the captain, judging by his actions, owned it. His wishes dominated everybody and everything.

In his "sailor's log," speaking of the year 1863, Captain R. D. Evans says, "It is difficult to convince anyone today of how completely the captain ruled things in the time of which I am writing. There was no law off soundings beyond the captain's will, unless you had an admiral on board, when his will became the law."

Today the captain exercises even greater authority. More, in many respects, because his control of a thirty-five-thousand-ton battleship, with twelve 14-inch guns, many thousands of horsepower, and a crew of fifteen hundred men, involves responsibilities far greater than those of the captain of an old sailing ship of one thousand tons, crewed by two hundred men.

But today the captain acts as the agent of a Navy Department with which he is in communication every day. There are still many emergencies and conditions not covered by specific orders from the department; but, in general, his discretion is controlled. On the other hand, the old-time skipper's acts were largely expressions of his own will, and were often not known in the Navy Department from which his authority stemmed.

In 1822, Commodore Isaac Hull granted Lieutenant John Percival eighteen months' leave of absence without even reporting the fact. Today a captain may not usually (except in emergencies) grant even a week's leave. He must forward a request for leave to higher authority.

The captain of whom I am now writing embodied the spirit of a past century. Though I did not relish opposing his wishes, my own self-respect as an officer forced me at times to protest against some order he had given. In all of these painful interviews he insisted on his right to consider officers merely as rational machines. He would interpret all regulations; we were to be guided wholly by his directions. The only thing to consider was the "efficiency of the ship."

"You will find I'm a Juggernaut if you get in my way," he once remarked. "If you do that I'll run over you and crush you. If you sit down on watch, day or night, I'll have you court-martialed."

Most of his orders would have been upheld by the Navy Department, although some of his memorandum orders were very vexatious. For instance, when at anchor in port he would not usually allow boats to be run after 6 P.M. He wanted officers and men to return to the ship before dinner, fresh for the next day's duties (the origination of the term "sundowner"). When undergoing overhaul in a Navy yard he required "heel-and-toe" watches, the same as when under way. This effectively prevented his watch officers from going home very often. He told me once that he was not interested in officers' wives, who, during long cruises lasting sometimes as long as three years, have to starve their affections on shore alone, except for those happy occasions when their husbands' ships come into their home ports. Unless, that is, the captain desires everyone on board by 6:00 P.M., no matter where they are.

But one may not quarrel with one's captain over little things. An officer may always appeal to the Navy Department, but an officer who would so appeal must have a real grievance. The captain will never be upheld if violating regulations or inflicting cruel or insulting treatment. Nor is he allowed to ignore accepted customs of the service. But, on the other hand, it is the custom of the Navy Department to support the lawful actions of officers whom it has placed in responsible positions. And, as might be assumed, most of the burden of proof rests with the complaining officer.

Our captain was undoubtedly of high personal character, but he was utterly regardless of our wishes. He would look out for what he thought we needed, insofar as his ship was concerned, but there his interest stopped and he erected an impervious wall.

In closing my remarks about this captain, who must, of course, remain nameless, I cannot say too strongly that he was at opposite poles from most officers in the Navy. He was an irrational disciplinarian beyond all bounds, even for those early days, and he was at least a century too late. In his own way, he may have been trying to be "efficient," though his judgment about how to achieve this may bear some criticism. In my opinion, he was not vindictive, though I'll admit I worried about this. In fitness reports to the Navy Department, he gave me all I deserved. But though he might say he had no objection to my serving under him again (he did check me off in this category), I fear I could not reciprocate.

It's also possible that the captain was afraid of what Father might write in his obligatory response to the mandated Navy Department inquiry if the captain had not given satisfactory fitness reports.

Some time later I spent a week as the guest of another captain aboard the dreadnought *North Dakota*. It seemed to me that his officers were all "automatons, mere intelligent machines." There was only one difference: neither they nor the captain knew it. It came from his natural leadership. He had the full confidence and admiration of his officers and men, and of the crews of the 14-inch naval guns that he later commanded in France.

Midshipmen in battalion formation in front of "New Quarters" in 1879. This building, completed in 1869, was home to the Battalion of Midshipmen until 1906, when the first and second wings of imposing Bancroft Hall were completed. "New Quarters" faced away from the Severn River, dimly seen in the right background, not far from the Tripolitan Monument. The slightly heavier midshipmen in a more ragged formation with their backs to the camera are no doubt "passed midshipmen," now back at Annapolis for final exams after two years sea duty.

Courtesy of U.S. Naval Academy

The USS *Constellation*, our second ship of that name, preparing to get under way. Naval cadets, all in uniform whites, are crowding the masts and yards. These lads are clearly already experienced topmen, but today's parents might look askance at similar training. Note the *Constellation*'s rounded stern, a nineteenth-century innovation. Father made his first midshipman cruise in this fine old ship at age seventeen, and she can be seen today, preserved at her permanent mooring in Baltimore.

U.S. Naval Institute Collection

A traditional photo of the class about to graduate, 1888 in this case, posed annually until wear and tear on Tecumseh, so-called in naval cadet lore, forced the academy to discontinue the practice in favor of the present bronze "God of 2.5" (the minimum passing grade). Cadet Beach is hanging off the statue near Tecumseh's head *(far left)*, fingers turned upward at his waistcoat. Distinguished classmates shown include future Commandant of the Marine Corps Lejeune, Fleet Commander Robison, Chief of Naval Operations Hughes, and Secretary of the Navy Wilbur.

Courtesy of U.S. Naval Academy

Graduating year photo of members of the class of 1888 showing off various athletic and official uniforms. On the far right is S. S. Robison, later fleet commander. C. F. Hughes, later chief of naval operations, is fourth from right. The equally tall midshipman with his left hand on Hughes's right shoulder is Curtis D. "Magical Mike" Wilbur, later secretary of the Navy. The extremely short midshipman standing just in front of Wilbur is Albert L. Norton, reputedly the shortest midshipman ever graduated (his annual physical exam allegedly included a rap on the head with a broom handle). Third from right is Frank Marble in midshipman's full dress wearing a regulation sword without tassel, since he is not yet a "passed midshipman." Father, with a sheathed fencing saber and a truculent look (he didn't like Marble and always beat him in fencing), is right behind him.

Courtesy of U.S. Naval Academy

As a "passed midshipman," Father was assigned to the obsolete but still hand-some Civil War steam sloop *Richmond*. Life aboard was never pleasant, though he grew to admire his somewhat peculiar captain. In 1890, when he returned to the Naval Academy for final examinations, he was amazed at how much he had benefited during the period, having become a true seaman and engineer, and above all, an experienced naval officer.

U.S. Naval Institute Collection

With an officer's tassel hanging from the hilt of his dress sword, Father is shown here as a full-fledged naval officer in the rank of Passed Assistant Engineer. The photo is from 1893 or 1894, and it was in this capacity that he fought at Manila Bay.

U.S. Naval Institute Collection

ALTIMORE SEP'T. 18-1900 —

683

In his memoir, Dad wrote about his participation in the 1 May 1898 Battle of Manila Bay in the cruiser *Baltimore*, shown here after the war, flying the traditional long homeward-bound pennant. His chapter on the battle is puckishly titled "The Battle of Irwin's Boots" because Assistant Engineer Beach's station was in an engine room, and he could see only upward through a heavy grating, upon which, tramping back and forth, were the boots of Ensign Noble Irwin, directing the fire of his broadside battery. Dad reported, however, that from beneath the grating, inspired by demands for "more news from the battle," he "sank" more enemy ships than anyone else.

U.S. Naval Institute Collection

Note the direct lineage from Ericsson's *Monitor* of 1862. *Nevada*, launched in 1899, exhibits nearly all the flaws and some of the advantages of her famous predecessor: Battleship-sized turret and guns, a conning tower immediately abaft the huge turret (this was one of the lessons of the 1862 battle), and very low freeboard, so that the sea itself protected her vitals (this and the revolving turret were Ericsson's two great innovations). All, or nearly all, living spaces were now above the waterline with good ventilation (found during the

war to be vital). Defects were low power, extraordinarily slow speed, inability to withstand heavy seas, and a propensity for quick and heavy rolling. As our Navy began seriously looking seaward rather than simply defending our harbors, monitors quickly fell into disfavor and we began designing some real ships.

U.S. Naval Institute Collection

USS *Vestal* being converted into the Navy's first big repair facility afloat. The rather severe modifications had not yet begun (coaling derrick masts and cargo holds are still evident), which suggests that Dad had probably not yet reported aboard. The ship was obviously large and well-found, worthy of the adulation he lavished on her as a good repair ship (right up his alley), and as a substitute warship during war games, a task he enjoyed thoroughly.

U.S. Naval Institute Collection

In 1915 Father served as skipper of the fine armored cruiser *Washington* (CA-11). As the aiguillettes indicate, he was also chief of staff to Rear Admiral William B. Caperton, commanding the Caribbean Cruiser Force, as the United States worked to maintain peace during one of Haiti's most violent revolutions. Through Dad's knowledge of French, his natural sympathy for the downtrodden Haitian people, and Caperton's decision to maintain "splendid isolation" aboard his flagship (he did not speak French), Father became his superior's instrument for ending the bloodshed. With Caperton's guidance and the full support of the U.S. Department of State, Dad negotiated the first useful treaty between Haiti and the United States, which endured for twenty-four years. Far better for Haiti had it endured an entire century and given our Marines and other forces a real opportunity to rebuild the country.

U.S. Naval Institute Collection

This photo and the one on the facing page depict the same ship, about three years apart, bearing many if not all the changes decreed by Teddy Roosevelt. The white-and-buff colored *Tennessee (above)* can hardly maneuver her guns on deck efficiently without first moving lifeboats, ventilator, anchor gear, and much else. Under Roosevelt she was greatly cleaned up, as the photo on the right shows.

U.S. Naval Institute Collection

Whoever master-minded this job for Roosevelt obviously had a clear eye for what a fighting ship needs at sea. Note the installation of the "cage" mast, intended to be more damage resistant than the simple "pole" mast it replaced. This mast became a trademark of our fighting ships for thirty years.

U.S. Naval Institute Collection

In father's own hand appears under this picture a caption he himself wrote for it: "A Naval Officer's duties are sometimes varied." Playing baseball in the rain certainly qualifies for this accolade, but Dad looks ready to throw a mean curve all the same.

U.S. Naval Institute Collection

Father, Mother, and me as a baby, taken about December 1918.

THE KING
SHAKING HANDS
WITH U.S.
OFFICERS

THE PRINCE OF
WALES SHAKING
HANDS WITH
U.S. OFFICERS

Having come aboard for lunch, King George V of England, wearing the uniform of a fleet admiral, shakes hands with officers of the *New York*. Also present are Admiral Sims, head of the U.S. naval forces in Europe, Admiral Rodman, commander of the American squadron, my father a few steps down the line, and several others. British Admiral Beattie, commander of the British Grand Fleet, and most of his accompanying officers are ranged less formally along the rail facing the Americans, who are pretty much "toeing a seam" for them.

Beloved.

Father wrote a single word at the bottom of this picture of his first wife Lucie, but it covers his feeling for her. "Beloved," he wrote, and elsewhere I have a many-paged handwritten document in which he wrote a veritable paean to the wonderful qualities she brought to their marriage. They were married in 1895 and she died in his arms twenty years later; the Navy had to break a few rules to get him there in time but except for personal comfort nothing could be done. Sadly, they had no children, but many years later certain thoughtful actions of Lucie's sister, May, caused me to wonder whether she might have begun to look on me as the son her sister might have wished for.

Father retired from active duty in the Navy in 1922, and this picture must have been taken about that time. He was an affectionate father and always gave his children a goodnight kiss with his brisk and wiry mustache, for which I recall bracing myself. I don't recall when Dad finally gave up and shaved it off (Mother might have had something to do with that), but it disappeared during my formative years and I never missed it.

U.S. Naval Institute Collection

Father, in a freshly pressed uniform, welcoming a somewhat frowzier Admiral Rodman to Mare Island during the latter's "inspection visit" in 1921. Each man has already taken the measure of his adversary, but Rodman might not yet have understood how deeply Dad was committed to preserving Mare Island: he retired from active naval duty to free himself for an all-out battle with his superior. For such a fray, halfway measures simply will not do. Father, be it noted, exudes more confidence than Rodman, reflecting perhaps his greater degree of planning and commitment. By this time he had published thirteen books about the Navy, and he was about to accept the professorship in history that Stanford had recently offered him.

U.S. Naval Institute Collection

With considerable help and encouragement from Mother, Father put on his uniform especially for this picture with me, taken early in 1942. I had just attained the eminent rank of lieutenant (junior grade) after two and a half years as an ensign aboard the old "four-piper" destroyer *Lea* (DD-118), which had been launched—literally—the same day I was. Father was already showing mental deterioration, and he died in December 1943.

14

AN ANNAPOLIS PROFESSOR
AND BACK TO SEA

The U.S. Naval Academy at Annapolis in 1901 and 1902 served two important purposes: first, to teach midshipmen the technical knowledge required by their profession and second, to soak them in naval tradition. The naval atmosphere, like a thick fog, settled on the Academy walls and almost shut out the rest of the world.

Officers were strenuously employed in teaching and drilling midshipmen. But, coming from sea, what did they know of belles-lettres and the liberal arts? They knew the subjects they had applied at sea; but in other fields they knew about as much as the midshipmen they were to teach, and little more. I was assigned to the department of "English Studies, History, and Law," covering in its own way a large part of human knowledge. No midshipman studied harder than "Professor" Beach.

Even now, after thirty years, I know that (according to *Hill's Rhetoric*) the five requisites of good English are clearness, force, ease, strength, and unity. Fine. Of course I agree, and I'm sure this autobiography is full of all those things. History, however, became a permanent and ever-increasing joy. Midshipmen had to memorize the Constitution of the United States, section by section. I had to do the same, and I learned a lot. I taught international law, which has always fascinated me, and I learned a lot there, too.

Social life began where studies ended. Hundreds of calls were paid and returned. Week in and week out there were dinner parties; throughout the year there were balls and hops (less formal dances). There were football and base-ball games, meetings of various kinds, and occasional lectures. Officers' wives participated in most of these activities, even attended some lectures, if they were not too technical. It was a happy time for all of us.

Besides the discussion of weightier subjects, there was always plenty of naval gossip: officers detached, new arrivals, ships in and out, some officer court-martialed, some old Navy bachelor married; excitement over this episode, indignation over that. At the Academy in those days there was a tremendous amount of mental activity, all relating to naval matters. Naturally, every hour seemed jammed with thoughts of some pending duty, either offi-cial or social.

After a year of this, our splendid head of department, J. P. Parker, was sent to sea. His successor was a professor, a scholar of attainments, a graduate of Yale, who earnestly desired to raise the standard of English instruction. So, he adopted new textbooks. In place of Hill's excellent rhetoric, which, with the instruction available, midshipmen learned by rote without understanding a word of it, he chose a "practical rhetoric" that applied knowledge we did not have.

One book had quotations, each a page long, from celebrated writers, whose style midshipmen were called upon to imitate. It took but one of these lessons to knock me out.

"Mr. Smith," said I, "imitate Hawthorne's style; Mr. Jones, imitate Shakespeare's; Mr. Brown, imitate Lord Macauley; Mr. Williams, imitate George Bancroft; Mr. White, imitate Thomas Jefferson."

These young gentlemen went to the blackboards and wrote rapidly. After some minutes I examined what they had written.

"My God, Mr. Smith!" I asked with unconcealed scorn, "is this your con-ception of Hawthorne's style?"

"Yes, indeed, sir; I'm sure I've quite caught it."

"That's rotten stuff! Rub it out! Try again!"

"Mr. Jones, do you think your effusion bears the slightest resemblance to Shakespeare?"

"Yes, sir; if you examine closely you will detect a striking similarity."

"Mr. Jones, if Shakespeare were in this room, dead in his coffin, he would rise to protest—and then drop dead again. Rub it all out!"

And then this midshipman delivered a solar plexus that knocked me out of the Naval Academy into salt water. He said: "Lieutenant Beach, would you please write a real imitation of Shakespeare's style so I'll know how to do it?"

My answer to this was, "Section dismissed!"

I also marched out, and wrote to the Navy Department asking for orders to sea. Not many days later I was ordered, as navigator and ordnance officer, to the monitor *Nevada*, which had just been completed and was fitting out at Portsmouth, New Hampshire.

My new orders thrilled me to the fingertips. As ordnance officer I had in my domain our primary battery, the turret with its big modern 12-inch guns, a secondary battery of 4-inch and 6-pounder guns, the powder magazines, and the shell rooms. As navigator I set courses, took sights and bearings, calculated positions, and did all the work necessary in directing the motions of the ship from port to port. I also controlled the electrical equipment.

These duties delighted me. My captain, T. B. Howard, was one of the Navy's famous electricians. As a navigator he was unsurpassed, and he had a thorough knowledge of gunnery. During our period of naval decay following the Civil War, he had been one of the few who kept abreast of foreign naval progress. By study, invention, and practical effort, he had been a leader in the conversion of our old wooden fleet with smooth-bore guns into the efficient modern Navy of great battleships and high-powered, breech-loading, rifled guns that fought Spain in 1898. Expert as he was, he nonetheless had a modest, kindly, helpful personality. Service with Tommy Howard inspired a keen desire to merit his approbation.

We were soon steaming south to test turret fastenings by firing our two 12-inch guns. Each shell weighed about 1,000 pounds, and a bag of powder charge 350. We fired the guns and came back rejoicing that our turret had stood the tests so well. But in discussing them afterward, Howard at some point asked the turret officer, Lieutenant Sawyer, point blank, "Are you satisfied? Was everything as it should have been?" Sawyer's answer surprised us all.

"No, sir; the powder bags were tagged 350 pounds, but they looked a little light, so this morning I weighed some to be sure about it, and found there must have been some mistake. I checked quite a number of them, and their average weight was only 289 pounds. They weren't even all exactly the same, and that's totally unsatisfactory!"

Captain Howard directed immediate re-weighing of the guns' propellant charges, and found Sawyer was right. We had to repeat the tests, and with sad results. Our turret fastenings were inadequate. Every one of them was torn away. This kept us several months longer at the Navy yard (which, I suspected, Lucie welcomed). So far as the Navy was concerned, however, though the next test was successful, a peculiar thing happened.

After the big guns were fired, Sawyer came to the bridge where I was. "Beach," he said, "I'm burned, but not badly. Just after firing, I opened the breech of one of those big guns, and a flame shot out into the rear of the turret. How were the guns pointing?"

I informed Sawyer that they had been pointing directly into the wind. "It seems," mused Sawyer, "that after a gun is fired, extremely hot gases from the propellant charge must stay in the bore for several seconds. If the gun is pointing to windward and the breech is opened for the next shot, as it would have to be during either battle or target practice, those hot gases will be blown into the turret chamber, where they'll burst into flame. That's mighty serious business!"

"Yes, somebody might get scorched worse than you were today."

"Somebody get scorched! Hell! If another powder charge were there, ready for loading, it would blow up and every man in the turret would be killed!"

He immediately began to work on an idea he had for gas ejectors. He invented a device by which, when the breech is opened, a jet of compressed air promptly clears the chamber of gases, blowing them out through the muzzle. This apparatus is now used by all important navies, including our own. Sawyer was granted patent rights, and receives royalties from all countries using the ejector, except the United States. With us, any invention by an officer in his own line of duty belongs, royalty free, to the government.

Readers of Father's 1913 novel, *Roger Paulding, Gunner*, will learn something—not much, it's true—about Lieutenant Sawyer's (Robert Drake's, in the novel) invention. Roger Paulding and his friend and superior officer, Lieutenant Drake, personally devised and installed the gas ejection equipment. Unidentified agents of an unknown foreign power were, of course, doing their best to find out the secret, only to meet frustration at every turn. The gas ejection apparatus is fairly well described in the novel, apparently with acquiescence of the Navy Department, but only partially. I once asked Father how this could have been allowed, and remember his answer. He stated that it was a life-saving invention that we made available to all nations with whom we were at peace. Personally, considering the actual date of the invention, our growing problems with Japan, and Dad's avoidance, in his novels, of any reference to that far eastern empire, it has occurred to me that the "bad guys" in all his novels, except *Dan Quin of the Navy* (1922), might have been modeled after Japan or the Japanese. If so, he went to pains to use unidentifiable names for all of them, and in other ways to conceal what nefarious foreign nation he might have had in mind. Historians will, of course, recall that the beginnings of our difficulties with Japan were in California, stemming largely from immigration of cheap labor during the last half of the nineteenth century. With Japan's sudden emergence as a world power, and her naval victories over China and Russia at the end of that century, the United States began to look on her as a serious rival in the eastern Pacific. War Plan Orange, a study of possible conflict with Japan, became the principal concern of our Naval War College in Newport, Rhode Island. If all of Father's novels, except *Dan Quin*, are re-read, substituting Japan and Japanese names and terms whenever possible, this speculation falls into place, and it is easy to imagine why he went to such effort to obfuscate this particular point in his novels.

Following our successful test we left for the drill grounds off Pensacola, Florida. Here we found an assemblage of our naval vessels, all preparing for target practice.

A new spirit had come into the fleet: one of helpful cooperation, combined with intense competition. Every officer was spurred to make improvements, to pass his best ideas to others, and to try out whatever suggestions or ideas he received in his turn. There was feverish work on the gun mechanisms and in drilling gun crews. And we held many conferences and discussions, formal and informal.

At this time, President Theodore Roosevelt was commander in chief; several rear admirals were flying their flags afloat; and seasoned captains, pacing the decks, were giving peremptory orders. Despite all this, it is equally true that a brown-bearded lieutenant dominated the hearts, minds, and ambitions of the officers and men of the fleet.

In reading military and naval history I had often seen references to the spirit of an admiral or general that pervaded an armed force and made victory inevitable. Like Tolstoy, however, I had always doubted the truth of this. But I now realized the influence of one man. In every group I joined the first name spoken seemed to be "Sims." Sims had done or said this, had advised so and so. Sims had suggested this innovation, or worked out that new principle. Sims had ordered reports to be made. I feel sure that the spirit of Sims, even in his absence, controlled the activities of the fleet. Here was leadership, leadership as effective as if this lieutenant had been admiral of the Navy.

The glorious naval victories of 1812 had created the impression that the methods of that day could not be surpassed. As late as 1901, I had given orders: "Away second riflemen!" "Away boarders!" "Stand by for a raking broadside!" "Lie down!" "Repel boarders!" "Charge pikemen!" "Cheer my lads, cheer!" This may have been suited to the days of Isaac Hull and Stephen Decatur, or even to the halcyon days of our Civil War. But the whole procedure was as out of date as Decatur's smooth-bore guns. Now, Sims blew our Navy into the twentieth century.

Older officers resisted change. For instance, the McCann Board of 1886, composed of high-ranking, distinguished officers, was appointed to prescribe the features to be designed into the new modern steel cruisers Congress had just authorized the famous "White Squadron" of 1890. Not content with modern triple-expansion engines, this board saw to it that each ship was also equipped with full sail power, and required to demonstrate the same during trials—resulting in an anachronistic photograph of the squadron under full sail, and barely moving. Likewise, new high-powered guns were provided, and old methods followed in training their crews.

Into this came Sims like a bolt out of the purest blue. His scathing criticisms outraged earnest, conservative, high-ranking captains and admirals, who had no interest in "Simian" theories. The Navy Department bureaus of ordnance and of navigation (so ran current gossip) would have none of him. It is said that Sims then addressed the secretary of the Navy—and was snubbed. This would have checked the average man. But Sims was no average naval officer, and he now put his very commission at stake. He addressed a letter to a stranger, one Theodore Roosevelt, who happened to be president of the United States, and mailed it to him direct. Perhaps Sims should have been court-martialed and dismissed for thus violating naval regulations, but Mr. Roosevelt was impressed. Besides, without Sims' knowledge, for years he had been reading Sims' voluminous letters and, as assistant secretary of the Navy, had even caused them to be circulated throughout the Navy Department.

———————————

It may even be surmised that Sims had learned of the special interest his voluminous letters and intelligence reports were creating in the Navy, and resolved to wager all on reaching directly to the (possibly suspected) basic source of much of it. It was a high risk, for such critical letters were always intercepted by staff even then; but "TR" had already given instructions that mail from Sims was to be handled specially.

———————————

The upshot, as previously mentioned, was that Roosevelt made Sims director of target practice. While the rest of the fleet was preparing to miss targets by the old method, Sims was given the *Indiana* to prove his arguments. After drilling his gun crews for six months, he went on the target range.

Meanwhile the other ships of the fleet each fired in turn at a flag lashed to a buoy. Observers in boats at both ends of the target range marked the fall of the shots by estimating the location of their splashes. Then diagrams were drawn tracing the path of the shot from gun to water, showing how near they came to the theoretical enemy ship that was their constructive target. Of course, the wobbling of the boats in the water probably lessened the value of these observations.

In the midst of all this, Sims and the *Indiana* came on the range. His goal was to score actual hits. He also emphasized speed, constantly preaching the maxim of "hits per gun per minute"—that a gun able to put two shots per minute into a target was twice as good as one that could hit it only once a minute.

A lengthier account of this incident is given in my *The United States Navy: 200 Years* (New York: Henry Holt, 1986, p. 399).

Instead of a stationary buoy with a flag, Sims had a tug tow a target raft across the firing range, so that, for the first time in our Navy, a battleship fired target practice at a moving target. *Indiana* was allowed twelve rounds for each of her 13-inch guns, firing only one gun on each firing run, and pausing for target inspection.

After twelve shots on *Indiana*'s first run, there were twelve holes in the target. After the second run, there were twenty-four holes. A new target had to be rigged for the third run; after which it showed twelve holes, and the fourth run made it twenty-four. The rapidity of shooting seemed beyond belief. Never before in history had there been such correct and rapid shooting. With the crash of the last shot, a great roar went up from every ship present, and this roar "was heard around the world."

It is only fair to say that Sims got many of his ideas from Sir Percy Scott of the British navy; but he developed these wonderfully. I have tried to describe this American revolution accurately. If not, a tall gray-bearded admiral can make any needed corrections.

Admiral Sims died in 1936, at age seventy-eight. Father wrote this passage prior thereto, and evidently failed to pick up on this point on later re-readings.

Sims had his own way of talking, as well as of shooting. The day after the *Nevada* reached the drill grounds area he came aboard.

"Beach," he asked, "have you received your telescopic gun sights?"

"Yes, this morning; but I haven't unpacked them yet."

"Open them up; I want to see them."

He examined one carefully, looking through it in both directions. "This sight is mostly parallax!" he exclaimed. "The man that passed this lot and sent them here should be shot dead and left in the hot sun—and then not buried!"

That was just like Sims. His speech sometimes lacked the elegance prescribed in Barbara Hill's textbook on rhetoric, but it never lacked elemental force.

At the start of these memorable drills off Pensacola, the guns' crews were clumsy and slow. But stopwatches were held on every operation. At the end of a few months the turret crews, once so clumsy, could load and fire twice a minute. Of course there was an element of danger in this speed. The 12-inch shells and the heavy powder bags were run up from the magazines to the breech of the guns by electrical hoists and were driven home by electrical rammers. There were fifty-six men in a turret crew.

The *Nevada* was to take her turn on the range after the *Missouri*, commanded by Captain W. C. Cowles. We therefore anchored a little in the rear of the course to be followed by the *Missouri*. She fired several shots from her 12-inch after turret. Just after the last shot there was a great burst of yellow flame, which completely enveloped the after part of the ship. It rose high, and was followed by a second burst, and a third.

Captain Howard was one of a group on our quarterdeck watching the practice. "Gentlemen," he said quietly, "There has been a terrible accident! Up anchor! Get boats ready to lower! Tell the surgeon and his assistants to come up on deck immediately!"

The *Missouri* now turned, heading at full speed across our bow for shallow water. The *Nevada* got under way and followed close under her starboard quarter. We all realized the danger to the *Missouri*'s magazines. If fire reached them, the ship would blow up, and Captain Cowles wanted to be in shallow water if that happened. In his own turn, our captain wanted to be well placed for rescue work in case that dreaded event took place. We saw men running aft with fire hoses and dropping into the turret. Then we saw inanimate burdens lifted out. Five officers and twenty-five enlisted men had lost their lives. But most of the crew and the ship had been saved.

With the special appliances fitted, the magazine doors had been promptly closed; and the magazines themselves had been flooded.

When the turret incident aboard the battleship *Missouri* occurred, Dad, as he describes, was aboard the monitor *Nevada*, which got under way to provide whatever assistance she could to her stricken fleet-mate. Medical aid to the injured was all she could do to help, but since all hands in the turret had been instantly killed there were relatively few for whom anything could be done. *Missouri*'s magazines did not explode and the ship was not destroyed, so there was no need for *Nevada*'s boats. As Father describes, the *Nevada*, which had been waiting her turn on the target range, shortly thereafter went on the firing line herself and turned in a good score.

Although my terse condensation of Father's language is rather prosaic, the severe accident badly shook our Navy of a hundred years ago, and it did, indeed, lead directly to our development of the gas-ejection apparatus that was subsequently fitted to all our big naval guns, and those of friendly foreign nations as well. As I've already pointed out, Father was not above fictionalizing his own experiences, or those of others, in his Navy novels, taking special care that descriptions and circumstances as he recounted them were accurate, but could not be identified with real persons, ships, or locations. In this instance, however, beyond his usual authenticity, he was either less careful in regard to particulars, or perhaps, because no foreign ship was involved, may have felt less need to conceal details. Beyond changing the names of the ships and individuals concerned, he pretty well told the whole story in *Roger Paulding, Gunner* (Philadelphia: Penn Publishing Co., 1913), exactly as it occurred. In the novel, Roger Paulding, Dad's protagonist, jumps into the threatened magazine of the battleship *Alabama* and slams shut a watertight door just in time to prevent flame from the exploding powder charges in the turret above from reaching the hundreds of similar powder charges in the magazine. Had this happened, as Father makes clear, all the charges in the magazine would probably have exploded, with truly disastrous consequences.

Technically there was no explosion; there was a horrible gunpowder-fed fire, and the press rightly called it one. The official death toll was thirty-six officers and men horribly burned, suffocated, or dead of smoke inhalation in the stricken turret. Three members of *Missouri's* crew had remained inside her after magazine, extinguishing the many burning powder granules that had gotten in before the door was shut, as did the fictional Paulding, and the Navy recognized their heroism by awarding each a Medal of Honor.

Aside from the dead and injured, there was one other person who suffered rather keenly from the catastrophe: the then Lieutenant Sims, who had persuaded President Theodore Roosevelt to allow him to change target practice rules. Sims had emphasized "hits per gun per minute" as his creed, and his detractors made much of the argument that undue emphasis on rapid firing was what had caused the accident. Sims spent a lot of time refuting this line of thought, pointing out, other things being equal, that a smaller ship able to hit a more powerful one more often than the bigger ship could hit back was in fact the superior in their primary mission. The real criticism, he stated with his usual failure to say unpleasant things tactfully, should be leveled at the designers who had failed in their duty to provide safe equipment. As to this, he provided unanswerable chapter and verse. (Shades of the future submarine torpedo controversy during World War II, of which this was a progenitor!) None of this added to Sims's popularity, of course, but it was halted by a typical presidential fiat: "The policy of this nation's Navy is to achieve the most possible hits per gun per minute!"

And then, only a few hours later, the *Nevada* went on the range and made a good score. A court of inquiry established the fact that the *Missouri* had been firing right into the wind. Apparently, just after the last gun fired, the breech was quickly opened; unconsumed hot gases had been blown to the rear; and these gases, igniting, had exploded a charge of powder held waiting for the reload. Sawyer had predicted exactly what occurred, and all navies of the world knew of it, and studied it.

15

AGAIN A PROFESSOR
AND BACK TO SEA

In 1904, the *Nevada* was placed, with the old battleship *Texas* and the monitors *Arkansas* and *Florida*, in a newly formed "Coast Squadron." The idea, faulty and now abandoned, was that, should war come, the Coast Squadron would protect the Atlantic coast. It is now realized that in war the supreme purpose of each of the opposing fleets will be to destroy the other, and that coast defense will depend upon the victory or the defeat of our fleet, wherever engaged.

The *Nevada* was busy every minute. The three monitors ran into all the bays, inlets, and river mouths from the Virginia Capes to Mobile Bay. Tons of never-to-be-used data relative to these coastal waters and the cities on them were collected and have slept the years away in the archives of the Navy Department. The officers of these monitors gained experience of an unusual kind: coast survey piloting, surf work, and navigation over bars where there was hardly a foot to spare.

One of the things that gave us a lot of fun in addition to personal and career satisfaction was the reenactment of the unsuccessful bombardment, by the British, of Fort McHenry during the War of 1812. There was to be a great celebration in Baltimore, where the old fort still exists. As is well known, this was the occasion of the writing by Francis Scott Key, an American detainee on one of the enemy ships, of a poem beginning, "Oh, say, can you see." In the absence of the flagship *Texas*, my old friend, John C. Fremont, captain of the *Florida*, was the senior officer present. Fremont, with his three monitors, arrived at dusk at the end of the navigable channel off the fort. After dark, his ships were to provide the "bombs bursting in air."

Being a thoughtful man, Fremont studied the charts. From his anchorage to the fort was mud—nice, soft mud, with thirteen feet of bay water over it at high tide. Night came on, impenetrably dark, with neither peeping moon nor stars. The three monitors silently got under way on a rising tide, and slowly, steadily, slid through mud. It comforted me, as navigator of the *Nevada*, to know that the *Florida* would stick before we did.

But, in this mock battle, Pathfinder, junior, equaled his father's record. Far from sticking, we got to the rear of the forts where none of their guns could be trained on us. We filled the air with bursting 12-inch "bombs," and it was well for Rotary Clubs and other patriotic organizations that Fremont did not command the attackers of 1814. For if he had, we might not today be singing, "Oh, say, can you see . . . ?"

Monitor officers happily allow Fremont at least one other claim to glory. The Navy Department had issued an order requiring officers to "dress" for dinner. This was well enough for battleships, with their laundries and other conveniences, and with every dinner a banquet. But for the seven officers squeezed into the mess rooms of monitors, the order was simply a nuisance.

John C., who was senior officer present, published the order to his squadron, as he was required to do with all such Navy Department-wide orders, and added: "Dinner aboard the monitors will be at 6:30 P.M. daily. Supper will be at 6:15 P.M. The uniform for supper will be the uniform of the day." This meant "undress" instead of "dress," and we all cheered ourselves hoarse. After that our evening meal was always supper.

In the meantime our captain, Tommy Howard, was relieved by Commander Alfred Reynolds, an old-time sailor man, rich in experiences. Though stern and determined in carrying out duties, he had a big, generous, understanding heart, and was the most companionable captain I have known.

My last target practice with the *Nevada* was held in St. Joseph's Bay, Florida, off what was once a thriving city of twenty thousand inhabitants, but is now a swamp. Our gun crews were thoroughly trained, and we were confident of making a good score. As usual, competition between ships was intense. Although our ships were not of the battleship class, our 12-inch guns were the same as theirs.

The day before target practice, Sawyer, still the turret officer, came to me. "Beach," he said, "keep all I'm saying quiet. You know that in firing at the target nearly two thousand yards away, we must elevate our guns about two degrees. Then, after firing, we must run them down to 'loading position,' parallel to the deck; load, and again elevate. This takes nearly ten seconds. Now, if you can arrange with the captain to fire on one side only, and with the chief engineer to shift coal to give us a list of two degrees, we shall always be in loading position, and can save ten seconds after each shot."

All this was done, and with amazing results. The *Nevada's* 12-inch turret guns made the highest score for their class in the Navy. All the world wondered—that is, except Captain Reynolds, Sawyer, and me.

After three years and four months in the *Nevada*, I was detached, given two weeks' leave, and ordered back to the Naval Academy. Here I found conditions much as before. At first I taught midshipmen the mathematics of "interior and exterior ballistics of guns," then, after several months, in honor of Alexis Delatour I was made head of the department of foreign languages.

In this capacity I was a member of the Academic Board. After the annual examinations, it was the duty of this board to go over the grades reported, and to recommend that certain midshipmen who had not achieved passing marks be dropped. Among these was Midshipman J. R. Barry, whose mark in mathematics was 2.36, or 59 per cent. The Academic Board made its recommendations and adjourned. Then I went to my quarters, an official residence on the Naval Academy grounds as befit the head of an academic department, where I was to entertain at luncheon the Board of Visitors appointed by the president to make a careful investigation of the Academy (an annual event). This was composed of distinguished personages, including members of both houses of Congress.

At this luncheon, hosted by Lucie and given in our home, they investigated carefully the softshell crabs and the canvasback ducks that make Maryland famous, as well as Smithfield hams, the pride of Virginia. To aid in the investigation was an amber colored liquid that "rained upward"—to borrow the expression of my son Johnny Beach, born many years later, when, at age seven he discovered ginger ale. This was not ginger ale, however. Though the crabs, ducks, and hams were not mentioned in the report, I have grounds to believe that the board found them satisfactory.

Before the luncheon a member of this board, knowing that the Academic Board had made its recommendations, asked me some pointed questions that I pointedly failed to answer. As we were sitting down to luncheon, this member asked permission to make a long-distance telephone call. He remained for some time at the telephone.

After the luncheon I received an order to report to the superintendent's office immediately. Here I found the Academic Board again assembling. The superintendent, Rear Admiral James H. Sands, greeted us and said, "Gentlemen, less than an hour ago I had a telephonic conversation of such importance that I called a stenographer and had it all taken down. This conversation was as follows." Sands began reading:

Voice: "The secretary of the Navy desires to speak with Admiral Sands."

"This is Admiral Sands."

"Admiral Sands, this is Secretary of the Navy [Victor H.] Metcalf. What is the recommendation of the Academic Board concerning Midshipman J. R. Barry?"

"Mr. Secretary, the Academic Board has found that Midshipman Barry has failed to meet the required Naval Academy passing standard. His mark in mathematics is 2.36; the passing mark is 2.50. Because of this failure, the Academic Board has recommended that he be dropped."

"Admiral, President Roosevelt wishes this midshipman to be passed."

"Mr. Secretary, I am sorry that the president will be disappointed."

"But, Admiral, this will not do! The president's wishes are orders. Midshipman Barry must be passed."

"Are you giving me an order, sir?"

"Not a technical order; but I am expressing to you a wish of the president of the United States. You will be guided by that, sir."

"Mr. Secretary, I am guided only by orders, not by wishes. Unless my present orders are changed, I shall approve the recommendations of the Academic Board, and Midshipman Barry will be dropped."

"You mustn't do that, Admiral. You must carry out as orders the wishes of the president."

"Then I must have an order, sir, not a wish."

"Admiral, please remain near your telephone."

"Admiral Sands?"

"This is Admiral Sands."

"This is President Roosevelt speaking. I am giving you now an executive order. The passing mark in the Naval Academy department in which Midshipman Barry has received 2.36 is, for this term only, changed to 2.35. This applies to all midshipmen's marks in this department. Do you require a written order?"

"No, sir; this order will be obeyed."

Admiral Sands had finished reading. Then, without further comment, he directed: "The Academic Board will reconvene; the previous recommendations will be reconsidered; the president's order will be carried out."

Admiral Sands was a good example of the naval officer of high rank who would not be swerved from his duty, as he saw it, by even the impetuous wishes of the president of the United States.

In passing, reference to the Naval Academy's *Register of Alumni* shows that Midshipman Barry, of the class of 1909, retired as a captain in 1946, and died in 1967. It is evident that Roosevelt's support at a low point in his career was not misplaced. It is not known, however, how many other near-bilgers of '09 also benefited. Undoubtedly some did. Father wrote thirteen novels about our Navy, its Naval Academy, and the service of young officers and enlisted men at sea, and it may be noted that the period covered by his books coincides with the youthful careers of admirals William F. Halsey, class of 1904, Chester W. Nimitz of 1905, and Raymond A. Spruance of 1907. His purpose was to describe the environment in which these revered naval leaders were formed.

This incident, however important or unimportant in itself, indicates the standard set long ago for naval officers. At first every officer, as such, was bound to defend his personal honor, and frequent duels resulted. But for many years past the Navy Department has assumed this obligation, since officers are expressly prohibited from sending or accepting challenges. For instance, soon after the 1898 Spanish-American War, an officer, in a public speech, attacked the personal honor of Captain Robley D. "Fighting Bob" Evans. The Navy Department called upon him to substantiate his statements. He was unable to do so. He was then court-martialed on charges of falsehood, was found guilty, and was dismissed from the naval service.

Conceivably the character of a boy appointed to the Naval Academy may be unformed. He is immediately impressed with the fact that the first requisite of an officer is personal integrity. A midshipman, or any officer, guilty of cheating, lying, or other dishonorable conduct, is instantly dismissed. There is no second chance for him. A standard court-martial charge covering such behavior is "conduct unbecoming an officer and a gentleman." Conviction means dismissal.

I do not mean that naval officers are paragons. They are very human. But the fact remains that an officer who does not rise to a high standard of personal honor must leave the service. He is made to realize that his honor is not only personal to him, but affects the whole naval service. His efficiency, his worth to the service, and his attention to his duties are all bound up with this obligation.

Admiral Sands displayed the true Navy spirit. Though unable to comply with the president's wishes because they violated the rules he had been sworn to uphold, he instantly obeyed a legitimate order from the commander in chief. And President Roosevelt displayed understanding too, in his own charismatic way.

In my naval service, shore duty was never so interesting as sea duty, even though it permits one to live nearly normally with one's family. At the Naval Academy there was always a lot going on, and officers' wives were frequently called upon to participate in official or semi-official capacities. For example, Admiral Sands wanted me to be his aide because his wife wanted Lucie to be her social assistant as the wife of his aide, a position frequently desired because of its social prominence. And Mrs. Sands sent for Lucie to help entertain the Duke de Abruzzie and other distinguished visitors when they came to Annapolis. It was a busy life for both of us, with many special privileges.

All the same, when on shore I was constantly thinking of going back to sea. There was my real job. One day, long before it was my turn for sea, a stocky individual walked into my house and said, "Beach, I am to have the new armored cruiser Montana. Will you come with me as navigator, to succeed as executive in a few months?"

I shouted, "You bet I will, Captain Reynolds!" Soon I was at Norfolk helping put a magnificent seventeen-thousand-ton armored cruiser in commission.

The great Confederate cavalry leader, General Forrest, asked how he managed always to win battles, is said to have answered in the language of his Tennessee mountains: "I allus gits thar fustest with the mostest guns." Though Forrest's English was amusing, Union generals did not find him so. In his reply he boiled down the principles of war tactics. In searching for the elements of victory, great American naval students—Mahan, Fiske, Sims, Frank M. Schofield, Frank Knox—have deduced its essentials, from history, as capable leadership, highly trained personnel, and superior weapons. Without the weapons the other elements will fail. Forrest's rule applied to the Navy means a superiority in speed and in gunfire. Mahan's great work aroused the world to this fact and brought about the race for naval supremacy.

The Montana was finished in 1908. She was the last word in armored cruisers. Making twenty-two knots, although actually capable of a little more, and mounting four 10-inch and sixteen 6-inch guns, she was indeed designed to "git thar fustest with the mostest guns."

Unfortunately, only a year later, other great powers were launching cruisers superior to the Montana; and we had to continue the mad race by improving on their designs. The only limit to naval construction was the inability of a country to provide funds. In 1922 Mare Island Navy Yard was building another, much larger Montana. This new ship was to displace forty-five thousand tons and cost, fully equipped, one thousand dollars a ton, or forty-five million dollars in all. At this time, despite President Woodrow Wilson's abhorrence of war, the United States was building twenty great battleships to cost nearly a billion dollars, a program quite beyond the financial capacity of any other nation.

One of the greatest acts of the world's history was the 1922 self-sacrificing surrender by the United States—by then the wealthiest nation in the world—of its potential supremacy in capital ships. We did this deliberately, in the cause of peace, when it would have been impossible for Great Britain, Japan, France, or any other country to match our building program. It is true that in so doing we may have averted a menace of immediate war. But in our sincere and whole-hearted effort to maintain peace, we literally threw more than three hundred million dollars, already spent, upon the scrap heap. No other nation has ever made a sacrifice comparable to this, as all Americans should remember when "apologizing" for their country. We should also note that the rest of the world was grateful within Talleyrand's famous definition: "Gratitude is a lively expectation of more favors to come."

The context of Father's "apologizing" statement is unknown. It's quite evident he was upset over the waste of money and the destruction of nearly completed warships. Possibly the apology was sarcastically aimed at the America Firsters, or "Peacenics," who were congenitally opposed to defense spending for any reason.

In digressing a moment from my story, I wished to emphasize the fact that, though the Montana, in 1908 when I joined her, was the newest and largest of armored cruisers, displacing seventeen thousand tons and developing 30,000 horsepower, she was supplanted in only fourteen years by the battle cruiser of forty thousand tons and 180,000 horsepower. Meanwhile the great battleship of fifteen thousand tons had been supplanted by the "super-dreadnought" of thirty-five thousand tons. In 1908, however, I was bursting with pride at serving in this magnificent Montana. As navigator, I also headed the electrical department, no small job in itself.

Our captain, Alfred Reynolds, formerly of the Nevada, was given six months to get everything in shape. Our executive officer—the captain's organizer, right-hand man, and spokesman—was Commander Joseph Strauss, an officer whose talents and character have brought him the highest naval rank. Strauss threw his soul into the work of organization and drill. He controlled the destinies of eleven hundred men, and, under the captain's direction, supervised speed trials, gunnery trials, and drills by day or by night. We steamed north, east, and south at sustained high speed, and would have steamed west but for the continent that interfered.

At the end of the six months, the Naval Inspection Board put the ship through her paces. This board of ten experienced officers took nothing for granted. They spent ten days testing guns, engines, and personnel. They looked everywhere and watched a hundred different drills. They scrutinized the report book, the doctor's records, the paymaster's accounts, and so on.

One afternoon the two 10-inch guns of the after turret were to be fired together, with shell and full powder charge. Reynolds, Strauss, and I were on the bridge. Most of the board members were in or about the turret. On the port side of our main deck, near the after turret, stood Commander George Evans, one of the board, with stopwatch in hand.

Then came the roar of the guns. Instantly the after part of the ship, including the after turret, was enveloped in black smoke. The fire alarm was sounded. Even before this, Strauss had left the bridge on a run and disappeared in the smoke. Someone shouted, "The turret has exploded!"

Captain Reynolds stood beside me. "The turret has not exploded," he remarked, "it's something else."

He was as cool and steady as a detective making an arrest. For my part, I was fairly calm too, for I had seen the terrible yellow fumes from the *Missouri's* turret, and also did not believe our black smoke was from an explosion. Hardly had the alarm been sounded before a half dozen hoses were sending streams of water through the smoke. During my naval service I have seen battle, shipwreck, fire, and explosion. Never have I seen an officer or enlisted man hesitate a second in doing whatever the emergency demanded.

Soon the murky cloud had cleared away. There stood George Evans, stopwatch in hand, imperturbably noting the time from the alarm to the first stream, and sedately recording other matters of interest. Aft, and on the starboard side, the deck was ablaze. The blast had burst tanks containing inflammables, like turpentine and alcohol, that according to Navy regulations must be kept on deck. This had caused the fire and smoke.

Some weeks later I happened to be in the cabin when a letter from the Navy Department was handed to Reynolds. This letter quoted a report of the Board of Inspection praising the *Montana* in every respect, and expressed the department's high commendation of Captain Reynolds. Such letters are treasured by officers, not only as keepsakes, but because they have a bearing on promotion.

Reynolds read me the letter, then sent for his stenographer and dictated a reply. He expressed his satisfaction in having the ship he commanded praised by the Navy Department, but added: "These conditions are directly and largely due to the splendid work of the executive officer, Commander Joseph Strauss.

I therefore return the department's letter, recommending and requesting that it be re-addressed to Commander Strauss and forwarded to him."

This is a good example of the spirit of fairness that permeates the Navy. In this connection, another incident is illuminative.

When the fleet that President Roosevelt had sent around the world was nearing home, early in 1909, the *Montana* steamed several hundred miles east of the capes of the Chesapeake, barked a noisy welcome, and tailed on behind, headed for Hampton Roads. Each ship was assigned an anchorage; and each captain knew that if he did not anchor in the exact spot designated, the commander in chief would hoist a disturbing signal of reprimand. The large number of capital ships made it necessary to anchor in a compact formation. Even with a slack tide in calm weather, this would have required careful maneuvering; but a strong gale was blowing, an ebb tide was running fiercely, and the *Montana*'s anchorage was particularly hard to reach. To get there we had to dodge several battleships that were backing and filling and others that were swinging directly athwart our course. Strauss stood near Reynolds and me on the bridge, conning the movements of the ship.

"How do you propose to get there, Strauss?" asked Reynolds.

In answer to Strauss's reply, Reynolds said, "You'll never get there that way. The *Montana* is 504 feet long; you are running into a strong cross eddy. You should run over to starboard, astern of the *Idaho*; then, with a quick hard-over helm, head for the *Ohio*'s bow; when near it, port the helm, head across the *Idaho*'s bow, and the tide will sweep you into position."

"I'd like to try my way, sir!" said Strauss.

"All right. Go ahead."

Strauss made three attempts. He might have reached his goal, but with the strong wind and fierce tide there was much danger of collision on every side. He skillfully averted disaster by backing, going ahead, and spinning this seventeen thousand ton ship on her keel, for he was too good a seaman to risk hitting, or being hit. After the third failure, he handed the speaking trumpet to Captain Reynolds, saying, "Captain, I don't seem to be able to make it. I wish you would try it, sir."

Reynolds ordered "full speed," headed for the *Idaho*'s stern, swung around the *Ohio*'s bow, cut across ahead of the *Idaho*, then ordered: "Let go the anchor!"

"Back full speed, both engines!"

He had gauged wind and tide exactly, and, within five minutes from the time he took charge, the *Montana* was on the required spot.

"All right, Strauss," he said. "Secure everything."

"Captain," said Strauss, "please excuse me. You are a better seaman than I am."

This typifies the way most of our ships are run: by officers of experience, with good feeling, and with mutual respect and reliance. Before long Strauss was detached and ordered to command the *Montgomery*, an older and smaller cruiser; she would be his first command, and Beach was raised to the Seventh Heaven by being made executive officer of our great *Montana*.

16

~

A COMMANDER

Soon the *Montana* was steaming for the naval base at Guantánamo, Cuba. While coaling ship there, the captain received sudden orders to proceed to Mersine, in Asia Minor, to protect American citizens. We were quickly on our way.

Passing through the Strait of Gibraltar, in a gale of wind, with heavy seas and a strong tide, I was reminded of the well-known story of an American warship, years ago, being towed through the strait in similar conditions. The tug captain, growing desperate, shouted through his trumpet to the captain of the tow:

> *If wind and tide do not abate,*
> *I cannot tow you through the strait!*

To which the American yelled back,

> *So long as you have steam and coal,*
> *You tow away, God damn your soul!*

In our effete days naval captains do not use such forceful language.

At Mersine, a Turkish town, with a population of Turks, Greeks, and Armenians, the sights were harrowing. Armenians were still being massacred in outlying districts. It was estimated that thirty thousand had been slaughtered in this vicinity; and many bodies came floating down the Sarus River, at the mouth of which we had anchored. Though order had been preserved in Mersine, Reynolds and I saw sad sights in the emergency hospitals there. Nor were Armenians the only sufferers. American missionaries from outlying districts had fled into the city and were existing under heavy privation; others had been murdered while endeavoring to protect Armenians.

The day after we arrived, the captain and I attended a meeting of missionaries, men and women who, for years, had devoted their lives to spreading the gospel of Jesus Christ. Their efforts had been confined to the Armenians. These good people had seen tens of thousands of their own pupils slaughtered before their very eyes. The Reverend Dr. Fuller had been killed in an effort to save Armenians. So had the Reverend Dr. Maurer. Thirty-three native Armenian pastors had also been killed. At this meeting, Reynolds and I heard the missionaries, one by one, tell of their experiences. They were all hysterical. Bursts of weeping, constantly growing wilder, greeted the dreadful reports made, one after another, by the survivors. I saw that in a few minutes these good people would lose all control of themselves; and I feared they would become grief-stricken maniacs. I nudged Reynolds, who was a wonderful storyteller, and said, "Captain, these folks are going plum crazy. You've got to stop them. Tell them a funny story!"

Reynolds jumped to his feet. "Look here, friends," he called out in his deep resonant voice, "you've all been doing a lot of talking. Don't you think you'd better give me a chance to say a few words?"

"Why, certainly, Captain!" replied seventy-five year old Dr. Christis. "We'll be real glad to hear from you."

"I've got something to say to you, and I want your advice. But first I must break your minds completely away from these sad thoughts. Until that is done you won't be in condition to give me the advice I need. So first I shall tell you a story."

And Reynolds not only told his story, but also acted it out. It was about a man who had taken several drinks too much; and the way the captain staggered and lurched about the room seemed terrible to these devoted ministers. They regarded him with fearful, fascinated eyes. He was a high-ranking captain in the

U.S. Navy, in full naval uniform, and for the moment there was no room in their minds except for what, then and there, they were seeing and hearing.

I cannot pretend to tell his story, but it was about as follows. The drunken man was trying to get home, and was making heavy weather of it. He made remarks to himself that, as given by the captain, were uproariously funny. For example,

> He grabbed a picket fence and could not see why it stopped him. He lurched against a lamp post, trying to pass it; but instead, swung completely around it.
>
> "What's the matter, my friend?" asked a gentleman who was passing.
>
> "Nothing, sir, except—*hic*—I can't get through these woods; wherever I go—*hic*—a tree bumps into me."
>
> "Well, tell me where you live, and I'll take you there."
>
> "Thank you, sir—*hic*—I'll go with you; but what's your name?"
>
> "My name is Paul. Come along."
>
> "All right, Paul. Say, Paul, I've read a lot about you and your travels, and your work and all that. I want to ask you a question. Will you answer my question, Paul?"
>
> "Yes, if I can. What is it?"
>
> "Paul, I want to know if you ever got an answer to the epistle you wrote the Ephesians."

My telling of the story is feeble. It is quite impossible to suggest Reynolds' inimitable portrayal. But it was received with shouts of laughter, and completely eliminated the hysteria. The group now settled down to making an estimate of the situation and to advising Reynolds of existing conditions. As a result of this meeting, we visited a number of Syrian ports where there were American missionaries.

One of these towns was Latakia. Here Reynolds and I attended another meeting of missionaries. Again, they were greatly upset. "Are you here to save us and our people?" asked one abruptly.

"My orders are to protect American citizens," replied the captain.

"Do you propose to let thousands of Armenians be slaughtered—men, women, and children—and to make no effort to prevent it?" was shouted at him.

"I will make every protest to Turkish officials. I will use my ship and its guns to protect American citizens. But I am under strict orders not to interfere between the Turkish government and its citizens."

He was now screamed at. "There is an Armenian town, Kessab, on the coast, only forty miles from here. A Turkish army is now marching upon it! And if you don't stop it, twelve thousand Armenians will be slaughtered by this time tomorrow evening! Are you, an American Navy captain, going to let this happen?"

"Are there American citizens in Kessab?"

"No. But there are God-serving Armenians there!"

For the moment these good people made no attempt to conceal their indignation. A powerful military force of their own country was refusing to help them, just at the time when, in their view, they needed it the most! But the American diplomatic position, and Captain Reynold's orders, were explicit. Exactly how explicit of, course, they did not know and, philanthropic God-fearing folk that they were, it would have made no difference anyway. But just then another missionary rushed into the room. He was addressed as "Brother Trowbridge." He had his own sad story to tell. Outside of Latakia he had been repeatedly fired upon; in his hat and clothes were bullet holes. After some minutes he remarked: "Miss Chambers has gone to Kessab. She'll be dead tomorrow!"

"Who is Miss Chambers?" asked Reynolds abruptly.

"An American missionary."

"Come on, Beach!" said the captain, starting up. "We'll leave for Kessab immediately. Ladies and gentlemen," he added, addressing the missionaries, "I cannot interfere between Turkey and her subjects, but I assure that I'll use every power I have, to the extent of destroying the Turkish army if I have to, before allowing Miss Chambers or any other American citizen to be endangered!"

We were no longer unpopular; but Reynolds was in a hurry to get back to the ship. By half past three the next morning we were anchored close to shore in a small bay. To the right were high, steep hills. To the left, perhaps three miles inland, was the Armenian city of Kessab, behind and flanking which were precipitous rocky mountains. Between these hills and the shore was a narrow strip of land. No force from the south could reach the city except around the hills to the right and along the sandy strip near the shore.

All hands were busy clearing ship for action; but the dawning day disclosed a peaceful scene. Rising abruptly in a compact mass, from a barren plain encircled by hills, were the white buildings of Kessab. After the ship had anchored, the captain gave me careful instructions: "Beach, if a Turkish army is really on the way to destroy Kessab, it must come around that hill over yonder. It can't reach Kessab any other way. It must pass within a half a mile of our guns. Take the Cuivass, go ashore, and be where you can meet that army, should it come. Get hold of its commanding officer. Tell him we are protecting Americans, and that there is an American citizen in Kessab. Say to him that if a single gun fires into Kessab, or if any attempt is made by him to enter that city, I will, without further notice, open fire upon his army with four 10-inch, sixteen 6-inch, twenty 3-inch rifled cannon, and with machine guns. Tell him I regard the presence of his army as a menace to American life, and that he must march away immediately. His presence here may cause wholesale slaughter, not of Armenians, but of Turkish soldiers, and may result in a war between Turkey and the United States!"

These instructions were given in the presence of an interpreter, whom the captain had referred to as "the Cuivass." This man was a "Druse," an attaché or employee of our consulate at Beirut. He was of great stature, and was the most fear-inspiring human being I have ever seen. He wore a queer bonnet and a remarkable gray robe, a sort of "Mother Hubbard," with divided skirts. He had fierce mustachios, and with sword, pistols, and daggers strapped to his body, was a veritable walking arsenal. Occasionally Reynolds and I would take him with us ashore to Turkish towns where conditions were unsettled. Usually we would walk in the middle of the street with the Cuivass several paces ahead. When approaching a Turk, he would always lunge toward him, with one hand outstretched in a menacing way, the other gripping a pistol.

By treaty, at that time the Turkish government permitted foreign legations to have an interpreter, known as a Cuivass, whose duties and person were entitled to respect. He was frequently a Druse, one of a tribe not accused of loving many people, but certainly hating Turks.

Early in the morning, the Cuivass and I reached the shore and waited, the two of us, for the approach of the Turkish army. An hour or so later a squadron of Turkish cavalry came dashing toward us. There we stood alone in the brilliant sunshine, the Cuivass with outstretched arms, an impressive figure, and

I, in my uniform, an unexpected one. And still more unexpected was the American warship, anchored close in, bristling with guns, all aimed at the shore, with many intent, white-robed sailors behind them.

The troop of cavalry halted suddenly. Then two officers rode up to us; and the Cuivass talked rapidly and emphatically. The officers made some reply, and dashed away. We now saw a long line of soldiers winding its way along the hillside toward Kessab.

"They have gone for the commanding general," the Cuivass informed me.

Either the general would yield, or he would persist in his attack on Kessab, and Reynolds would open fire. In this case it might not be pleasant for the Cuivass and me.

Some minutes later a party of mounted officers, including the two we had first seen, came trotting up. "Here is the General!" remarked the Cuivass.

The general, whose rank, I discovered, was "general-captain," was polite and kindly in manner. He wanted to talk to me, but the Cuivass, now in his element, was hard to hold down. He had plenty to say for himself, and talked vigorously. Finally, however, we got him to interpret. I gave Captain Reynolds' message to the general, and it plainly caused consternation to him and to his staff. Their eyes constantly turned toward the *Montana*, which, with its mighty broadside, could not have looked reassuring. They retired for a private talk, then delivered an answer.

The general-captain was grieved to the heart that my captain would imagine that he would permit, much less order, any cruel action. The Turks, he explained, were good people. They merely acted as any other people would act when threatened by treason within and attacks from without. He had come to investigate certain reports against people in Kessab, not to kill. His country felt warm admiration and friendship for the American people. Far be it from him in any way to disturb these excellent relations, or to create any misunderstanding. To prove which, he would proceed no further against Kessab, but would retire with his army and would not return.

I told him my commanding officer would much appreciate this action, and would now, through me, express his earnest thanks. And, with kindly words, the general-captain and his staff dashed away. His army of fifteen thousand men, which had halted, marched back in the direction from which it came.

Here was a modest naval captain, who, without shooting, or getting shot at, caused an army to give up a raid and saved twelve thousand people from being massacred. Kessab should remember Alfred Reynolds.

Readers of Father's 1911 novel, *Ensign Ralph Osborn*, will find, near the end of the book, a fictional description of this incident. Miss Chambers becomes Gladys Bollup, Ralph's fiancée. Ralph and his classmate Tom Bollup are ordered to Kessab and Adana to represent the American government, and the armored cruiser *Montana* is converted to the battleship USS *Illinois*, anchored off the town of Mersine. In the novel, Father's part as executive officer was played by a Lieutenant Commander Hale, who stayed very much in the background. The Cuivass does not appear at all, but the secret ruler of the Druses (a description of which may be found in comprehensive dictionaries and large encyclopedias) figures dramatically. In Father's novel there is no Turkish army headed to butcher Armenians; instead, a troop of Turkish cavalry, led by a British Major Doty, who, I suspect, may have been a true-life person, gallops everywhere in Adana rescuing endangered people from frenzied, but not fully identified, rioters. Father did not, however, fictionalize the orders apparently received by the skipper of his hero's battleship: they were identical to those actually received by Captain Reynolds.

But Captain Pegfield did not put the *Illinois* alongside the road to Kessab, as Reynolds in actual fact did with the *Montana*. The confrontation with the Turkish army detachment in which Dad participated—which would have served as dramatic purpose in the novel as it did in real life—was left out entirely. It is also evident that Dad's fictional role for the Turkish cavalry was more acceptable to American mores than were perhaps the actual intentions of the real Turkish army, whatever its general may have told Father during the confrontation. As I experienced with my own books about Navy life, clearance sometimes had to be sought from naval intelligence and related agencies, and there might have been pressure to avoid too explicit a narrative.

In this third novel in the Ralph Osborn series, where I found the fictionalized story about Kessab and the Druses, the major portion of the book concerns Ralph's tribulations in the engineering department of the old battleship *Illinois*. As already noted, Father spent the first ten years of his career as an engineering officer. His participation in the famous Battle of Manila Bay was in that capacity, because the engineering and line branches were not combined until 1900. One of the principal reasons for his writing about the Navy, a motivation which I've also inherited, was to describe the hard-working ingenuity, integrity, and general worthwhileness of the American sailor and officer, while at the same time giving a true picture of duties and life on board ship. His descriptions of our Navy for the period about which he wrote were as accurate as he could make them. In reading them, one has confidence that although the story must be fiction, as stated, yet the milieu in which it was situated was as near to historical truth as Father could devise.

I, too, have hued to that ideal, finding that the romance of the actuality exceeds that of the inactuality every time. This is a fact that some writers of fiction apparently have not grasped. Some seem to believe the functions of material things like ships and machinery can be novelized as legitimately as can the purposes, capabilities, and ideas, not to say "ideals," of men and women. Fictional characters can always be manipulated to fit an author's intentions, but whatever the plot, the mechanics of the ships, aircraft, and submarines in which it is laid cannot be. These must be as true to life as possible, and all authors owe it to their readers to make this an inviolate rule. Father's ulterior motive was always to "teach" about the Navy, and mine has been the same. One can be sure that the descriptions of operating the main engines of the USS *Illinois*, or of stoking her coal-fired boilers, were as close to the real thing as it was possible to make them.

———————

In 1910 I was promoted to the grade of commander and was ordered to the Boston Navy Yard as an engineer officer. Life at sea was so full of interest that

I was sorry to go ashore. The commandant at Boston was my old friend, John C. Fremont, and he was now an admiral.

As engineer officer I had general charge of a number of shops employing several thousand men in machine, blacksmith, electrical, pattern shops and others, as well as a power plant, steel rolling mill, and drafting room. Under me were various assistants. The Navy Department had made a great effort to modernize the methods at its Navy yards, basing the improved methods on studies by efficiency engineers. A Navy yard works only for the Navy, or, in special cases, for other branches of the government. It builds and repairs ships. In the building of a ship, almost every mechanical trade is involved.

All civilian employees are under Civil Service rules. When additional workmen are called in, they are chosen by Civil Service officials. When lay-offs occur, those discharged are selected according to official records, with the least useful being the first to go. The purpose of the law was to put appointments and discharges solely on a merit basis, and to prevent the injection of any political or other favoritism. If it were desirable to ignore these rules, it would be difficult to do so, but not impossible, as I shall show.

Layoffs occur when the money appropriated by law for certain U.S. Navy purposes is exhausted. These appropriations are made annually, and specify the exact sums and the purposes for which they are to be applied. When money runs out, men must go. It has been hard for politicians and others to realize that "special pull" will not land a man in a job, nor keep him there, nor influence his official record. Naval officers, like Civil Service officials, are not in politics. Their interest is not local or personal, but federal. They work for the interests of the United States as a whole, and they also know that if favoritism is shown somewhere, then what should be called "prejudice" must appear somewhere else.

My problems at the Boston Navy Yard never came from work given me to do, but from the attitude of persons who thought that because of their special pull they could dictate matters of employment and discharge, favoritism and prejudice. For example, soon after my arrival, a big layoff occurred. A committee of five men, representing an association in Boston, paid me a visit. Their manner was friendly.

"Commander Beach," began the spokesman, "we represent some of the men employed in your shops. We know you are about to have a big layoff. I am handing you a list of workmen. Our organization vouches for the character and ability of every man on that list; and we ask you not to discharge any of them."

I read them the naval regulations bearing on the matter of discharges. "Oh, we know all about that!" was the reply. "And we know that when it comes to discharges, it's you who picks out the men. We simply ask that you don't lay off any of the men on that list."

"I will not accept your list. It will not influence me in any way."

"Commander Beach, we desire to be friendly; but frankly, these men must not be discharged. If you discharge them, you will be lifted out of your job. We'll see that you don't remain here."

"Hurrah!" I shouted, jumping up and rushing to shake hands with each of them. "Thank you! Thank you! I didn't want to come here. When do you think you'll be able to fix up my detachment?" That was the end of that particular episode.

Another day, the following conversation over the telephone occurred. "Commander Beach?"

"Yes, Beach speaking."

"This is Senator Lodge."

"Yes, Senator."

"I am informed you are having a layoff and are discharging a man named so-and-so. I am much interested in this man. He is in all respects a fine character, and, I believe, a good workman. I particularly ask you not to discharge him."

"Senator Lodge, you surely know the laws of Congress governing Navy yard discharges. If I do as you request, I violate those laws and the Navy regulations. I'm sorry to refuse you, senator, but there is nothing else I can do."

"I'm very sorry." And he hung up.

Some days later, at a reception, I was introduced to Senator Henry Cabot Lodge.

"Commander Beach," he began, "I have an apology to make to you. I myself wrote the law regulating Navy yard discharges. I knew you would make the reply you did. But consider my position: one of my most earnest supporters and loyal friends, a man I am very grateful to, sat by me at my home in Nahant while I was telephoning to you. He was greatly distressed; and came to me confident of my friendship and my help. I explained the law, but he implored me to telephone to you. We great statesmen are sometimes very human, Commander Beach!"

And so are naval officers. We shook hands with mutual admiration and respect. One day Admiral Fremont called me to his office.

"Beach," said he, "here is a handwritten letter to me from Secretary of the Navy Meyer. It encloses a personal note to him from the vice president of the United States. Read both of them."

The letter from Vice President James S. Sherman stated that I had discharged a workman whose brother was his strong political supporter and friend. He asked Secretary George von L. Meyer to have him reinstated. The secretary asked Fremont to do this.

"You'd better put him back," said the commandant.

"All right, Admiral, I'll cancel his discharge. But I want these letters kept. If I am court-martialed, my star witnesses will be the vice president of the United States, and the secretary of the Navy."

Fremont laughed heartily. "I hope you will be court-martialed. That would be the best joke ever. Rest assured, these letters will be kept."

The man was reemployed. The first thing he did was come to see me. Not to thank me, however. He was scornful and sneering.

"You thought you were pretty big, didn't you?" he said. "Let me warn you to leave me alone. If you dare to bother me again, you'll get knocked down again. You'd better not monkey with a friend of the vice president of the United States!"

"My friend," I rejoined, "that was only round one. Now the second has begun. You are again discharged. Get out of my office! Go to your friend, the vice president, and see what he can do for you this time!"

I stated the circumstances in a letter to Fremont, asking him to forward the letter, with his own comments, to the vice president. A letter from the latter was received in which my action was heartily approved.

One day a man of fine appearance came to my office. He was in his early thirties. I liked him instantly. "I am Curley, mayor of Boston," he began. "Now, look here, Commander Beach, we politicians must look out for our friends. I'm trying to the best of my ability to give Boston a good, clean, honest, economical government. I must have the backing of my friends, or I fail. And I must help my friends, or they won't back me. I do stand by them. In fact, I once spent three months in jail for a friend. Jail didn't keep me from going to Congress, nor from being made mayor of Boston. Now, look here, Beach; you're going to have a layoff; here's a list of good friends of mine who work in your shops. I'm asking you to see that none of them are discharged."

"Mr. Mayor," I replied, "you shouldn't bother with a subordinate officer. Go with your list of names direct to the commandant, Admiral Fremont."

"Hell!" said the mayor of Boston. "I'll never go to see that gentleman! Why, only last week Congressman Billy Murray of the Charlestown district went to see him. 'Mr. Commandant,' said Billy, 'I'm Congressman Murray from this district.' 'Mr. Congressman Murray,' said your Admiral Fremont, 'will you kindly take off your hat when you enter my private office?' Beach, do you think the mayor of Boston should go to see a duck like that?"

We both laughed. I was sorry, but I couldn't help him. And he understood.

Once I was hauled up on the carpet by the G.A.R. (Grand Army of the Republic) for discharging a Civil War veteran employed as a sweeper for two dollars a day. The veteran was the only witness I called in my defense. I proved that the only use he made of his broom was as a crutch to keep him from falling. Another time I discharged eighty-six-year-old Frank Mitchell, whose claim to Navy yard employment was that he was a member of the crew of the *Kearsarge* in 1864 when she sank the Confederate raider *Alabama*. For awhile this looked serious. But by Navy Department records I was able to prove that Mitchell had enlisted aboard the *Kearsarge* in 1867. That let me out, and Frank Mitchell also.

A man runs against many snags ashore that he never meets on blue water. I was glad indeed in the spring of 1913 to receive preparatory orders to report to the USS *Vestal* as her new commanding officer. She would be my first command.

17

FIRST COMMAND

The USS Vestal

A captain taking his first command frequently amuses his juniors by showing his joy. He is up and down, to and fro, in and out, at all hours of the
day and night. To him, at least, his ship is a thing of beauty. After years of sub-
ordination, he now says to one, "Come!" and he cometh; to another, "Go!"
and he goeth. His "yes" or "no" is final. Upon him lie a thousand responsibilities; and to meet these he has, as detailed in the regulations, a thousand powers. Smokeless powder must be inspected, boilers must be tested, safety valves
lifted, engines overhauled, brasses fitted, lost motion taken up, coal and oil
consumption analyzed, guns examined, all mechanisms tried, all electrical
devices constantly observed.

The Navy Department does not, however, take the doing of these things
for granted; specific reports are required. These reports are carefully checked
in Washington by experienced officers, mostly former skippers themselves.
Should they find abnormal or less-than-satisfactory conditions—too much
sickness, bad discipline, poor work at target practice, excessive consumption
of fuel, poor working of the engines, or undue loss of equipment (to name only

some of the possibilities)—pointed queries, detailed instructions, or even a court of inquiry, may follow.

At intervals an inspection board descends upon a ship and tests it, or examines her from stem to stern and from fighting tops to keel. I once saw Commander C. F. Hughes, later senior admiral of the Navy (that is, chief of naval operations), squirming for hours under the boilers of a ship, investigating defects in an inaccessible place.

The captain is responsible for everything; but is thrilled to the fingertips with his new duties and powers.

The *Vestal* had been built as a Navy collier; but was converted into a fleet repair ship. As her first skipper after the conversion, I was happy with the knowledge that she had been selected for it because of the solid structure of her hull (she had been built to deliver coal at high speed directly to warships that would come right alongside), and the power and dependability of her engine. She was the size of a battleship and could make battleship speed (in those days sixteen knots, which was a very respectable speed for a fleet auxiliary). She carried no armor, and her few small guns were for emergency defense only. Prior to this, the Navy had proved the worth of several small supply ships, and now had the ambitious purpose of supplying a floating, miniature, Navy yard. We crew members of the *Vestal*, however, used to say proudly that our main battery, our extensive and highly capable collection of master shops, was as valuable to the fleet as the guns of any battleship.

Father's background as an engineering officer showed clearly in his detailed description of the shops on board the *Vestal*, and what he could do with them. His selection for this assignment was very likely due to growing recognition in the Navy of his special abilities in this field. Father's pride in his first command charmed me, his young son who now, many years later, is preparing his autobiography for publication. One of his special delights occurred when, for purposes of fleet maneuvers, *Vestal*, the size of a battleship, was designated as such, and deployed in the battle line. He spoke of this fairly often, usually in response to my persistent questions, and wrote of it in his autobiography. It may also be mentioned, in passing, that under a later skipper *Vestal* distinguished herself at Pearl Harbor on 7 December 1941, when the Japanese attacked.

———————

We had on board mechanics of all trades. The plant included a machine shop, with turret and other lathes, and with shapers, slotters, drills, planers, and other power tools. We had a foundry capable of making five-ton castings; and an electric shop that could build and wind the largest armature to be found on any naval vessel. There were also carpenter, blacksmith, pattern, coppersmith, and boiler making shops, all of them top grade.

At times, when at anchor, or alongside a pier, one had to be reminded that the *Vestal* was a ship. Sometimes twenty-four hours a day, one heard the pounding of steam hammers or the tap—tap—tap of compressed air riveting machines. In the foundry men stripped to the waist poured melted iron, or brass, copper, or lead, into molds. Pipes were brazed by the coppersmiths. In the machine shop, a hundred machine tools, some large, some small, were grinding, punching, cutting, and milling pieces, sometimes large castings, of the hardest iron and steel. Large dynamo armatures were rewound. Boilerplates were rolled, and boiler tubes bent to specific curves. Whenever we were with the fleet, mechanics from the other ships would come aboard for special jobs. At such times the *Vestal* was like an industrial plant ashore. We could do anything, and loved to show off. In addition, the ship was equipped with large store rooms, and with a refrigerating room to carry huge amounts of frozen meats for the fleet.

In the fall of 1913 we shoved off from the Boston Navy Yard for Guacanayabo Gulf, some 160 miles west of Guantánamo Bay. This curve in the Cuban coast, better known to sailors of my day as "Hungry Gulf," was an area to which Navy ships usually retired in winter for intensive work that the public knew little of. Unlike Guantánamo, a fine, well-protected deep-water harbor on the south coast of Cuba, Guacanayabo Gulf is a very large indentation in the coastline in which sailing warships could anchor essentially right on station, or proceed easily to sea with almost any wind. It is well suited to revictualing or more recently coaling our warships because of high ground to the north that pretty much protected the gulf from bad weather. Food spoilage in the Caribbean climate, however, in the early days of its use brought about its unappetizing name.

In Hungry Gulf we found Rear Admiral Clifford J. Bush, with a squadron of battleships conducting target practice. Navy regulations require the captain of a ship falling in with a fleet commander to report immediately aboard the flagship. Accordingly, as soon as we anchored, I lowered a cutter and tried to pay my official call. But before I could reach the flagship, it steamed away. Returning, we had a three mile pull to windward. I then wrote a note to Admiral Bush explaining my failure to call, and dispatched it that evening by the guard boat, a large launch that makes the rounds of the fleet for mail. That night a wireless message came from the admiral: "Not satisfactory."

This message puzzled me, but it also made me angry. I deserved no such reprimand. On top of that, it was generally a "given" that an admiral's pronouncement of "not satisfactory" might finish the career of a captain under him. The injustice of this treatment surprised me, for I had known Bush twenty-five years. Such a peremptory message was unlike him.

Next morning, early, I was in a steam launch headed full speed for the flagship, now miles away. Admiral Bush received me with his usual warm-hearted cordiality. I was too much disturbed to reciprocate, something he immediately noticed. "What's the matter, Beach?" he asked.

"I exceedingly regret you should have found it necessary to send me this radiogram, sir," I replied.

He read it carefully; then sent his Marine orderly to fetch his original message from the flagship's radio room. A moment later he handed it to me with a grin, saying, "This is what I sent, Beach." The message, in his own handwriting, was: "Note satisfactory."

This little incident indicates the effect of adverse criticism on a naval officer. His reputation for character and efficiency is his invested capital. Take this away and his usefulness is gone. Living closely together, officers know the ins and outs of each other's lives. No one is more "touchy" about his professional reputation than a naval officer. A small thing, but an important one.

When the business about the official call was adjusted to everyone's satisfaction, our ship delivered stores and provisions to various fleet units, then heaved up her anchor to steam for the island of Culebra, off the east coast of Puerto Rico, where the fleet was to hold target practice. Just as we were starting to go through the water, however, Paymaster Fred McMillan came rushing to me much excited. "Captain!" he cried, "we've got to break off and go into Santiago de Cuba! Our ice machine has had a big accident. It's totally smashed! In this hot weather down here, our frozen meat will spoil in a day!"

"Paymaster," I replied, "We're to report to the commander in chief at Culebra at a particular time and have not an hour to spare. This ship is to take the place of an absent battleship in an attack on Culebra by a hostile fleet. We will not stop at Santiago, no matter what, even if our meat rots long before we get to Culebra."

The paymaster, who was also in effect the fleet's commissary officer, was insistent. The fleet was expecting fresh meat from us, and failure to supply it would bring each of us a reprimand. He certainly had a good point. On the other hand, I felt my usefulness would be ended if I failed to report with my ship at the designated time. And, it must be admitted, I would have gone to almost any lengths to prevent losing my chance of commanding a battleship, even a spurious one, in a fleet problem.

We now descended to the ice machine room where I found my executive officer, Connelly, and my chief engineer, Oberlin. The cylinders had cracked, thus demolishing the machine. We could easily build a new one on board, but the meat would spoil while we were doing it. I knew how popular I would be if we arrived with one hundred thousand pounds of rotten meat for a fleet of battleships that wanted nothing so much as a good, filling dinner (that had been promised for weeks) after the strain of target practice.

As always, Connelly's brain worked quickly. Once, as noted later, it worked too quickly, but that's another yarn that will be told in its place. "Captain," he said, "we can make a new machine out of some junk we have stored below. And we'll have it going in six or eight hours."

He kept his word. The only deviation was that we built three machines instead of one. They saved the meat; and we arrived at Culebra on time.

Connelly utilized the principle that if compressed air is chilled and then allowed to expand freely, in the process of expansion it absorbs heat; that is, it produces "cold." Accordingly, he dug out two discarded feed pumps and an old steam launch engine from the stock of used parts that all naval ships, especially repair ships, routinely carry in case of unexpected need. He set them up as "ice machines" by running them on compressed air, supplied by an air compressor, instead of the usual steam. This air, hot when it left the compressor, was first chilled somewhat by passing it through an old steam coil hung over the ship's side in the sea water. Then it was further chilled by doing work (expanding against pressure) in the cylinders of the machines. Because heat and energy are convertible, this work involved loss of heat—and Connelly optimized these results by having the feed pump valves cut off at half stroke. The discharge of these pumps, which drew water from casks, was throttled down to increase the work. The launch engine was an expansive, compound engine instead of the simpler feed pumps, but he hooked it up exactly the same way, except for the timing of the cut-off.

Finally, the exhaust from these three air engines (this of course was what we were interested in, not the "work" they supposedly accomplished) was led through holes in a bulkhead into the refrigerating room. Free expansion of the chilled compressed air produced a freezing temperature, and five minutes after the machines started, the exhaust orifices were covered with heavy frost. Wild was our exultation.

We had hardly reached the fleet when its boats were alongside, presenting peremptory requisitions for fresh meat. They all got what they wanted, and we got shrieks of laughter at the most miserable looking ice machines ever built by man. Soon the whole fleet heard of our rattletrap machines. Lieutenants, captains, and admirals—and some ship's engineering officers—came piling aboard to poke fun at us, and deliver many hearty slaps on the back.

We were satisfied. The fleet got its frozen meat in good condition; the *Vestal* was on time, and everybody loved us. Next day the ships steamed out to attack the inoffensive target island of Culebra, which in fact lived on annual "attacks" by the U.S. Navy. We provided mountains of used target practice ammunition that was salvageable for all sorts of purposes, and much unused or discarded food, all available to Puerto Rican foraging parties that came over whenever the Navy let them. Colonel George Barnett, USMC, with a few Marines, had the duty of defending that unhappy, useless, usually uninhabited island.

A plan of attack had been carefully worked out, the object being to effect a landing without being discovered. There was plenty of deep water if, with the aid of buoys and landmarks, one could find it. My job was to reach a designated landing place in the dead of night, behind the reefs, islets, and rocks; lower boats; and land a thousand fully armed and equipped imaginary men.

But if fire opened on the landing force before it reached the shore, the attack at this point would be defeated.

I believed at the time that we were assigned the most difficult task of all the ships present because it would look better in the newspapers to have a repair ship aground than a battleship. But since we were of battleship size, and drew just as much water as one of our "wagons," doing the job was just as difficult for us as for any of the real battleships.

Lieutenant J. D. Willson, my navigator, and I studied the charts with intense concern, and planned our intrusion. The night was more than dark; it was jet black. Neither moon nor stars were out. We could see nothing. When we drew near to the island, I was indignant with Barnett. He had extinguished the lights of the lighthouses. I could not see Culebra or any other of the many islets I had to dodge. His zeal made things especially tough for us, not to mention really hazardous for *Vestal's* more thinly plated bottom. At dead slow speed we crept in, twisting about, barely missing half a dozen big rocks, while I cursed Barnett's duty-bound hide every time we nearly impaled ourselves. All the same, finally we were close in to shore, able to fix our position by the dim lines of hills I had studied and knew well. By great good luck, we arrived in exactly the right spot, just the right place to land our troops.

We lowered the boats and started for the shore. I was jubilant. No one could expect a ship as big as ours to slip in to such an impossible roadstead in such a gloomy blackness. I had done well, as well as any battleship commander could have. Mentally, I compared my feat with that of Wolfe at the Heights of Abraham. He was a great commander, had put his troops ashore exactly as planned, and so, by golly, had I!

But suddenly the whole shoreline flashed fire, and "Cannon to the right of me, Cannon to the left of me, Cannon in front of me, volleyed and thundered." Colonel George "Napoleon" Barnett was there with his heavy artillery. My language was unprintable. I got back the boats, with their crews and the thousand fictional men, and tried to get out. And, what is more, we did get out, but it was hard work.

I had one more string to my bow. My orders were, if repulsed, to try another spot on the northeast end of the island where no reasonable man would expect any other reasonable man to land.

We ran full speed to this new point of attack, but reached it only after dawn, only to have Napoleon Barnett arrive first, and give us a royal salute of more than 101 guns. I was forced to retire without laurels, but was pleased to learn that all the other ships had had the same luck. This U.S. Marine Corps' Napoleon had "allus got there fustest" with a few Marines.

George Barnett later became commandant of the Marine Corps, from 1914 to 1920, and it's evident that Father thought he fully merited that assignment. His successor in that post, from 1920 to 1929, was none other than John Archer "Gabe" Lejeune, Father's old roommate at Annapolis.

Culebra came near to finishing an important member of my crew, my steward Watson, the kindliest, most devoted darky [sic] I ever knew. He had served me in the *Nevada* and *Montana,* and was now my cabin steward in the *Vestal.* Like Alexis Delatour and my one-time landlady, he had but one fault. In Watson's case, it was an excessive love of liquor. I could keep him sober for three months at a time by keeping him aboard ship; but at the end of this term he was entitled by regulations to shore leave. He would always return ahead of time, and would always follow the same routine.

He would enter my cabin with a brush, pretend to dust, then say, "Mistah Beach, suh, yo' sees ah comes back clean an' sobah, suh—"

"You're drunk again, Watson. Be at mast tomorrow morning for punishment!" My own routine was also always the same. The U.S. Navy could never forgive such dereliction of duty.

"No, suh! May Gawd A'mighty in his infinite mehsey fo'give yo', suh, for aspiratin' mah charactah, suh; ah's a membah ob de charch, suh. Ah had cramps in mah stomach, suh, Mistah Beach, suh; an' Saint Paul in his pistol tells me ter take a little wine fo' mah stomach's sake, suh. Yes, suh, dat's de trufe, Mistah Beach, suh."

"Watson, get into your hammock immediately, or I'll put you in the brig!"

"Yes, suh; thank yo' Mistah Beach, suh. An' I'se goin' ter thank A'mighty Gawd dat yo's de mos' nobles' and de mos' grandes' an' de mos' handsomes' captain in de Navy. Thank yew, suh, Mistah Beach, suh."

But at Culebra, Watson had been aboard for more than three months, since no shore going was allowed there, or at Guacanayabo Bay. He felt abused. On our arrival at Culebra, I had put a bottle of bay rum on a rack in my bathroom, and forgot about it. (Only the captain rates a private bathroom aboard a Navy ship. It's one of the wonderful perks of command.) The next day I noticed that Watson was acting as he always did after returning from shore leave. I also noticed that my bottle of bay rum was half empty.

"Watson," I called out, "You've been drinking my bay rum!"

"Mistah Beach, suh, ah swear wid uplifted han' befo' all de angels ob Heavin dat ah ain't tech'd one drap ob yo' bay rum. An', Mistah Beach, ah asks A'mighty Gawd ter strike me dead as I stan' ef ah has drunk yo' bay rum. No, suh!—"

"Watson, since you have defended yourself so emphatically, I accept your statement. Now, tell me what became of my bay rum."

"Well, suh, since yo' puts it *dat* way, suh, I tells you confidentiary dat ah jest squacked him right down. But Mistah Beach, suh, doan' yo' go an' tell Mr. Connelly, suh. Mr. Connelly am a powerful fine officer, suh, but I fears, suh, he doan' read de Bible, an' doan' know dat Saint Paul in his pistols tells us believers ter take a little bay rum fer our stomach's sake, suh. Yes, suh, Mistah Beach, suh, dat's de trufe, suh."

Poor Watson. A few years later, he survived a convulsion of nature that destroyed a mighty warship. Then, getting ashore, he drank a bottle of bay rum that killed him.

About a month later the *Vestal* steamed back into the naval station at Guantánamo, Cuba, where the entire North Atlantic fleet had assembled. That afternoon I received an invitation from Captain Niblack and the officers of the *Michigan* to come, with the other officers of the *Vestal*, to a smoker. I sent for Connelly and gave him the invitation.

"Pass this around," I said. "We'll leave here at eight o'clock."

"Very well, sir," replied Connelly, "but of course I'll not go."

"Why 'of course'? You're executive officer, and we're all invited. Why won't you go?"

"Captain, I entered the Navy as an apprentice boy, and served for years as an enlisted man. Through the great kindness of officers I was given a commission, and now I'm a lieutenant commander. But, Captain, you know, and I know, that these social affairs are for graduates of the Naval Academy and staff officers, not for fellows that came up from the ranks."

This made me indignant. "You should be ashamed to say that," I fired back. "You know you were promoted by the laws of our country just like any other officer. You are criticizing your brother officers, making them out to be a lot of snobs. Connelly, I tell you plainly, if you are not fit to go into the society of other officers, you are not fit to be a lieutenant commander, or the executive officer of this ship!"

Connelly had a temper. His eyes flashed. "I'm as fit as any of them!" he cried. "I just felt that I wasn't wanted."

"Of course you're as fit, and of course you are wanted. Now drop these foolish notions and be ready to leave at eight o'clock!"

We have a number of officers in our Navy who entered as enlisted men and won commissions, not by chance, but on sheer merit. Once commissioned they mold their own futures. One hundred enlisted apprentices each year are sent to the Naval Academy. Others who have become "warrant" officers, not Academy men, are commissioned from time to time. It is not the Naval Academy, but the Navy itself that is the great teacher.

Although this is absolutely true, prior to World War II most officers of our Navy came from the Naval Academy. During that terrible conflict there were many others taken in from all sources, and leavened by the presence of "trade school boys," their performance was everything that could have been expected. Since then, the greatly increased size of the Navy has mandated a much bigger officer corps than the Naval Academy could maintain on its own, with the result that it is far more diversified.

Another conversation with Connelly, later, when the ship was at Vera Cruz, pops into my recollection. We were in my cabin after dinner. Without much forethought, I suddenly remarked: "Connelly, let's go ashore and call on the Gurleÿs."

Connelly jumped up, ablaze with indignation. "You insult me, sir! Captain Beach, I don't understand you for suggesting such a thing! I don't know and I don't care to know that kind of people!"

I was astounded—and then a light broke upon me. "Connelly," I said, "Mr. and Mrs. Gurley are two fine young people, refugees from Guadalajara, where they ran some kind of school. Their little baby is ailing; their small house is a hot box. I thought we'd call on them and take them a cake of ice. Now that our ice machines are running again, we have a lot of this. Perhaps you've made a mistake. Their name is spelled 'G-u-r-l-e-y.'"

Poor Connelly choked. "Captain," he said, "I should have known better. I humbly beg your pardon. Can you forgive me, sir?"

"On one condition," I replied, "—if you'll go with me tonight to call on them." We went, with ice, spent a pleasant evening, and were morally certain that the Gurley baby benefited too.

In April 1914, the *Vestal* was at the Norfolk Navy Yard. Trouble between the United States and Mexico was brewing. General Victoriano Huerta had seized control of the government and had deposed the president, Francisco Madero, who was later assassinated.

President Wilson refused to recognize Huerta as chief of the Mexican government; and things began to happen. Two American naval officers were arrested and jailed in Tampico. A big German freighter, the *Ypiranga*, loaded with war munitions from American factories, was speeding to Vera Cruz to land them into the hands of Huerta's henchmen. Our North Atlantic fleet was dispatched to that port with orders to seize the customhouse, because it was feared that this cargo of ammunition might be used against Americans.

The *Vestal* was ordered to leave Norfolk and join the fleet at Vera Cruz, where we arrived a few days after the American ships had captured the customhouse and the rest of Vera Cruz. Only two of the smaller ships had used their guns, firing to protect our landing force from hordes of snipers in the windows and on the roofs of buildings. If the great guns of the fleet had been also used, the result would have been a holocaust. As it was, only two buildings were seriously damaged. Several hundred Mexicans were killed, and eighteen of our men.

See Father's *Dan Quin of the Navy* for a fictional account of this episode.

Shortly after midnight on the day following our arrival, an orderly woke me with a request from the commander in chief to report to him at once. I was soon talking with Admiral Charles Badger aboard the flagship *Wyoming*.

"Beach," he began, "A piston of one of the cylinders of our ice machine is broken. I am told that if this machine is not running within twelve hours we shall have to transfer our frozen meat to some other ship. Can you make and install a new piston within that time?"

"Yes, sir, if I may take the broken piston with me to use as a pattern."

I delivered the new piston within the twelve hours. Then the admiral said, "Beach, I have several gun boats that need extensive repairs, some of which will require dry docking. In the Navy yard over at San Juan de Ulloa there is a floating dry dock which, I am told, the Mexicans have recently used. I had about determined to send the *Nashville* north, for she needs docking and new boilers. Do you know how to operate a floating dry dock?"

"Yes, sir; it's easy. To sink it, you simply have to fill the tanks; to raise it, you pump them out."

As a matter of fact, I had never in my life even seen a floating dry dock, though I knew, at least theoretically, how it was supposed to function.

"Do you know how to build boilers?"

"Yes, indeed, Admiral. Give me an examination on Wilson's 'Boilers,' and I will prove that I do."

"Can the *Vestal* undertake work of that magnitude?"

"Yes, sir, we are especially fitted to build boilers for the gunboat *Nashville*."

"That's good news. Tomorrow you will receive orders to move to the inner harbor and to assume command of the old fortress of San Juan de Ulloa, with its prison and Navy yard. Get the floating dock ready for the *Nashville*; and after she leaves the dock, bring her alongside the *Vestal* and rebuild her boilers. I'm glad I won't have to send the *Nashville* away. One reason is, I need her. Another is, I want to keep her long-legged, red-haired captain, Commander Bostwick, near me. I'm sure you know him. Didn't you serve with him in the *Philadelphia*? Finish work on the *Nashville* as soon as you can. Is there any order I can give to expedite her repairs?"

"Yes, Admiral; if you will send me every boiler maker in the fleet, we'll work on her twenty-four hours a day, in three eight-hour shifts."

The *Vestal* was soon moored bow and stern in the inner harbor. The dry dock I gave to our navigator, Willson, whose navigating expertise would not be needed for a while. He knew as much about floating docks as I did, and no more.

But that was enough. He pumped out her tanks, and she rose; he filled them, and down she went. He brought her up; fitted the blocks for the *Nashville*'s bottom; sank her; received the *Nashville*, again raised her with the *Nashville* inside. It has been my experience that a naval officer is willing to accept any task that needs doing, and will make every possible effort to accomplish it.

The *Nashville* was soon back in the water and moored alongside the *Vestal*, and her boilers were rebuilt. After that we took the scout cruiser *Salem* alongside and made extensive repairs to her. Smaller ships and tugs followed.

The day I assumed command of San Juan de Ulloa, a Mexican steamer came in. She was bringing to Vera Cruz 102 recruits for the Mexican army, commanded by a lieutenant named Rojas. As war between the United States and Mexico was possible, Admiral Badger did not intend to let these recruits join the Mexican army. Instead, he sent them over to be confined in the fortress of San Juan de Ulloa.

Cortez landed in 1518 on the reef where the fortress was later built; and his ships were burned there. The fortress had sponsons for some four hundred guns on an encircling wall. To seaward was a moat of clear sea water, now only three feet deep.

Those recruits were the dirtiest, raggedest lot I ever saw. They were emaciated and looked hungry. In a storeroom of the fortress was a quantity of underwear, outer clothing, shoes, and hats, evidently intended for Mexican soldiers. I had Marines herd these woebegone Mexicans to the moat, make them undress, drive them into the water, and give each one some "salt water soap." Some of them, apparently never having seen real soap, at first bit rabidly into it. But they enjoyed the warm sea water, and were soon having a great time soaping themselves. They didn't want to come out; and when dressed in the clean clothes provided, they were quite a decent-looking set of young men.

I had also provided for them a great lot of beans and bread. And, watching them eat ravenously, I knew why they had looked so hungry.

The next day, Professor Carlos Cusacks, who spoke Spanish, came from the flagship with an order to investigate each recruit. They were of Indian blood, and had all come from jails in the province of Tabasco. This struck me as an amazing method of recruiting. Each man was questioned as to the reason for being in jail. Twenty-nine stated that they had been convicted of murder and sentenced to life imprisonment. Only one of the twenty-nine claimed innocence. As I remember, all the rest had been jailed for admitted crimes of violence.

I kept them at work for five hours a day, cleaning the old fortress as it had not been cleaned for three hundred years. They bathed daily in the moat, and they had all the good Mexican food they could eat. In the afternoons they were allowed to gambol in the open prison yard, and at night they slept in the barracks. Soon they were a happy, contented set of men. When I went to the old fortress I would hear shouts of, "*El commandante viene!*" (The commandante is coming.) I soon realized that they regarded me as the source of good food, good quarters, and easy work, hence a friend.

At this time Mexico was in the throes of the 1910 Revolution—a revolution that would last until 1918.

A fictional version of U.S. occupation of Vera Cruz, the full Mexican name of which, according to Father, was *Tres Veces Heroique Veracruz* (Three Times Heroic True Cross), combined with a fairly accurate account of the 102 former prisoners and their care, may be found in *Dan Quin of the Navy*. Father's own duties in command of the old fortress San Juan de Ulloa are fictionally taken up by Captain Gaunt of the fictional battleship *Montana*—bigger than, but otherwise similar to the armored cruiser in which Father had served. As commandant of Mare Island Navy Yard, in 1919, Father supervised launching of the great new battleship *California*, the same which was so badly damaged at Pearl Harbor in 1941. Immediately thereafter construction began on the new *Montana*, far bigger than Father's old ship, bigger even than the magnificent *California*. The choice of names for Father's fictional ships was thus somewhat predictable; and the tiny, silver-plated riveting hammer with which he ceremoniously "tested" the first rivets in *Montana*'s keel, later somewhat damaged in my own basement workshop, is now on exhibit in the U.S. Naval Institute's new headquarters.

This new, great *Montana*, however, was never completed. Construction was halted by the Naval Treaty of 1922, and I can still recall seeing huge rusty plates that had been piled up near her building ways. She would have been half again the size of the *Arizona* sunk at Pearl Harbor, and to the battleship lovers of her day would have been absolutely magnificent, though anachronistic too. In view of the coming debacle at the hands of Japanese Naval Air, it's just as well that she never served, except as a source of steel plates needed for battle-damage repair in World War II.

18

SAN JUAN DE ULLOA

We went through some heavy "northers" at Vera Cruz. These storms come up with great suddenness and raise tremendous seas. Inside the harbor, we were snug and secure. Outside, the battleships had to keep steam up during the norther, drop a second anchor, veer chain to get a better "bite" on the ground, and sometimes, even with extra anchors down, keep the engines turning.

During one of these storms a big deep-draft merchant ship, laden with stores of which the admiral was in immediate need, was in the offing. Admiral Badger directed the ship to proceed through the reefs to the customhouse to discharge these stores. The captain of the merchant ship emphatically refused, saying it could not be done. The admiral signaled to my Naval Academy classmate, Commander Herman Stickney, his collector of customs for Vera Cruz, to secure a local pilot to help bring the ship in. All the local pilots refused. "Too risky," they said.

Stickney took a tug; steered it through reefs enveloped in spindrift, and in columns of water driven by the hurricane; reached the merchantman; climbed up the Jacob's ladder trailing astern—by this time he and his uniform were soaking wet—and ordered, "Up anchor!" "Full speed ahead!" "Hard a-star-board!" Standing on the merchantman's bridge, water pouring out of his clothes, he brought the ship safely through several miles of reefs to the inner harbor.

As in the case of Willson and the floating dry dock, if a thing must be done, a naval officer will usually have the nerve, and the self-confidence, to give it his best effort. After I had been at San Juan de Ulloa about two months, Stickney was called to Norfolk; and I, designated by the admiral, appointed by the commanding general, Frederick Funston, became collector of customs during Stickney's absence. Stickney had found the customhouse in a dreadful mess. All the Mexican employees had left. American bluejackets, totally ignorant of even the basic needs of accounting procedures, had camped in the place for days. Records had been piled helter-skelter, used to keep tent bottoms dry or for insulation, unwittingly taken away, even carelessly destroyed. Their officers, not realizing what was happening until too late, had given poor guidance.

Stickney knew nothing about customhouses, but had been assigned a job. His orders were to reorganize the customhouse, employ necessary clerks and laborers, and administer it according to the Mexican laws. In a few days he had brought order out of chaos. The Mexican government had forbidden Mexicans, under threat of punishment, to work for Americans. Stickney hired American refugees and certain Mexicans proscribed by their government. They may have had their problems with other bosses, but they worked for Stickney. Freighters were constantly unloading, and import dues were collected.

Relieving Stickney, I found he had created a thoroughly organized, going concern. This Vera Cruz customhouse was one of the most important institutions of the Republic of Mexico. Almost all Mexican imports were landed there. The warehouses occupied half a mile along the waterfront. When I first sat at my desk I examined some papers written in Spanish. Soon I was floundering. Seated close to me, head down, typing hard, was a beautiful young woman of Spanish extraction. She was perhaps twenty years old. I looked at her, seeking help with a Spanish phrase; but she continued to hammer away, oblivious of my existence, or, apparently, that I was her boss.

I said, "Senorita!"

She jumped up like a shot out of a gun. "Mi Capitan?"

Those lovely eyes pierced me through and through. Why not say frankly that I quite forgot what I had intended to ask her. "The light that lies in woman's eyes . . . ," etc.

She waited. Something pouring out of those eyes held me speechless. And then, in soft, heart-stirring words, she said, "Mi Capitan, my name is Lola. I only get half enough pay here!"

I was instantly convinced of the shameful injustice being done Lola, not that I had the faintest idea what her wages were. Lola excused herself, and disappeared; in a few minutes she reappeared with another vision of blue-eyed loveliness, a girl of about eighteen.

"Mi Capitan," said Lola, "this is my sister, Pat. She, too, is getting only half as much as she ought to have!"

These girls belonged to a family of close friends of President Madero and therefore were not popular with the Huertistas. Both had been educated in the United States. I became a grandpa to the sisters. A few months later Lola was married aboard the battleship *Georgia* to an American oilman named Stephens. A year later Pat was married aboard the *Machias* to Ensign Addoms, an officer of that gunboat.

Father must have checked Lola and Pat's married names carefully. Addoms is correctly spelled. He retired as a captain in 1946.

From the American refugees, Stickney had chosen for his assistants men high in the railroad and mining affairs of Mexico. With their active daily help, the customhouse ran on roller bearings. Nevertheless, there were always difficult problems to solve.

Once an indignant protest was made by a firm that was importing mining machinery. We always collected all import duties in cash before permitting the importer to take possession of his materials, whatever they were. I also knew, of course, that eleven miles beyond the lines occupied by General Funston's forces a Huertista customhouse also collected duties in cash, and evidently used fairly persuasive methods in the process.

My demand for import duties on this mining machinery, amounting to 120,000 Mexican pesos, or $60,000, was met with the statement that they had been paid before we took charge. But they had no record of such payment, and in any case, this would have been contrary to the procedures Stickney had put in place. It took a little time, and some difficulty, but finally I found a complete record disproving this claim. The importers then came down with a battery of lawyers from Mexico City, vehemently demanding relief from import duties because they would have to pay a second time. But a naval officer who has received explicit orders is not open to legal argument, especially when he holds proof to the contrary.

When I announced that I would, as required by Mexican law, sell the mining machinery at public auction, they became very upset. Not only had they misrepresented the facts of their payment in the first place and ignored the papers I'd found showing they had not paid, they continued to argue that I was unfairly forcing them to pay a second time. However, I had no recourse. If skullduggery of any kind was involved, bribery perhaps, that was none of my affair. I was applying the laws of Mexico. I stuck to my guns—that was all I could do—and finally, they paid.

We kept a strict account, for the Mexican government, of every centavo received. The U.S. Navy was acting merely as a trustee. Whether the Mexican government later returned the duties collected by Huerta, if any had indeed been collected, I cannot say. In the case of this mining machinery, a cablegram from Secretary of State William Jennings Bryan called for a full report of the transaction; and another, later, gave word that my course was approved.

One day a tall, dignified-looking gentleman appeared, with a very heavy suitcase. "I am Senor Ascaragua," he said. "I was administrador de la aduana (customs) when you Americans drove us out, and in fact, this room was my office. One difficulty here has been to prevent the contrabanding of gold and silver coin. It is a crime by Mexican law to send such coin out of the country. You can sell in your country, for one dollar, a gold coin that you buy here for seventy-six cents. That is an unnatural depreciation—gold is gold everywhere—but it has resulted from the financial conditions of several years past.

"A contraband runner fills a suitcase with Mexican gold coin, gets to the United States, melts it down, and on every $1,000.00 of this bullion he makes a criminal profit of $240.00.

"Shortly before you came, I learned that an American living in Mexico named McManus was leaving on the Ward Line steamer *Esperanza*, and was carrying contraband gold coin. I personally went aboard this steamer and found two bags of gold in his suitcase, which I seized, giving him a receipt. I placed the gold in this safe just behind you. At the time of your assault upon Vera Cruz, not knowing what might happen, and fearing for the safety of this money, I carried it away with me. I have now brought it back. I will ask you to count it and to give me your official custom house receipt for it."

Senor Ascaragua then took two canvas bags from his suitcase, each filled with gold coin. I felt like the Count of Monte Cristo. Each bag held exactly twenty-eight thousand pesos in gold coin.

A few days after this, Mr. McManus came to call upon me. He wanted me to give him fifty-six thousand gold pesos. He said he had been robbed of his money; and he expected that his own country, having in its possession the very coins stolen from him, would return them. He was abusively angry when I refused, and stormed at me when he left.

McManus could be, when he pleased, attractive in manner and appearance. He made friends quickly and easily, and soon managed to become friendly with General Funston. About a week later, the general's judge advocate general, Major John Biddle Porter, of the U.S. Army, whom I knew well, came to see me. He was laboring under stress of deep feeling.

"Captain Beach," he began, "I have had a bad break with General Funston. High words have passed between us. He has signed, and handed to Mr. McManus, an order directing you to deliver to him the fifty-six thousand pesos now in your possession. I protested against this. I told the general I had investigated the facts of the case. In the first place, McManus is a criminal by the laws of Mexico. No matter to whom the money belonged, it is a crime to take it out of the country. Mexico has a perfect right to enact such a law. Further, the money never belonged to McManus; he was simply employed by a gang of scoundrels as a contraband runner. This money was properly seized by Senor Ascaragua, and its disposition is now in the hands of a Mexican court. I told General Funston he had no right to give you such an order. This is a matter that may cause serious trouble between Mexico and the United States, and we shall be entirely, and, I will add, shamefully, in the wrong. General Funston disdains my advice. I have told him that my duty as an American would cause me to use every effort to prevent this; and that I would inform you of everything that has passed between him and me about it."

"Thank you, Major," I replied, "but now I must ask your legal advice. Must I obey General Funston's order and deliver this gold to McManus?"

"I'm afraid you must," he mournfully answered, "but I wouldn't do it on the order McManus is bringing you. I would suggest for your own protection that you insist that his order state it is caused by imperative military necessity; that it is peremptory; that you have no option except to obey it immediately; and that you, as an officer of the customhouse, are relieved of all responsibility in obeying this imperative military order."

I jotted all this down, and Major Porter left: a downcast, worried, and indignant officer of the U.S. Army. And then the debonair McManus came in. "Captain Beach," he began, "I'll have the fifty-six thousand pesos that were stolen from me and that are now in your possession, if you don't mind!"

He then added in triumphant tones, "And to induce you to hurry, I'll give you this little order from Major General Funston." This order was addressed to me as collector of customs. I read it carefully. It directed me to deliver to McManus the fifty-six thousand gold pesos in my possession, which had been stolen from him.

I handed it back to McManus, saying quietly but distinctly, "I refuse to accept this order."

McManus again exploded. He threatened everything about me.

"Mr. McManus," I said when I had a moment, "I refuse to discuss this matter with you. You will please excuse me from further conversation."

He left, shouting I would soon hear from General Funston—which I did. But in the meantime I prepared an order from him addressed to myself, along the lines advised by Major Porter.

Soon a soldier, General Funston's orderly, came to see me.

"Sir, are you the collector of customs?"

"Yes."

"General Funston directs you to report to him immediately, sir."

I found the general in what a novelist might call "a towering rage." "Commander Beach, you are under my orders! Do you disobey the orders of your commanding general?" he shouted.

"I obey your proper orders, General."

"I'll order you court-martialed for disobeying my orders!"

"But that wouldn't settle the matter, sir."

"What do you mean?"

"I mean that I will prove in my defense, before any court, that your written order is an improper one. I am the custodian of a large sum of money which I hold in trust. I know that it was seized, in accordance with the law, by the Mexican government, from a reputed contrabandist, McManus. It was not stolen from him. If I am court-martialed I will summon Major Porter to testify as to the legal advice and information he has given you. And I will have plenty of evidence to show the character of this McManus."

The general was more enraged than ever. "I'll dismiss you, sir. I won't have an officer who defies me!"

"But that won't help you, sir. You can only appoint a naval officer nominated by the commander in chief, in compliance with the law governing a joint Army and Navy occupation of a foreign port. I would demand a court of inquiry that would bring to light every fact connected with this matter."

"Commander Beach, I have no desire or intention to give an improper order. I have the power and authority, as a military necessity, to have my orders obeyed. If my order is not correctly worded, I will change it. Do you intend to obey my order?"

"Not the one I sent back to you, sir."

"How do you want the order worded?"

I handed him the order I had written. He signed it immediately and returned it to me.

"Commander Beach," he said, now in a kindly tone, "I am here to protect American citizens. We have in our possession a large sum of money violently torn from McManus, an American. I have reason to believe it was his own property. Americans in Mexico have been robbed and murdered by the hundreds; their property has been destroyed; endless litigation has followed. The dead are not restored to life; the survivors demand recompense that never comes. Diplomats and lawyers argue for years, and nothing results. I cannot work that way. It has been my lifetime object to rectify wrongs immediately, whenever I have the chance. I hope and believe I am right in my judgment of McManus. I do know the money was taken from him. Whether or not it was his, the Mexicans would never return it, no matter what. If he has no right to it—well, I hope he'll keep them arguing as long as they have kept our people arguing in other cases.

"Now let's forget any feeling we have had. I am well satisfied with my collector of customs. And if you'll invite me to dinner aboard your ship sometime soon, I'll bring with me a Russian officer who wishes to go over that big fortress of yours."

So McManus got the money the next day. He was in such haste that, beyond opening the bags, he made no count before signing a receipt for the gold, and I never did discover what happened to it after that.

I was a busy man at Vera Cruz. All day and all night my ship shops were busy hammering, grinding, cutting, and drilling. I discussed every job with the officer in charge of it, and each day inspected each job in progress.

The admiral's chief of staff, my classmate Charles Frederic Hughes, came on board frequently. He gave me the admiral's orders, and wanted to know many things. How that old walrus found time to sleep, I cannot imagine. Every radiogram and cablegram addressed to the commander in chief was delivered to Hughes as soon as it was received. About a hundred of these came each night. No wonder the old boy became the senior four-starred admiral of the Navy. Since we had been at Annapolis, back in the stone age, he has averaged about twenty-four hours of work a day, some twelve hours more than the rest of us were good for. I have been told that when he commanded the *Birmingham* he was in the double bottoms, or under a boiler, when not on the bridge; and in the terrific Atlantic hurricane of 1911, his tremendous force of personality and superior seamanship saved his ship. As used to be said in the days of sail, every hair of his head is a rope yarn, and when he sweats he sweats tar. And with all of this, he has a heart, too.

Besides ship work, I spent an hour or more daily at the fortress. While Stickney was away, I was at the customhouse at nine each morning. Soon after my painful talk with General Funston, which—thank goodness—had ended with friendly words, the general sent for me.

"Beach," he began, "the Huertistas and Carranzistas have been fighting near here. The latter were defeated and chased into our lines. Major Porter advises me that I must intern them; that they cannot evade capture by surrendering to us and then go out and fight the Huertistas again. Whatever our relations with Mexico as a whole, we are neutral as between these contending factions. But I have no place to keep these refugees. Can you confine them in your fortress? This will be a great help to me. There are nine officers and ninety-odd men. You may use your judgment as to paroling the officers."

"Yes, General, I can take care of them."

At eleven o'clock the next day I took a tug to the terminal wharf, where the Carranzistas were delivered to me. They were gaunt, lean, and sad in appearance. Obviously they had been having hard times. There was no luggage.

We shoved off, heading first for the entrance to the harbor, with the grim old fortress on our port hand. The Carranzistas seemed intensely interested in the warships visible outside. Then suddenly, to come up broadside to the landing at San Juan de Ulloa, I put the helm hard a-starboard (i.e., rudder left, or port), and slowed down.

There was great excitement among the men to be interned. Some grew hysterical. "San Juan de Ulloa! Oh, Dios! Dios! Oh, el Inferno!" were among the despairing cries I heard. For years the fortress had been infamous as a prison. Tales of those murky dungeons had traveled far.

The nine officers came to me. Their colonel, Beltrano, a fine looking fellow, said, in a very troubled way, "Captain, two years ago my regiment had more than a thousand men. These are all that are left. We were killed in battle, we froze on the table lands, we thirsted in the desert, we succumbed in the jungles, we starved all the time. But would to God we had died as men under the open sky, Captain, rather than as beasts in these awful dungeons! Oh, God! Oh, God! Do you have to lock us up there? Can't you just let us die in a more decent place?"

Officers and men were weeping. They were desperate. Their grief affected me so that for a moment I could not see; and even now, many years later, as I write of that scene, a film comes over my eyes. I reassured them. "Caballeros, no tienen ustedes miedo! Vengan conmigo. Soy vuestro amigo." (Comrades, I have nothing against you! Come with me. I am your friend.)

The tug was tied up; the soldiers were marched to the barracks where a bountiful Mexican meal awaited them. Then, followed by the nine officers, I entered the fort. Not a word was spoken. We crossed the Navy yard, and passed through a passageway to the prison yard. Ahead of us was the great sea wall of the fortress. Reaching this, I mounted stone steps to the top. Close at hand were the spacious, inviting quarters recently occupied by the Mexican major general in command of the fort and the prison. These quarters, on top of the wall, opened on a garden beautiful with palms, shrubs, and flowers.

Inside were many connecting rooms, comfortably furnished, all open to the breezes from seaward. The first apartment was a lounging room; next to it was a dining room, with a table at which nine places were set. There was clean napery, and a profusion of foods: roast meats of several kinds, green vegetables, beans, tortillas, chile con carne, bread, butter, dulces, and cigarettes. Also, I must confess, there were nine quarts of rich red wine.

"Gentlemen," I said, "this is your dungeon, and your home while with me. This afternoon I want you to eat and sleep and rest. I will be here to make other arrangements with you at five this afternoon. Your soldiers are being well cared for."

These officers were seemingly stunned. For the moment they could not comprehend. Then there were wild cries of joy, and I left. I saw these men daily until I left Vera Cruz. At all times I was made to realize their warm affection for me.

A year later, after I had left the *Vestal* and had become captain of the big armored cruiser *Washington*, I was walking one afternoon on the main street of Vera Cruz with Señora de Reyes, mother of Lola and Pat, both now happily married. Of a sudden I was seized from behind; my arms were pinned to my body; my ribs were crushed. Then I was kissed repeatedly by a hairy monster, first on one cheek, then on the other, with hoarse shouts of, "Mi Capitan! Mi Capitan!" It was Beltrano, now a general. Huerta was gone, and Venustiano Carranza's star was high in the heavens.

19

A CAPTAIN

The History of the Haitian Republic

The *Vestal* left Vera Cruz late in 1914. In December I received a document from the president of the United States, who said that reposing special trust in my fidelity, valor, etc., he had, by and with the advice and consent of the Senate, appointed me to be a captain in the Navy. With a razor blade I eagerly cut off the silver leaves from my most-used uniforms, pinned on new eagles, and gave the rest of my uniform jackets to *Vestal's* tailor shop for a professional "sew-on" job. Soon another letter, signed by Josephus Daniels, secretary of the Navy, directed me to leave the *Vestal* and report to command the armored cruiser *Washington*, sister ship to the wonderful *Montana* in which I'd served as executive officer for Alfred Reynolds a few years earlier. The *Washington* was the flagship of Rear Admiral William B. Caperton, commander of the cruiser force in the Caribbean Sea; within days I found myself again at Vera Cruz.

I have yet to meet a more lovable man than my new admiral. He combined a winning personality with keen judgment that guided him safely through great and unexpected responsibilities. He had only one fault: an innate modesty, a self-deprecation that had to be pierced, before one appreciated the bigness of his soul. I'll have more to say on this subject later.

One stormy day, with a fierce norther blowing and the harbor waters boiling, he sent for me. "Beach," he said, "here is a radiogram from the gunboat *Machias*, at Progreso, saying that a German named Galler has been sentenced by drumhead court-martial to be shot tomorrow morning. Marshall, skipper of the *Machias*, earnestly urges further investigation before the sentence is carried out. Now, you speak Spanish—" (I really didn't, but by this time I could limp along). "Go over to General Carranza in the lighthouse down there at the entrance to the harbor, and make a request of him in my name. Tell him that the sentence of death after this sort of drumhead trial is hardly the way for Mexico to build up her image in the world, and since the Germans have no representative here, because of the war in Europe, I am acting as the German minister would act were there one." As he spoke, I thought of McNamee, and "the regrets his government would have, if it knew."

The admiral went on, "Tell him I ask that Galler's execution be delayed until after investigation, and then not until Carranza himself has personally approved it."

Taking our biggest motor boat, I lost myself in clouds of spray driven by the hurricane over the reefs and across the winding passages. Finally I reached Carranza's headquarters, which were, indeed, in a lighthouse—under the circumstances in Mexico at the time, it might as well have been termed his "lair." In the lighthouse I found an earnest, kindly seeming gentleman of distinguished appearance, and delivered Admiral Caperton's message.

"Tell your admiral," said he, "that I am glad to accede to his request. I shall telegraph the necessary orders immediately."

Two years later, in February 1917, I was returning from Vera Cruz on a passenger steamer. We stopped at Progreso to take passengers aboard, among them a tall, fine looking man with a mustache and a pointed brown beard, who particularly impressed me. He told me in conversation that he was superintendent of the English Railway Company of Merida. From this, and also from "the cut of his jib," which had the earmarks of London tailoring, I took him to be an Englishman.

The evening of our departure from Progreso, in the smoking room where the passengers gathered, I told of the Galler incident, since it had taken place in the port from which we had just departed. He seemed keenly interested and asked many questions. I remarked, finally, that I had never heard anything about Galler after this, and wondered if he had been shot after all, or if my intercession for him had been successful.

A broad smile was my answer. "No, my friend," he said. "Thanks to you, Marshall, and your admiral, Galler was not shot. I am Galler!"

Then he ordered a bottle of liquid that "rained upwards," and we pledged each other, having not the slightest idea that in two months his American friends would become his American enemies.

Returning to Vera Cruz and 1915: by that time Americans and Mexicans were again friendly. But, as usual, revolutions were in progress. Now there were Carranzistas, Palezistas, Narvelistas, Zapatistas, Villaistas, and so on. I doubt if they understood, any better than I, what they were fighting for.

One day Carranza took me to see the departure of his army for battle. On railway tracks were various trains, each composed of many boxcars; all were awaiting Carranza's signal to start. On the roof of each car were soldiers; under each car were slung canvas hammocks, similar to naval hammocks, each providing a soldier with a precarious place to sleep. Inside each car, as I could see through the wide-open doors, the floor space was crowded with women and small children. Mexicans, I was told, would not go to battle unless their wives went too. While the men fought, the wives scrounged food and cooked meals, and the children played.

The *Washington*'s job was to protect Americans; but as there were no complaints, it seemed there were no Americans being molested, and in due course we departed.

Late in June 1915, Admiral Caperton was ordered to take the *Washington* to the north coast of Haiti, where yet another revolution had started in that revolution-prone country. A Dr. Rosalvo Bobo, a Haitian politician, had hired the traditional revolutionary army, consisting of peasant Caco woodcutters of the north, and declared a "revolution" against the government under the sitting president, Vilbrün Guillaume, who had been in office only a few months. Americans residing in Haiti, in fact all foreigners, were uneasy. There was something different about the way this revolution was developing. It was somehow less cut-and-dried than its predecessors. For one thing, it was widely sensed that Guillaume, sometimes known as "President Sam," might not follow the standard pattern. This, in brief, amounted to transferring the national treasury to his own credit in a foreign bank, and leaving the country as soon as the coastal city of St. Marc surrendered to the advancing Caco army, march-ing southward from the north coast city of Cap Haitien. Port-au-Prince, cap-ital of Haiti, some fifty miles south of St. Marc, by custom surrendered when St. Marc did. Basically, the whole revolution was a war of maneuver, not of battle. Even in Cap Haitien and St. Marc, the bellwethers of success, there was rarely any real fighting.

Guillaume, however, appeared to have ambitions to remain in office more than just a few months. Perhaps he hoped to give the Haitian treasury time to collect a whole year's revenue before transferring it to an overseas bank. In any case, he was a tougher individual than most of his predecessors, and there were indications he might fight the traditionally automatic defeat signaled by the fall of St. Marc.

On the first of July, the *Washington* anchored off the ancient port of Cap Haitien, on the north coast of Haiti. Only some three months earlier, Guillaume, a former convict sentenced to life imprisonment by President Nord Alexis for embezzlement of government funds and promptly pardoned by Alexis' successor, Antoine Simon, had borrowed fifty thousand dollars from his uncle, former president Simon Sam (who expected the money back very soon, with good interest). Guillaume then paid the required fee to the Caco chieftains for three thousand Caco woodcutters to march south and install him as president. This they proceeded to do. Everyone followed the ritual for such matters, and so far as is known, not many Haitians, if any at all, were hurt. Now, Dr. Bobo, like Guillaume, agonized at the wrongs inflicted on his beloved country by a series of rapacious presidents, was following in the foot-steps of Guillaume, Téodor Davilmar, Orestes Zamor, Michel Oreste, Antoine Simon, Nord Alexis, Cincinnatus Le Conte—seven presidents in eight years—not to mention Guillaume's uncle, a few years earlier still. Each revo-lutionary candidate invariably claimed that his only intention was to rescue Haiti from its monumental, ever-increasing, fiscal depression by sequestering the national income—virtually all resulting from customs duties—in Swiss or French banks, where it would be safe.

The only problem was that the name on the account was always that of the president. Although it was the impoverished country's entire revenue for the period, and was supposedly administered by the foreign-owned bank that col-lected it at the customhouse source, treated in this way it also constituted the president's personal proceeds from his term in office. It was, in fact, the entire reason for the continuous series of revolts that had bedeviled the country for years. Payment of interest on the huge national debt, still mainly owed to France, was collected and distributed by the Banque Nationale de Paris before any money was turned over to the national government representative. These two distributions—one of them legal, the other simple embezzlement—normally absorbed Haiti's entire annual revenue. The embezzled money would provide the former president luxurious living in Europe, although much of it usually found its final depository in the gambling casinos of Monaco, and elsewhere.

Haiti has had a tragic history. By the Treaty of Ryswick in 1697, the western third of the island of San Domingo, for centuries known as the "Pearl of the Caribbean," was awarded to France. Spain retained the eastern two-thirds.

And French St. Domingue became the most productive tropical real estate in the world. In 1788 it supplied all tropical imports into the rest of Europe. A third of the merchant tonnage of France, eighty thousand tons in those old days, was employed solely in this trade. Intensively cultivated, Haiti was a veritable garden. There was no wasted space. The entire area of ten thousand square miles was divided into seven thousand productive plantations.

Life was wonderful for the forty thousand French colonists. Of the forty-four thousand mulattos, the men were mostly overseers and accountants for their French fathers, and the women were favored household help. But life was harsh indeed for the 450,000 black slaves brought over to replace the native Indians found there by Christopher Columbus, who had mostly succumbed to smallpox brought in by their colonial invaders.

Haiti was thus a paradise for the fortunate few whites and highly placed mulattos of those days, but few of them, if any, could appreciate the gathering power of the racial storm that was brewing as the eighteenth century neared its end. Some social historians suggest that the difference in types of slaves brought in ultimately made the difference. Slaves brought to the North American colonies were more docile, less warlike, than the fiercer blacks brought to the Caribbean islands. There was some idea, at the time, that the different tribes "adjusted better" in these different locations.

Whatever the reason, there was no successful slave revolt in the northern continent. But in 1789, when the General Assembly in Paris adopted "Liberté, Fraternité, Egalité" as the motto for the new Republic of France, it also declared that all men were equal. The black slaves, who had made Haiti bloom with the produce Europe was so willing to pay for, said to each other, "Why, that means us!" It took thirteen years of human butchery to prove that it did indeed mean them. Aided by French soldiers, the colonists tried to crush the aspirations of the slaves by wholesale slaughter. At one time Lieutenant General Rochambeau, the same man who had supported George Washington in our American Revolution, drove twelve hundred black men, women, and children into Port de Paix. There, herded upon barges with arms pinioned and stones tied to their bodies or around their necks, they were dumped shrieking into the bay. There were many such occurrences. But the blacks were eager imitators, who could also kill in original ways, and without conscience.

The brutalities on both sides, as chronicled by Robert Heinl and Nancy Heinl in their extraordinary book, *Written in Blood* (Boston: Houghton-Mifflin, 1978), are truly beyond belief.

And the climate, with the assistance of the dreaded yellow fever, could kill better than anything, or anyone, else. One French army after another was destroyed by yellow fever. Napoleon finally sent over General Le Clerc, husband of his sister, Pauline Bonaparte (who accompanied him), with an army of thirty thousand Frenchmen. Le Clerc's orders were to make a quick end of the rebellion using any methods deemed necessary, and return to Europe before the yellow fever season. But the black resistance was formidable, and Le Clerc could not move fast enough. Of his army, twenty-eight thousand, including Le Clerc himself, died in Haiti, nearly all from "la fièvre jaune." Pauline survived. General Rochambeau, following after him, did his best to live up to Napoleon's orders, but unsuccessfully, except to become emblazoned on Haiti's lists of monstrously cruel whites.

In 1802, finally tiring of the struggle, France acknowledged the independence of Haiti, which assumed a debt to France of thirty million dollars. This was twice what President Thomas Jefferson paid Napoleon a year later for the Louisiana Purchase of nearly one hundred times the area! At the beginning of the nineteenth century, France thus valued an average acre of Haitian land at about two hundred times the price it placed on any of the acreage in the entire Louisiana real estate deal!

Slaves and yellow fever, together, had conquered the great Napoleon. In the years of destruction, all buildings, bridges, and plantations, all technical development such as electricity or improved methods of agriculture, virtually all roads and railroads, were destroyed, terminated, or set back many years. Nearly all whites were killed, or fled the country. In 1802, only nineteen whites remained alive in Haiti. An undetermined number escaped to other parts of the Caribbean, and some to Louisiana; only a few families ever returned. The land was in ashes. The blacks had won their war, but in the process they had turned their small verdant country into a desert. There is no doubt they loved Haiti, but they had no idea how to manage their victory, and at this bitter point, it would be surprising if many of them thought about managing anything.

Starting with nothing, the new republic found it a terribly difficult journey to rise from desolation. A large percentage of the population, not long removed from primitive African savagery, simply reverted to it. Under the circumstances, could anything else have been expected? But a century's record shows that Haitians have unrealized potentialities. What they need is generous, altruistic help to get on their feet. Not money, but infrastructure such as roads and power lines, and above all, education. The French policy, it may be noted in passing, was to keep the black element of the country's population, by far the biggest portion, in total bondage. Blacks were completely prevented from getting any education at all; and, by and large, even in the most abject poverty, they didn't need much merely to stay alive. In Haiti, living is easy if one's basic needs are few. This outlook seems to have sunk deep roots. With a wonderful climate and rich soil, life was certainly easier than in Africa itself, from where their ancestors had been so brutally torn.

Haitians are, I believe, the only slaves in the world's history who, without outside aid, without allies or help of any kind, lifted themselves to international independence. They have been shamefully treated by foreign governments: by Germany in the Luders case; by England in the Peters case, and so on. But Haiti does not cringe at the sight of a hostile fleet of warships, and has kept her flag always mastheaded, though not always to her advantage. In comparison, five times in the equivalent hundred years, roughly the whole of the nineteenth century, the Dominican Republic, occupying the eastern two-thirds of the island, has hauled down its flag in surrender and hoisted foreign colors. Perhaps the more Hispanic Dominicans were wiser.

It is not surprising that independent Haiti, nearly solidly black, was anathema to the huge slave-holding country immediately to the north. Until 1861 the United States refused even to acknowledge its existence, let alone its independence. Haiti was just a gap in the map, a cipher, so far as we were concerned. Yet, until the revolution of 1915, when I arrived there in the *Washington*, it had never failed to pay the interest on its huge foreign debt. As mentioned, the Banque Nationale collected the customs revenues before permitting Haitian politicians to touch funds, and all of Haiti's wealthy upper-class society was deeply, often illegally, involved in politics. Politics, in fact, was literally their life's blood.

———————

Those who have progressed this far in Father's autobiography will recognize that he has become a sympathetic advocate of Haiti. It was there that he met my mother, Alice, the orphaned granddaughter of French importers who fled to Louisiana at the beginning of the nineteenth century and were among the few who returned after that terrible time of troubles. Her parents had died of yellow fever within the same month. Her mother cared for her father until he died, and then came down with the dread disease herself. This was not unusual, because there was no one else to care for the sick. The role of the mosquito in spreading the illness was as yet unknown, nor were means of combating it. Young Alice Fouché was brought up by the Carlstroem family, Norwegian cousins who must have felt some responsibility for the loss of her small inheritance at the predatory hands of one of their number. After Father's first wife Lucie died, he met Alice and she became his wife on 1 April 1917. Because of Mother, the interest he already had in Haitian history, and its misfortunes as an independent nation, ballooned. It's also possible that ungenerous criticisms levied on him by unscrupulous Haitian politicians, who seized upon the American occupation to excuse their own shortcomings, brought out his inherent supportive feelings about our efforts to help that benighted country. Far from "interfering with the 'normal succession' of presidents," as one Haitian account described it (i.e., by bought and paid for "revolution" after a year or so in office), he and Admiral Caperton set up one of the few honest governments Haiti has ever had. It may not have been perfect (Admiral Caperton's successors and assigns were sometimes less liberal-minded than he and Father), but all the same it was modern Haiti's best time. The text of this book will show how they did this, and how they felt about that poor country.

Sadly, after our Navy and the Marine Corps departed, about twenty years after their entry in 1915, Haiti reverted to its previous habits. This was most recently exemplified by the two Duvalier regimes, in which virtually all of the tiny nation's revenue was diverted into the bank accounts of "Papa Doc" and his cohorts.

On the first page of Father's 1922 novel, *Dan Quin of the Navy,* one reads, "Dan Quin is speaking to you, Dan Quin of the United States Navy. If you wish to know who Dan Quin is and happen to be in Mexico, ask any prominent citizen from Vera Cruz. If in Haiti, ask President Dartiguenave or Secretary of State Louis Borno. In Santo Domingo inquire of Archbishop Noel, or Don Frederico Velasquez."

Dartiguenave and Borno were true figures, like Aguinaldo of the Philippines; and I believe Noel and Velasquez probably were also. In addition to the letter from Aguinaldo, mentioned earlier, Father once showed me a letter from Borno, emotionally written in excellent English, commiserating on the loss of the *Memphis,* formerly the *Tennessee,* sister to the *Washington* and *Montana.* Father continued to incorporate fictionalized renditions of his own experiences into his novels. I have the unfinished manuscript of a second Dan Quin book, set in Haiti, describing how Dan managed to prevent corrupt politicians from stealing the national treasury. Dad was up to his old tricks, since Dan's adventures are evidently a fictional conversion of what Father actually accomplished in 1915.

———

The friends of Haiti cannot forget the country's heroism in lifting herself from slavery to independent nationhood, and in maintaining that independence.

They soft-pedal raucous noises, and denature bad smells with French perfumes. Her detractors, with unctuous superiority and cramped minds, can see nothing but voodooism, hear nothing but the tom-tom, record nothing but bloody acts of military despots. Many bad things happened there, of course, but Haiti is no different from the rest of the world in such history.

All the same, Haiti has been cursed by the visitor of a few days who collects all sorts of weird tales, and with self-assured authority writes articles for newspapers and magazines that, to be published, must be excitingly colored. Many years ago this was even more in vogue than today. Having visited Haiti a number of times, with several protracted stays, and having studied the country at some length, I may say that the fairest book on Haiti that I know is *Black Democracy*, by H. P. Davis. Other books fall usually into two classes: defending, written in French; and denouncing, in English. Thank you, my dear Davis, for *Black Democracy*!

Father is referring to Davis's *Black Democracy: The Story of Haiti* (New York: Dodge Publishing Company, 1936). Whatever Father's opinion of H. P. Davis, it was not shared by everyone. The Heinls, for example, characterized him as "a commercial adventurer."

My picture would be somewhat as follows: "The Haitian peasant is a happy, amiable, generous, embodiment of lazy ignorance. The limits of his foresight are reached when he provides food for tomorrow; but all the same he will give that food to any hungry stranger. He started in 1802 with ten thousand square miles of ashes and a debt of thirty million. His traditions were African savagery, Haitian slavery, and an ocean of blood."

When the *Washington* reached Cap Haitien, on 1 July 1915, there were indications that the ocean of blood might be about to overflow yet once again. Admiral Caperton was directed to prevent this if he could. The small French cruiser *Descartes* had already arrived at the north coast city of Cap Haitien, apparently the focal point of the trouble, and one of Caperton's problems was to carry out the Monroe Doctrine—in other words, get rid of the *Descartes*—without causing an international incident. The *Washington* was a much bigger ship, carrying many more U.S. Marines than the *Descartes* could accommodate. French marines had already landed, but Caperton sensed that the French skipper might be glad to get out of the tricky situation. Indeed, he recalled his troops on board when the *Washington* came on the scene. Official calls, with punctilious protocol, were exchanged between the senior officers present of the U.S. and French navies, during which each quietly asked the other, in amiable language, how far he and his country were prepared to go. Captain Lafrogne of the *Descartes* wanted to know if Admiral Caperton's instructions "interfered" with his remaining at Cap Haitien. Assured that they did not, he then received the diplomatic hint that the United States was extremely grateful for everything he had done during the few days the French ship had been there prior to arrival of the *Washington*. Now, however, Caperton's much bigger crew could take over the peacekeeping obligation that the French cruiser had handled so well. Both officers were alert to the unstated under-currents, and when Lafrogne asked Caperton's "permission" to depart the area, it was granted with the utmost of good will on both sides.

According to David Healy, who made quite a study of the U.S. inter-vention in Haiti (*The U.S. Navy in Haiti, 1915–1916*, Madison: University of Wisconsin Press, 1976), there was considerably more to this incident. The Heinls' 1978 *Written in Blood* very much agrees. Short of coal and becoming a bit anxious, Captain Lafrogne did indeed desire to leave, particularly in view of the possibility of difficulty with the United States, but he had as yet received no instructions from France. Admiral Caperton, in the meantime, had come to the con-clusion that the French cruiser must depart, and if she needed stronger hints, it was up to him to provide them. He therefore informed the French captain in their next meeting that the United States "had now assumed charge of protecting all foreign interests," and that his con-tinued presence "would be undesirable on account of the primary interests of the United States in the neutrality of Haiti." The implied invocation of the well-known Monroe Doctrine was all that was nec-essary, and although *Descartes* remained anchored at Cap Haitien for a few more days waiting for instructions (and coal), relations remained most amicable. Captain Lafrogne did not find it necessary to re-land his French marines.

Caperton's dispatch orders from the U.S. State Department were to secure the safety of all life and property (i.e., of all foreigners, and of the local populace as well). Therefore he decided to prevent all combat in that part of the country, or, at least, as far around Cap Haitien as his influence could be made to extend. To this end he sent Father on a dangerous and virtually unprecedented mission behind revolutionary lines, deep into the Caco country, to seek out Dr. Bobo, leader of the new revolt, and hand him an official letter. Composed with all the formality he and Father, acting as his chief of staff, could muster, the letter put Bobo on notice that the United States would not tolerate any fighting of any kind in the city, and their big cruiser, the *Washington*, had the guns, ammunition, and purpose to prevent the same. In many ways the situation was reminiscent of the similar one a few years earlier, when as executive officer of the *Montana* Dad halted the advance of a Turkish army toward the city of Kessab, in Syria (see chapter 16). I have read several accounts of Father's second such mission, this time in Haiti. The two best are Healy's and the Heinls' books, but there have been a number of others, too. Nearly all cite Father's story, reproduced below and available in the National Archives under the title, "Admiral Caperton in Haiti." Although the Navy Department, perhaps fearing some sort of State Department reaction, refused clearance for publication in 1919, whatever considerations existed back then can hardly be important now. I have Dad's own bound typescript, exactly as he wrote it in 1919, and am exercising my editorial and filial prerogatives by including it here. Father wrote it, these are his words, and this, his last book, is where they belong.

First, however, it's necessary to remark at his sometimes apparently forced exclusion of any specific mention of himself in this particular passage, even though it's clear enough where he figures in the story. I have no idea what that reason might have been; so, to set the record as straight as possible, I've inserted a few personal pronouns where they seemed needed.

Father's 1919 account, which he called "The Revolution of Dr. Bobo," is as follows.

_____

On 30 June 1915, while at Guantánamo Bay, Admiral Caperton sent for me. "Let's relax a little," he said. "This is June thirtieth, our birthday, yours and mine. You are forty-eight years old today. I am sixty. Let's celebrate." We did.

There's no indication of what they did to "celebrate," but Caperton had Dad's birthday right, and I checked on his. In any case, they didn't have much time to celebrate anything.

Soon came a cable informing us that a revolution had broken out in the north of Haiti. Coal was taken on board, and the *Washington* left, arriving at Cape Haitien on 2 July. Admiral Caperton first proceeded to investigate conditions, which were as follows.

Dr. Bobo, a former cabinet minister, after a certain private interview (undescribed but doubtless related to finance), with certain persons, went to northeast Haiti, and there, in a passionate proclamation filled with patriotic asseverations reciting the terrible wrongs the current president was inflicting upon Beloved Haiti, he proclaimed himself "Chief of the Executive Power," and asked all true patriotic Haitians to join him in freeing Haiti from the tyrant who was so misgoverning her. (This was the standard method of starting a "revolution.")

Several thousand Cacos, the same identical woodchoppers who had installed and later ejected the previous eight or nine presidents, and only a few months before had installed the present one, Vilbrün Guillaume, were either also indignant at the wrongs Haiti was suffering, or else glad to make fifteen gourdes each for a few weeks of easy work. With little persuasion, they joined the mission of kicking out their most recent chief of the executive power, replacing him with Dr. Bobo. But it seemed that Guillaume intended this time to make a strenuous resistance. Cap Haitien believed real danger threatened the city, and the lives and property of foreign residents there. Dr. Bobo and his forces were said to be at the town of Petit Anse, three or four miles distant across the bay, and ready to attack.

Admiral Caperton proposed to take whatever steps were necessary to prevent this. There was a road, leading across a sort of swamp but in part close to reasonably deep water, that Dr. Bobo's Cacos would have to traverse to reach Cap Haitien. The *Eagle*, a small gunboat, formerly a light-draft yacht, was directed to anchor close to this road and keep it constantly illuminated by searchlight, so that her guns could control it completely, day and night. At the end of the town was a railroad station, a dock, and a water connection. There a company of Marines was stationed, with rifles and machine guns. With these forces in place, it was impossible for Cacos to get into Cap Haitien except at the cost of many lives.

But Caperton wished to accomplish his mission without having to kill anyone from either side. So, he sent [me] to Petit Anse with a letter to Dr. Bobo that he and I had laboriously written in French, stating in unmistakable terms that no assault on Cap Haitien would be permitted. [I] was to accentuate this in verbal conversation, but was not to remain with Bobo or his forces after nightfall. Early on Monday, 5 July, [I] set out with Dr. Livingston, the U.S. consul at Cap Haitien, who was an American [black], and a small group of Marines consisting of an officer and six privates. Dr. Livingston had been for many years an important fixture at Cap Haitien. He came along because of his intimate knowledge of the Creole tongue, the only language known by the Cacos.

The letter was probably largely composed by Father, because Caperton did not know French.

But the town of Petit Anse was completely deserted. The only living thing in it was a lonely donkey. The party walked through the one long street of the empty village. On either side of the road were small but well-built brick houses, all appearing to have been hurriedly abandoned. Several Marines were directed to follow the road for some distance, and come back immediately if anyone was seen. Soon they returned, reporting they had seen an armed sentry. So now the party started out again, except for Dr. Livingston who, because of the obvious risk, awaited their return offshore in the launch in which they had all come.

The road now ran into houseless country. At first it was wide, but it gradually narrowed. The sentry was found. He understood no French, but when the word "Bobo" was said, he pointed in the direction the road led. More sentries were passed, each pointing onward upon hearing "Bobo." The road became a trail, winding about in a dense tropical jungle, and it was soon obvious that many men were following the American party. It was not an inviting situation, but Admiral Caperton's letter had to be delivered, and there was nothing to do but go on.

We continued for several miles, during which time it was evident that the number of men ahead and behind the party constantly increased; nor was their appearance reassuring. A more villainous looking set of men was never gathered together. All were but slightly clad, and each was armed with a musket, a pistol, a sword, and a long, viciously sharp knife.

Without warning, the path suddenly opened into a wide enclosure in which were many hundreds of men; it was now realized that the American party had stumbled into a main Caco camp. It is impossible to adequately describe the appearance of these men. Each was a veritable arsenal. On each person was a number of different weapons. Each man looked to be a real devil, capable of unimaginable horrors.

"Keep your men together, guns ready for use," [I] whispered to the Marine captain, an instruction, as he put it, that was entirely unnecessary.

A well-dressed man, evidently a general who had been apprised of our coming, addressed us courteously in French. He said Dr. Bobo was away but had been sent for and would be present in a few moments. He would be glad to meet the Americans. Stools were brought, and the party sat down.

The Haitian officer was disposed to be friendly, but obviously was also trying to kill time. He talked at length about Dr. Bobo's patriotism, his purpose in this revolution, his erudition, and his fine personality. Asked if he could deliver the letter to Dr. Bobo, he answered yes, but he preferred that the Americans should give it to the chief of the executive power personally, thus adding to its significance.

A Haitian woman brought up some hot coffee. Sir Spencer St. John's tales of secret poisoning were remembered, but the day was hot, the walk had been long and dusty; so the coffee was drunk. It is not likely that there ever was better coffee. Then some oranges were produced, green in skin but wonderfully sweet and refreshing. The Cacos, standing about, were all talking and laughing. But soon ammunition cartridges were served out to all of them, which did not help the flavor of the oranges.

It was explained to the Haitian general that any attack upon Cap Haitien was forbidden by the American admiral, that he had full power to prevent this, and that he would use whatever measures were necessary, no matter how severe, to ensure that no attack was made. The general did not like this at all.

The American party now started to leave. It was beginning to get dark, and we had been at this camp for a long time. The letter was given to the Haitian general. The latter peremptorily and emphatically now said that he could not permit us to leave, that we must wait to see Dr. Bobo. In reply to this, the Haitian was firmly told that the purpose of our visit would be accomplished when the letter was given to Dr. Bobo; and that we must leave. About this there would be no argument.

Then the Haitian general changed his manner to a pleading tone. He thanked the Americans for their visit. The Haitians had been honored by it, he was truly sorry we had not seen Dr. Bobo, but he would deliver the letter and the message. He regretted that conditions had made it impossible to show the Americans more hospitality, but would they kindly accept a little present as a token of the good feeling he bore them? And then the woman who had brought the coffee gave the [departing party] a great, fat, beautifully dressed turkey, most probably prepared for the dinner we had, in effect, declined.

This little incident, unimportant as it may seem, is indicative on our side of the habit Admiral Caperton had, under some conditions, of letting people know his intentions so that trouble might be averted. Also, it is a sample of the hospitality and kindness that one always finds in Haitians, whether of the educated class or peasants.

And in this connection, there is another point. To Father, the situation looked ominous; anything might have been expected to happen. But later, after becoming better acquainted with Haitian customs, he used to say that he had never been safer in his life than when surrounded by these Cacos. He had no need of weapons or guard. The coffee, oranges, and turkey were expressions of a kindly hospitality that is never found wanting in Haiti. The assembly in force of Cacos, and the distribution of ammunition, was meant simply to impress on him that Bobo had soldiers and the arms and means to fight. It was not intended to intimidate him personally but to spread the knowledge of Bobo's formidable force. The Haitian general made no real attempt to detain Father. He probably felt

Dr. Bobo might reproach him for not inducing the American to remain longer, and it is entirely possible that Bobo's delay in appearing may have been intended as a sort of social gambit over dinner to establish his personal superiority as a future president of Haiti. It's also possible that he had been watching the whole business from some hidden vantage point. This might have been a logical move for a slightly addled man, as Admiral Caperton and his people had already begun to think of him. It was not much different from Guillaume's similar escapade, described in nearly all accounts of this period, in which he first played the formally dressed doorkeeper, then disappeared, replaced his doorkeeper's jacket with a resplendent full-dress uniform coat and a big ceremonial sword, and, now accoutered as president, formally received his visitors.

To an American of short residence in Haiti, conditions always look fearful, for he hears lurid tales. But nothing of this sort happened; quite the opposite, it should not be forgotten that in Haiti's history as an independent nation, no white civilian has ever been molested, either in person or in property. This was not true, of course, during her earlier wars for independence.

Although Guillaume Sam never appreciated this, Caperton's measures to protect Cap Haitien all the same effectively derailed Bobo's revolution. This was not the admiral's purpose, of course, because between Dr. Bobo and President Guillaume, he was careful always to be neutral and impartial. But his protection of Cap Haitien meant that Dr. Bobo's forces had failed in the initial step of their campaign. The Cacos could not enter that city, even without a fight, as was the general custom, and this caused Bobo's revolution to collapse before it really began.

Had Guillaume not pushed too hard, too far, and too revengefully, he might have been able to remain in power awhile longer. For the moment, perhaps Bobo did not understand this. Yet he must finally have realized it, because, erratic as he may have been, his mentality was keen, and he knew, as everyone did, that the first requisite of success for a revolution starting in the north was the capture of Cap Haitien. If Cap Haitien was not captured, the bought-and-paid-for revolution was blocked. While this may have been a bit beyond Caperton's specific instructions, he thus defeated, without cost of a single American or Haitian life, some three thousand mercenary revolutionists animated solely by money paid to them.

Although Caperton kept the Navy Department informed of his actions in official dispatches and written reports, he did not draw attention to the immediate result on Dr. Bobo's revolution; and this statement, written in these pages, is probably the first announcement of what that result was.

***

Because Father sat up late nearly every night with the admiral composing reports, and making plans for the next few days' activities, he could state this with certain knowledge. It is also likely that someone, somewhere, may have felt that he knew too much, that his opinion was too authoritative. All Father ever knew was that publication clearance was denied. The "The Revolution of Dr. Bobo" manuscript remained on file in the National Archives, however, where it was accessed years later by a number of researchers. This is how Dad wrote it in 1919, four years after it happened.

***

In the meantime, now back in Port-au-Prince, Guillaume was making a desperate effort to maintain himself in power. He had been president only four months, and did not propose to be driven out so soon by Dr. Bobo or anyone else. So he gathered troops and prepared to attack Bobo in the north. Cap Haitien was garrisoned, as were other points. Guillaume also knew that, in Port-au-Prince, disaffection was in the air and that conspiracies, as always, were hatching. So he arrested the men he suspected of being political enemies, in addition to male members of their families, and had them confined in the city jail.

Most of these prisoners were innocent of any conspiracy, but among them were some who might have been guilty of something (among the intelligentsia this was endemic), and some who had the potential, perhaps, of conspiring later. The governor of Port-au-Prince, Charles Oscar Étienne, had orders from Guillaume to kill every one of these special prisoners in case he, the president of Haiti, should be attacked, or, in fact, if a single revolutionary shot were to be fired.

When the arrests of political suspects began, many Haitians, feeling insecure for whatever reason, took refuge in different foreign legations and consulates, as was their habit. These were crowded. Charles Delva, a former chief of police of the city, had been given asylum in the Portuguese consulate. In the early morning of 27 July, having laid his plans, he stole out of the consulate, which lay on the outskirts of the city, and accompanied by only thirty-seven other men followed the dry bed of the river Bois de Chêne that leads into Port-au-Prince near the presidential palace.

The Heinls say he was joined by sixteen additional men led by Ermane Robin. Together they arrived right in the rear of Guillaume's defenses.

Guillaume had thought himself secure, having stationed numerous, well-armed guards to defend the presidential palace, but Delva, beginning his attack on the palace at four in the morning, caught them from the rear by surprise. It seems easy to tell about it now, but although the entire force of the government was against him, he overcame all obstacles. First he captured the machine guns the president had emplaced in the palace grounds, then used them on the palace guards, causing them to flee in disorder. By 8:30 in the morning about seventy of Guillaume's defenders had been killed, and the rest surrendered. Vilbrün Guillaume, with a leg wound, scrambled over the fence that separated the palace grounds from the French legation next door (he had the key to the gate but it would not turn the rusty lock), and claimed asylum.

While this fighting was going on, Étienne was busy executing the order he had received the day before. At 4 A.M. he began slaughtering the political prisoners, and not satisfied with those in the jail, he sought out and murdered some in their homes. By eight o'clock he had killed somewhere between 165 and 170 (precise figures do not exist). At about nine o'clock Étienne heard that the rioters had been successful and that the president had fled and taken refuge in the French legation; so he went to the Dominican legation to seek the same for himself. This did not help him much, however, for the elderly Edmond Polynice, a distinguished former senator whose three sons had just been murdered in the jail, donned his most formal clothing, put a pistol in his pocket, went to the Dominican legation, sent in his calling card, and asked for him. When the unsuspecting Étienne appeared, perhaps not actually aware that Polynice's sons had been among his victims, the former senator suggested they step outside for a talk, and then suddenly shot him three times, once for each of his sons. Étienne's body, changed into a shapeless, bloody mass, lay before the legation front door for twenty-four hours, riddled with thousands of bullets. Every passerby vented his fury by using it as a target.

Guillaume's soldiers had entirely lost heart by 8 A.M. and were in the mood to accept Delva's authority. Both foreigners and Haitians in general say that as chief of police he had been severe to law-breakers and was held in great fear by them, but that he had always been absolutely straight and could not be bribed. Following his own sudden and successful revolution, he was in complete military power, but his conduct was not at all according to Haitian precedent. Instead of using that power for his own benefit, he did nothing for personal advancement. He is remembered in Haiti as a man of forceful integrity, honest and unselfish, a true patriot.

He, and others, formed a committee of public safety and telegraphed news of the revolt to Cap Haitien, where Caperton instantly realized that his presence was needed in the capital. Getting under way immediately, he brought the *Washington* into Port-au-Prince at noon on 28 July.

As described in *Salt and Steel*, the *Washington* was seen through binoculars by young Alice Fouché, as the big cruiser raced dramatically into the harbor with "a bone in her teeth," backed her engines, and anchored.

20

THE DEATH OF
VILBRÜN GUILLAUME

In a lecture at the Naval War College, quite a number of years ago, a distinguished international lawyer said that much international law had been made by naval officers who, in protecting the interests of the United States, were at times called upon to make sudden decisions, and to act without specific instructions.

A number of such incidents, mostly forgotten except by historians, come to mind. David Porter's actions in the Marquesas Islands, and at Fajardo, Puerto Rico, have been mentioned. In 1853 Commodore Perry induced Japan to open her ports to foreign nations. It is true, of course, that he had been sent for this express purpose by the U.S. government, but on the spot he was beyond communication with Washington except by slow mail boat, and had to think and act for himself. The lengthy reports he had to write, and the ever-present possibility of presidential disapproval, no doubt exercised restraining influence over whatever he did, but the fact remains that he had to generate his own agenda, with only basic instructions from Washington to guide him.

In 1854 an American commodore at Asunción, Paraguay, induced that country to accord just treatment to Americans. About 1855, before the British had hoisted their flag over the Fiji Islands, the U.S. sloop-of-war *St. Mary's* "made war" upon them to protect Americans. I use the phrase, "made war" advisedly, well knowing that, so far as the United States is concerned, only Congress can declare war. There was violence done. Guns were fired, and in the process of protecting Americans, some people were killed, though not many. In 1854, Captain T. F. Kane, in the *Galena*, broke up a revolution on the Isthmus of Panama.

In 1869 American warships bombarded Japanese forts, again with a view to protecting American citizens. Twice, once in the 1870s and again in 1886, American warships attacked Korean fortifications. In 1882 Lieutenant Littleton W. T. Waller, acting under the orders of his captain, landed at Alexandria, Egypt, to preserve order.

In 1889 Commander R. P. Leary of the *Adams* prevented a German squadron from subjugating the Samoan Islands. In 1893 Captain Gilbert Wiltse, commanding the USS *Boston*, landed troops in Honolulu, resulting in the overthrow of the government of Queen Liliuokulani. In 1894, in the harbor of Rio de Janeiro, Admiral Andrew Benham, by his own sudden act, brought a great revolution to an end. In 1898 the *Philadelphia* landed blue-jackets and Marines in the Samoan Islands. The final result was that Tutuila became an American possession.

In 1915 Admiral Caperton, at a time of wholesale massacre and anarchy, landed troops in Haiti; restored and maintained order; and, by request of the best elements of the Haitian people, gave protection to the lawmakers of that country. He encouraged these best elements to establish their own government; and, demanding nothing for his own country, brought comfort to an overwrought and harassed people. Of this I know whereof I write, for I was his chief of staff as well as captain of his flagship, and became his instrument for all of this. In the process, I learned a lot about Haiti, and know it still needs a lot of help.

In 1916 Admiral Caperton landed troops in Santo Domingo, restored order, broke up a country-wide brigandage, protected American and foreign residents, and brought hope to the best people of the Dominican Republic. The situation was much the same as in Haiti, though with less anarchy and bloodshed. With his prior experience in the smaller one-third of that once green, blooming, island, Caperton was able to bring order out of chaos and set the nation's economy back to rights. When we left, things were as they should be, although, sadly, the country has not been able steadily to maintain the balanced course we marked out for it. To my disappointment, I was not able to follow this particular campaign to its end, for reasons that will become clear.

I speak, however, with personal knowledge of what this admiral accomplished in both Haiti and Santo Domingo; and shall now describe these operations in Haiti, also known in the press as the "Black Republic."

On the night of 27 July 1915, while we were anchored off Cap Haitien, on the north coast of Haiti, Caperton received a cablegram from Washington. After studying it, he directed me to proceed at once with our ship to Port-au-Prince, and to be ready to land troops on our arrival at about noon the next day. We went full speed, and I was up most of the night.

Soon after we anchored, the secretary of the American legation, Beale Davis, the British charge d'affairs, a man named Kohn, and an American contractor, Harry Berlin, came aboard. From them we learned details of the previous day's wholesale butchery of political prisoners by order of the president, Vilbrun Guillaume.

Firing squads went from cell to cell, poked rifles through the bars, and shot down the men inside. When all in a cell were down, they entered and finished the work with bayonets and knives. Then they moved on to the next cell.

Around the time of the *Washington*'s arrival, a party of about forty Haitians of the best class—far from an ordinary mob but in a state of extreme agitation—accosted the French minister, Monsieur Girard. They demanded that their president, who had proved himself such a horrible monster, be ejected from the French legation.

Citing the international rights of asylum, the minister politely refused, but this was small impediment in their fevered state of mind. They brushed him aside, stormed into the French legation mansion and searched it. Led there by the strong odor of iodine Guillaume had used to treat his relatively minor injury, they found him hiding in an upstairs toilet. By this time totally deaf to any expostulations about violation of French diplomatic rights, they seized their quarry and dragged him down the stairs and through the house, breaking his arm in the process. Outside the building, observance of diplomatic niceties extended only to dragging him without further injury (so it was said) through the legation grounds to the street, where a much bigger and far less inhibited mob awaited in the full fury of knowledge about the prison atrocity. Once in their hands, the Haitian president lived less than a minute.

In *Written in Blood*, the Heinls say Guillaume was killed in the legation grounds before his body was pitched over the fence, and I tend to believe this version, since he might conceivably have had some of his former bodyguard there.

Minister Girard, holding that the French legation had been violated, international law and the custom of nations transgressed, and his country insulted, hauled down the French flag. He requested troops be landed for his protection from a French warship in the harbor.

The warship was the *Descartes*, just down from Cap Haitien. Landing French marines temporarily for the protection of the French legation was acceptable under the Monroe Doctrine. They were taken back on board when Caperton arrived.

As all this was happening, the *Washington* was anchoring, and Caperton ordered me to send our landing party ashore. He prepared explicit orders for Van Orden, the Marine officer in command. This landing party was composed of bluejackets and Marines, 330 men in all. Caperton also gave me a written message to deliver to the committee of safety at Port-au-Prince. It stated that he was sending troops into the city merely to protect life and property, that he came and should be regarded as a friend, and that the United States had no designs whatever on the integrity and independence of Haiti, and would not interfere in any way with the normal processes of the government.

"Beach," he said to me, "I want you to go ashore as soon as possible. I cannot give you detailed instructions but I have confidence in your judgment. The important thing is that this committee of safety, which is supposed to be running things, must understand that we come as friends. We are marching troops into the city but not in a hostile spirit. They are coming only to help the local authorities restore order. They must not be fired upon nor attacked in any way. Be sure the committee understands this.

"Now get ashore as soon as you can; make any statement that seems necessary; and give any orders in your name, or in my name, that you consider advisable."

After giving hurried orders to McDowell, the ship's executive officer, and to Van Orden for his Marines, I left the ship accompanied by Lieutenant John N. Ferguson, the admiral's flag lieutenant. Caperton's position was indeed difficult and delicate. Here, on an island republic close to the United States, anarchy reigned. It was Caperton's job to protect the lives and property of Americans; and, at a time like this, of all other foreigners. In addition, simple humanity demanded that he also do what he could for the Haitians. Into a large city of one hundred thousand people, crazed with horror, he was throwing a paltry force of a few hundred men. For the moment he could know but little of the conditions ashore; and what he knew was not reassuring.

The presence of French forces made Caperton's position more delicate still. It has been the history of foreign occupations that once a great power lands troops in a weak country, these troops remain there a long time. Haiti was, of course, a very weak country, situated very close to the United States. A further complication was that the French legation had been violated, and, as they viewed it, the French flag desecrated. Then there were the economic aspects. French investors held Haitian bonds amounting to millions of dollars on which the interest was overdue. This, in itself, involved many dangers.

Caperton had to think not only of American and foreign lives, but also of the Monroe Doctrine, a shifting rule of political conduct as precarious as quicksand. He had to judge for himself the things to be done, the best ways of doing these things, and the probable attitude of his home government toward his efforts.

With unerring judgment he decided each question as it arose. Later, in recognition of his services, he was given the rank of full admiral (four stars) as opposed to the rear admiral (two star) rank he then held. This is the highest rank that exists in our Navy.

Father wrote this in about 1935. The permanent rank of fleet admiral, five stars, was created for those who led our fleets during World War II. Its holders having now passed away, the five-star rank is again in disuse.

With the most tactful courtesy, Caperton demanded that the French warship withdraw its troops from shore. That night the Frenchmen would sleep on board. Meanwhile, I had reached the dock at Port-au-Prince, found a cabman, and had him drive me to the presidential palace, a magnificent structure, spacious but badly run down, that had been built by France more than a hundred years previously.

From many conversations during my previous visits to Haiti and from personal observation when Guillaume overthrew Téodor Davilmar, I knew the unwritten law of Haitian revolutions. As soon as the Caco woodchoppers have finished their job, the old president resigns and flees the country, taking the treasury with him. Then a committee of public safety is appointed, or appoints itself, and this controls the government until a new president is elected. A standardized technique for revolutions had evolved. I knew I would find such a committee somewhere in Port-au-Prince, exercising whatever control there was.

It was a weird drive to the palace. Crowds of citizens were rushing about, some shooting weapons mostly pointed upwards. Soldiers wearing dungarees with red stripes on collars, sleeves, and trousers were running up and down, also shooting into the air—although I guessed that some of the shots I heard were directed more specifically, and that a lot of looting and revenge-taking was happening too. Officers on small horses were dashing aimlessly through the streets.

At the palace I found the committee, headed by Charles Delva, leader of the band, small at first, that in open battle with Guillaume's guard of five hundred had overthrown the villainous president. The presidential guard had lost its stomach for fighting after seventy-two of its number had been killed or wounded, and the mob, rallying to Delva's support, had tripled its size and fury.

If I remember correctly, the committee was composed of six members: Delva, Polynice, Mont Pom, Robans, Charles Zamor, and Chevalier. Presenting Admiral Caperton's letter, I announced that our troops were landing at the suburb of Bizoton, several miles distant, and were coming as friends, to protect Americans and foreigners, but with no intention of harming Haitians. I also made it clear that if any Haitians were so foolish as to attack our forces, we were prepared to defend ourselves; and that although we would deplore any need to use the big guns of the *Washington*, now moored with bow and stern anchors close in to shore where her guns could decisively control everything around her for several miles, that was what they were there for.

"What do you wish us to do?" asked Delva abruptly.

"Which of you commands the Haitian troops in Port-au-Prince?" I asked.

"I am the general in command," replied Robans.

"Then," I replied, "I ask the committee to order General Robans to compel every Haitian soldier to go into his barracks immediately. There are thousands of soldiers, mad with bad rum, rushing about and shooting their rifles. Your whole city is overwhelmed with grief because of the terrible events of yesterday. After you confine the troops, you must also advise the townspeople to go to their homes and remain in them. Tell them the Americans are coming as friends; that no hostility must be shown them; that the results of any hostile act would be bad. And one thing more: I ask that you have General Robans meet the American forces that will reach the city in three or four hours, and direct them to a suitable camping place for the night."

There were many Haitians standing about, listening to what I said. I was well aware from their looks, and from their words, that they heard me with relief and joy.

Comments in frenzied tones, in Haitian patois, which I could not understand, were hurled at the committee. These people had seen terrible sights and had suffered agonies of grief. With French troops on shore, with another armed body marching into their city, with a great warship training its guns on them, they had been almost crazed by worry and exhaustion. And here they were offered kindness and friendship.

An elderly man of the committee, Polynice, now spoke. "Tell the admiral," he said, "that we thank him and that we accept his word that he is coming as a friend to help us. We need help and we need friendship. We promise that all you ask shall be done."

"I thank the committee," I replied. "I will be at the American legation tomorrow morning at eight o'clock. I ask that the whole committee meet me there at that time."

This was agreed; we parted with friendly words; and Ferguson and I were soon back on board the *Washington*.

Father did not learn until several days after this that three of Polynice's sons had been killed the day before in the prison massacre, and that Polynice himself had killed Étienne.

Our landing force did not march into Port-au-Prince until dusk. It was met outside the city by Robans and several of his officers, who conducted them to camping places: an empty, disused hospital building, a vacant field (the "Champs de Mars"), and the market.

Van Orden and his officers and men were ready for anything. There was some desultory firing upon them, and, at one time, a sharp, short attack in which six Haitians were killed. But there was evidence that the Haitian soldiers were restrained, and there was no concerted action against us.

That evening the admiral's two aides, Lieutenants Coffey and Ferguson, went ashore and visited different parts of the city. They called upon some of the foreign residents, visited the different American camps, and mixed with a number of persons who, contrary to orders, had failed to remain indoors. Their reports were reassuring.

Except as mentioned above, not much was happening. The great majority of the people, exhausted by the wracking horrors of the two previous days, relieved by the coming of the Americans, who, they rightly felt, would take charge and put things in order, had simply gone to bed.

By this time Caperton had learned much of the existing conditions. He talked with us until 3 A.M., outlining in general the policies he wished us to carry out.

"Beach, you will be in the American legation early; the minister, Blanchard, is away on six months' leave. All the foreigners and diplomats here, and many prominent Haitians, are asking me to take charge, and I judge there is nothing else for me to do. But I shall remain on board ship, where I can stay in instant communication with Washington, and will try to maintain a position of benevolent isolation. Please take up your quarters at the legation, but come back often, and by all means keep me informed by whatever means seem to work best.

"First, tomorrow morning, get that committee of safety to agree to govern the city, for the time being, in accordance with my orders. And if they agree, check up on them. Find out if they are keeping faith. You won't be able to refer everything to me; so don't hesitate to give what orders you deem necessary.

"In general, do not kill, and do not get killed. Do not shoot unless there is absolute necessity. Under no circumstances haul down any Haitian flag, whatever the provocation. Under all circumstances be kind and considerate. Avoid in every way the attitude of a military tyrant. Remember, we have promised friendship; and also remember we are acting so far without specific orders. Be careful to do nothing that will embarrass the United States or our Navy Department. Go to the two newspapers and tell them to interview you, to ask you any kind of question. Convince the editors of our friendly purpose. Arrange for meetings at private houses, talk to any group you can get together. Find out where the government money is kept. Take any necessary measures to protect it. Find out who controls the Haitian soldiers; consider carefully the answers you get to that question. Find out how many soldiers there are, what weapons and ammunition are in the city, and where they are kept. Talk with all the Americans you can find, and with other foreign residents too. We need to earn the confidence of everyone in this city."

I believe the admiral successfully indoctrinated me with his own spirit and purpose. In the days that followed, I gave many orders, some with specific directions, some without; and had reason to believe that he was well satisfied. After the first day, radiograms from Washington came frequently; and each night, after my lengthy oral report, Caperton sent back full information.

At eight o'clock the second morning, the revolutionary committee of safety greeted me with friendly handshakes. I tried to learn things from them; but found that, while answering some questions, they would dodge others, and that they were chary of volunteering information. I could get nothing explicit about the government funds, nor about the soldiers, and only little as to what the committee was actually doing. Clearly, they were up to something.

But it wasn't difficult to learn one thing: with the possible exception of Polynice, they were all supporters of Dr. Bobo, who controlled three thousand

Cacos in the north. The chief interest of this committee of public safety was to convince me that Guillaume had been eliminated for the purpose of having Dr. Bobo made president, and that we Americans were honor bound, after our professions of friendship, not to interfere with Bobo's election in the normal Haitian manner. But I emphatically refused to discuss Haitian politics with these people.

From other sources I at once began to acquire much information differing from what the committee was telling me. Many Haitians, some of them prominent figures, called on me and told me about the different political factions and their controlling personalities. Also, I received private requests to call on various Haitians who might find it embarrassing publicly to pay a call on me. And I called on many of them. Some seemed anxious to impress me with their views for selfish purposes, while others seemed wholly patriotic and disinterested. Many were heartsick at the shameful acts of some of their compatriots. All wanted to know if the United States intended to establish a protectorate over Haiti, or if, in accordance with our previous interest, St. Nicholas Mole would be taken for a naval station. But the chief question was: Would the United States permit Bobo to be elected president?

I answered every question as frankly as possible. I could promise nothing. I knew nothing of the intentions of my country toward Haiti or even if we had any intentions. St. Nicholas Mole, a fine harbor, was no longer needed because we now had an equally fine harbor in Guantánamo, not too far away. Admiral Caperton had come on a friendly mission without specific orders.

I learned also that Mont Pom was a Caco chief, employed to install Bobo as president, and that Robans was associated with Mont Pom. Of these two men I promptly conceived a strong distrust.

There were, of course, other problems too. In the afternoon of my first day, I posted on the walls of buildings a printed notice forbidding any persons from carrying arms in the city of Port-au-Prince. That evening Beale Davis handed me a letter that read: "The German minister requests to be informed by what right and by what authority Captain Beach has presumed to give orders forbidding the carrying of weapons by anyone in the city of Port-au-Prince."

"Suppose you answer this," said Mr. Davis. I agreed this was proper, and wrote: "In answer to the request of the German minister that he be informed by what right and by what authority Captain Beach has presumed to give orders forbidding anyone in Port-au-Prince from carrying weapons, he is informed that it is by that right and that authority which the German minister recognized when he asked for, received, and still retains, a guard of sixteen American Marines for his protection."

The German minister did not answer this letter; but he very sensibly retained his Marine guard. I heard nothing more from him on this subject.

My sources of information multiplied. Every afternoon and evening, by request, I met with different groups of Haitians in private homes. Prominent men, hearing of these discussions, wanted to talk with the American naval officer on shore and to expound to him their views as to what should be the relations between our two countries. They always asked, "What would the United States insist upon?" "How soon would the Haitian parliament be allowed to convene to elect a president?"

Through the many discussions in these group meetings I gained some insight into Haitian thought. While answering some questions, I asked many; and got more answers than I gave. I soon realized that the major interest—natural to the educated people, who lived and breathed politics—was in the presidency. The government for years had been the will of the president, so his identity and policies were paramount.

Another source of information, of which only one Haitian knew, was from a member of the Haitian parliament, a man of no great standing; he called privately upon me. "Mon Capitaine," he began,

I ask you not to talk to any Haitian of what I am to say. I realize that my country must accept whatever your country decides to do. I have no political ambitions. My purpose is purely to serve my country. As I see it, there are two things vitally necessary for the future of Haiti, and only two. One, that independence be maintained; the other, that government by revolution cease.

We have now in Port-au-Prince 126 members of the Haitian parliament, senators and deputies, out of a total of 141. The great majority of us earnestly wish to elect a president as soon as possible. Until then we have no country. But we hope that this time we shall not be coerced, and will be allowed to vote without looking down the barrel of a rifle.

All Haitian revolutions follow the same course. The revolution succeeds; Port-au-Prince fills up with Cacos; each senator and deputy is forced, under threat of being shot, to go to the parliament house; there a rifle is held on him while he votes; and it is certain to go off unless he votes for the revolutionary chief who has paid for their services. This person is of course unanimously elected, and thus becomes president of Haiti.

Now here is the present situation: Mont Pom is the Caco chief, paid to elect Dr. Bobo; Robans is concerned in this and commands the troops. Charles Zamor, brother of ex-president Zamor, recently butchered in the Port-au-Prince jail, Charles Delva, and Andre Chevalier, are all interested in the election of Bobo. Polynice is neutral.

These men are planning to force the parliament to meet to elect a president. If they can get us there, Robans and Mont Pom will fill the place with armed men, and Bobo will be promptly chosen.

But we members of parliament, senators and deputies, have decided to attend no meeting unless you will assure us of the protection of American troops while we vote. And that's what Bobo's friends object to. With you here they dare not use force to bring about a session. They dare not hold the election unless the rifles are in Caco instead of American hands.

Bobo's friends cannot force us to meet, and we will not unless you are there to protect us while voting!

I at once saw that this gave the United States power—not to elect the president, which we would not do, but to delay the election to suit our pleasure. It was inconceivable that the United States would acquiesce to the parliament's convening under Caco guns to elect a revolutionist president, thus continuing government by cynically bought-and-paid-for upheaval.

On the other hand, before the United States gave the protection needed to secure peace, order, freedom, and a legal election, it would be well to know the characters and records of the probable candidates. We could best serve the interests of Haiti by playing a waiting game. It now became my business to find out who would be elected in a free election, and whether he would be the man Haiti needed.

I here and now asseverate that I never named to any Haitian a man who would be favored by the United States. There was no bargaining, no exchange of promises, no influence of any kind to secure the presidency for any particular person. But I did go about constantly preaching to Haitians the need of choosing, for themselves, a man of proven character, ability, and unselfish patriotism.

I had frequent conferences with this unnamed member of parliament. From

him I received daily information as to the men considered and their probable strength. It was easy, having the names, to find out all I pleased about
them.

In a day or two I had reason to believe that the committee was not living
up to its agreement with me. They threw men into jail; they released others.
Robans was moving arms and ammunition. They were threatening senators
and deputies. Almost obsessively, possibly hoping to avoid another "pay day"
to the Caco chieftains, they urged Bobo upon me. On my third day I saw that
I had to act, and act quickly. I therefore organized a conspiracy on my own
account by calling on Harry Berlin, who was paving the downtown streets of
Port-au-Prince.

"How many trucks have you?"

"Eight."

"How many mules?"

"Forty."

"Will you lend these all to me, with drivers, tomorrow morning at half past
eight? And will you keep this request quiet?"

"I certainly will," he replied.

The six committeemen came before me at 8:30 the next morning. I had a
long docket, especially arranged for the occasion. I asked many questions, gave
much advice, and entered into long discussions. Ten o'clock came, and I was
beginning to worry. But I went on talking, now against time; and a few minutes later a Marine orderly brought me an eagerly awaited note.

"Gentlemen," I said to the committee, "I have to inform you that this
morning I have had taken from your barracks three thousand Mauser rifles and
four million rounds of ammunition. Also, I have had all the soldiers in these
barracks marched out of town, told them they were discharged from the army
and ordered them not to return to the city in uniform. And lastly, you are
excused from coming to see me anymore. You are warned not to give any
orders in this city nor to exercise authority of any kind!"

This came as a thunderbolt. Their army had been torn from under their
feet. Their power had gone in an instant. Their "army," drafted Haitian style
and dragged into ranks with ropes, had been disbanded and was already happily heading homeward. The United States, which they thought they had
been bamboozling, had found them out and crossed them up! They jumped up
and rushed out of the room like men suddenly crazed.

And now, to my heartfelt relief, a whole regiment of U.S. Marines landed, brought in by the battleship *Connecticut*. The town had been cleared of native soldiers, arms, and ammunition. Thinking Haitians, I had reason to know, understood that my purpose was helpful.

Now came reiterated, insistent demands from the best elements in the city for the admiral to set a day when, with American protection, the parliament could meet and choose a president. But the admiral was not quite ready. Unknown to others, he and I were studying the records of the candidates, and I continued my preaching.

Finally a new name appeared on the list and my reports were that this candidate was gaining strength by jumps. His name was Sudre Dartiguenave. I had not yet met him. A member of the parliament for thirty years, he had never been in a scandal, a conspiracy, or a revolution, and had never belonged to a political faction. I called upon him. He insisted that he was not a candidate by his own choice, and that he fervently wished to escape the troubles of a Haitian president.

At length I said to him, "Senator Dartiguenave, in case you should become president of Haiti what would be your attitude toward the United States?"

He replied, "Should I be thus unfortunate, my attitude toward the United States would be to carry out, to the best of my ability, the constitution and the laws of the Republic of Haiti."

That night I reported this answer to Caperton. A few days later the election was held. There were armed men present, but none in the parliament chambers. They were standing in military fashion outside of the building, wearing the uniforms of the U.S. Marine Corps. Their guns were not pointed at anyone, but they were ready if needed. Sudre Dartiguenave was elected by a vote of 94 out of a 121, in the first free election, in accordance with its own laws, held by Haiti in many a year. I can say, with complete knowledge of all the circumstances, that the only promise Dartiguenave ever made to any representative of the United States was as here recorded.

21

MORE ABOUT HAITI

The election of Dartiguenave occurred on 12 August 1915. On the morning of the eleventh, the day before it was scheduled, threatening warnings in heavy letters had appeared on walls around the city. These denounced the impending election, and declared that the only true candidate was Dr. Bobo.

As previously stated, the influential people of Port-au-Prince had for some time been urging that a president be elected and that the government resume its functions. But as this representative element, many of whom were also members of the parliament, emphatically refused to have an election without American protection, the election took place in the presence of U.S. Marines, who, as the Cacos would have been, were armed. The difference was that the Marines were outside the building, thus ensuring that the parliament could vote in peace rather than while facing a rifle or pistol held by a Caco woodcutter standing in the election hall.

I personally carried out Admiral Caperton's instructions and am therefore competent to state the following: the presence of the Marines was in compliance with the request of the best elements of the Haitian people; their sole

purpose was to prevent coercion; no representative of the American government in any way indicated a preference for any candidate; the election was
conducted without pressure of any kind; and no understanding of any nature
existed between any candidate for the presidency and any American official.
It is necessary to say this because of loose assertions that a bargain existed
between Dartiguenave and the United States.

Immediately after the election he took the oath of office; and then,
descending from the platform, he came directly to where I was sitting, next to
Senator Sansarique, a distinguished Haitian. Dartiguenave, holding my hand
in his, made an impressive speech. He spoke of Haiti, of her troubles, of her
hopes; and referred to the unselfish help recently received from the United
States. He followed this by saying that he realized, and that every Haitian
should realize, that in building up Haiti to the position she should occupy, he
and others would need the active, sympathetic help of the great republic to
the north.

I have always believed that Dartiguenave intended this as a public notice
of what his policy would be. Since my only superior in the service of the
United States was Admiral Caperton, who felt it necessary to maintain his
heretofore "benevolent seclusion" so as to remain free of even the appearance
of applying any influence or pressure, as second in command I was our "point
man."

Parliament then adjourned for the day; and it was announced that the new
president would hold a reception at the home of Deputy Cham. Senators and
deputies with their families, and many other prestigious Haitians, were invited.

Pouring out of the chamber and into the carriages and automobiles, the
crowd made its way to the home of the heavy-bearded Cham. I hunted up my
efficient assistant. "Oberlin," I said, "get to Fort Alexander as soon as you can,
and fire the national salute of twenty-one guns, to let Port-au-Prince know
Haiti has a president!"

Oberlin hurried off. The salute was delayed because he had to load the
saluting guns himself. For want of wadding, he successfully used the fine
Haitian mud. And he fired each round himself. Give an American naval officer something to do, and it will usually be done.

And now, as my duties were over, I found my carriage, intending to return
immediately to the *Washington,* to report to Admiral Caperton. But my carriage was hemmed in. I would have to wait until the inaugural procession

started. It was so long in starting that I became impatient. Finally I noticed a senator, Sudre Villar, walking down the street looking into each vehicle he passed. When he saw me, he approached rapidly.

"Captain," he said, "President Dartiguenave is waiting for you. He says his inaugural procession will not start until you are with him."

So I went along, wondering why he wanted me. When I reached his auto he asked me to step into it. Then the procession started, winding about the streets of Haiti's capital.

It was an interesting experience. Finally we reached the home of Deputy Cham where a raised platform had been improvised; and here the president of the Republic of Haiti and an ordinary officer of the U.S. Navy received congratulations.

I am told that, when Caperton heard of this, he laughed heartily and remarked, "Well, when Beach comes aboard, hoist the Haitian flag to the main truck, man the rail, have the Marine guard up, and give him twenty-one guns!"

That night the admiral received a radiogram containing the treaty that the American government proposed to Haiti. I handed it to Dartiguenave and his six ministers of state two days later. It has controlled the relations between the two countries since 1915.

The treaty breathes helpfulness. Our government agrees to promote the commerce, the industries, and the agriculture of Haiti; to collect Haitian customs; and to appoint a financial adviser to the island republic. It assumes the obligation, in case of disorder, to land armed forces, if necessary, and to suppress it. It also agrees to officer and train a Haitian constabulary.

This treaty was to expire in 1935, and was in fact set aside a year earlier, when our Marines were removed from Haiti. It gave us much less authority over Haiti than we have exercised in the past over Cuba.

When I returned to the *Washington* after delivering the treaty, Admiral Caperton came to me with a radiogram, which he himself gently put in my hands. The contents frightened me. The message was personal, and carried very bad news.

"I am so sorry, Beach," this dear friend said. "You must hope for the best. I have ordered steam on a tug; as soon as you get on board it will leave for Santiago de Cuba. You can take a train there for Havana."

In everything then, as at all other times, Caperton had gone to the limit in his kindly and understanding consideration. In Boston, where Lucie was ill, I was overwhelmed with grief and desolation. Nothing could be done for my beloved wife. Brave woman that she was, she had concealed from me the terrible news given her by her doctors until nearly the end, when she was in fact bed-ridden. We had a few precious days of leave-taking, and, in the middle of September, she died in my grieving embrace. In its inarticulate way, the Navy did the best it could for me. I was formally detached from the *Washington*, ordered to New York with only nominal duty, and informed that I would later be assigned to the Naval War College.

Father's first wife, Lucie Quin Beach, suffering from breast cancer, died on 17 September 1915.

But a month later a telegram came directing me to report to Secretary of the Navy Daniels. I took an early morning train; and expecting to return the same afternoon, carried no baggage. In Washington Daniels said to me, "Secretary of State Lansing wishes to talk with you about Haiti. Go see him."

I spent an hour with Secretary Robert Lansing. "Captain Beach," said he, "the treaty you handed President Dartiguenave has been ratified by the Haitian deputies, but great opposition to it has arisen in their Senate. I am informed that but twelve senators are sure to vote for it; also, that representative Haitians feel you are friendly to their country. I am therefore asking the secretary of the Navy to return you to Haiti, and to request Admiral Caperton to assign you to special duty in connection with the ratification of this treaty. I hope you will be able to go by the first train."

After a talk about conditions in Haiti, I returned to Daniels' office. Here orders were given me to report to Admiral Caperton for duty as captain of my old ship, the *Washington*. Meanwhile, the admiral was directed to employ me specially as desired by Secretary Lansing.

I was told to get to Key West in a hurry; but, though I had to run for my train, I had time to buy a toothbrush. On the run down I bought collars and handkerchiefs. Arriving at Key West on a Wednesday morning, I was much disappointed to find that on Wednesdays no steamer left for Havana. I rushed to the one-legged commandant of the naval station and showed him my orders. (In those days, an officer who was injured in action could remain on active duty if he could perform all the duties of his office; this rule permitted the famous Robley D. "Fighting Bob" Evans, severely injured in the Civil War, to stay on the active list and retire as an admiral, full of honors, in 1908.)

"Captain Hayden," I announced, "you've got to send me to Havana immediately!"

"I have nothing but steam launches, Beach," he replied; "nothing fit for the crossing to Havana."

"Then please get steam on your biggest launch. I've got to go today!"

Hayden jumped about on his one leg as fast as the ordinary commandant did on two. A river launch was made ready; coaled and provisioned, steam was raised, and we cast off for Cuba.

Two hours later, off Sand Key lighthouse, the lieutenant in charge of the launch came to me in great excitement and concern. "Captain," he cried, "we've got to go back! I didn't need a compass to Sand Key light and didn't look for one. But I've just taken the cover off the binnacle. The compass isn't there! We've got to go back!"

"We'll do nothing of the kind!" I replied. "We're going straight to Havana— at least, we'll be able to hit Cuba!" Using a chart we took our departure from the lighthouse in a direction that, I judged, would land us somewhere near Havana.

But a new trouble arose. It had started to blow hard, and a heavy sea was running from the south. As our river launch had its stern largely cut away, with a great hollow propeller well (the better to retrieve practice torpedoes), the rudder could not hold it on course in the worsening weather. We cut figures of eight; and, though the launch was speedy, the way she would sweep through sixteen points of the compass was disheartening. I could only guess what course we were making good.

The lieutenant begged to go back, but I persisted. "No! We're on our way to Cuba!"

Noon, afternoon, and night came. At midnight, the lieutenant, worried sick, told me we were out of fresh water; and just then, for lack of feed water, we had to shut off the boiler, and the engine was stopped. Here was a mess. No compass; no fixed course; a new heading each second; and now, no fresh water to make steam with!

I directed a thorough search for fresh water; and, to my joy and relief, several full tanks and breakers were found forward. We soon got this into the feed tank, restarted the boiler and the engine, and again began our wide-sweeping course.

At about one or two o'clock we thought we saw land ahead. Soon we made out mountains and headed for them. In the lee of this land the wind and sea calmed down. The lieutenant, now happy, was positive he recognized the land.

"I know exactly where we are!" he exclaimed. "Havana is twenty odd miles to the east."

"I believe Havana is to the west," I replied.

But he was so certain that I agreed to let him head east, and in two hours we picked up a green light, a red light, and some others that, as the chart showed, were near Matanzas, well to the east of Havana. Swearing softly (though audibly) I swung the launch back to the westward.

At six o'clock, with gray dawn breaking, we were running into Havana harbor. In the inner harbor a Cuban launch drew near; and men in it shouted at us. Standing in the stern of our boat, I turned the rays of a lantern on the stars and stripes. We dashed past the Cuban launch which I now recognized as a government police boat. A dozen Cuban policemen were yelling at me; but as they did not shoot, I kept on. Soon another launch pointed toward us. By its great yellow stripes I recognized it as a quarantine boat. More shouting. But I was determined to make a landing and kept on. At a customs dock I left the launch. Here some policemen tried to question me; but I kept on. At the visa office of the customhouse, men were sweeping; the doors were open. An official tried to expound the laws of the Cuban Republic that I was violating.

"Wake up President Menocal! I'll talk with him, not with you!" I answered. This horrified him.

"But you can't leave without having your baggage inspected!"

"Here's my card," I said. "And here's all the baggage I've got. I'll make you a present of it!"

I handed him my toothbrush and handkerchiefs and hurried on, caught a train for Santiago de Cuba, and arrived there the next day.

A month or two later I received a letter from the secretary of the Navy enclosing a copy of a protest of the government of Cuba against the lawless acts of El Capitan Beach, who had defied and violated the police laws, the quarantine laws, and the customhouse laws of the Republic of Cuba. The American State Department requested the Navy Department to call my attention severely to my outrageous conduct. In the same mail was a personal note from Secretary of State Lansing which said, rather humorously I thought, that the evidence was overwhelming that Captain Beach was a hard man to stop when he was "a-going" to Cuba.

On 25 October 1915 I reported to Admiral Caperton. And for just a month, in carrying out the specific orders and directions of my beloved chief, I did "all manner of things," as required in my commission. In the middle of November the Haitian senate ratified the treaty by a vote of twenty-five to fourteen—at least, this is my recollection. In writing these memoirs I have no notes of any kind to bother me.

The next thing, according to a message from Washington, was to request Haiti to agree to a modus vivendi. Though now a self-created veteran diplomat, I must confess I had no idea what a modus vivendi was. In due course, however, I learned that it meant a working agreement with respect to the treaty, pending its ratification by our senate.

A meeting was therefore called by the American minister, Mr. Bailly Blanchard, who had returned to his post. Present for the Americans were Blanchard, Caperton, Colonel Waller (U.S. Marine Corps), Conard, Oberlin, and myself. The Haitian secretary of state for foreign affairs, Mr. Louis Borno, a very highly respected person later to become president in his own right, represented Haiti. He asked different individuals to suggest the forms of a modus vivendi; and in each case answered with an emphatic "No!" Oberlin ventured a proposal. "Not as bad as the others; but not satisfactory." Then Captain Conard tried his hand.

"Haiti will agree to that," said Borno.

"Just dictate that to me, Captain Conard," said Minister Resident Blanchard.

And I can still see this kindly gentleman using the stub of a lead pencil to copy Conard's modus vivendi. A few days later Conard and I were in the legation. Blanchard hauled us into a corner, and, beaming with pleasure, read to us a highly commendatory cablegram from the State Department congratulating him on his insight and wisdom in framing the terms of the modus vivendi. I do not know what his reply was.

Following that I was appointed acting financial adviser of Haiti, and Conard acting receiver of customs. With Conard alongside, my efficiency in this position surprised everyone except Conard and me. Fiscal matters were in a mess. But Conard reorganized every customhouse in Haiti, and order began to reign in Haitian finances.

A week or two later, Admiral Caperton summoned the two of us. "Here's a job," he remarked. "Haiti has a double currency: dollars and Haitian gourdes. Our Treasury Department says this causes confusion; and the Navy Department directs me to propose a method for reorganizing money matters. I know nothing of finance except that involved in making my pay cover my expenses and sixty-five dollars a month for insurance premiums. Now, you two fellows understand Haitian finances. Get me up a report and a recommendation!"

Which we did. Conard went at the problem hard. His greatest difficulty was in making me understand. We took our report to Caperton. Conard explained, while I looked as wise as I could.

"All right," replied the admiral. "It's all Greek to me; but I'll sign it and send it by radio."

Soon afterwards Caperton was highly commended by the Treasury Department for his understanding of financial matters and his special skill in solving the currency problem. He gave credit where it was due, however, and it was no accident that Captain Charles Conard, Supply Corps, U.S. Navy, was later one of the wizards concerned with the preparation of the annual budget of the United States.

In those days Colonel Littleton Waller Tazewell Waller was in command of the several thousand Marines stationed in Haiti. He was the personification of those qualities that have made the Marine Corps famous. He was busy restoring peace and order throughout Haiti, but faced insurrection in the north, where the Cacos resented the loss of their power to install new presidents and the special source of income it represented. I didn't have the privilege of participating in, or observing, his response to the challenge presented by the Cacos, but all the reports I heard about it confirmed his reputation as a tough Marine who carried out his orders with firmness and dispatch, and was not the kind of officer one could trifle with. It was he who finally destroyed the Caco power, even though much was later reassembled under the "Ton Ton Macoute" brand.

In February 1916, I was detached from the *Washington*, and ordered to command the *Tennessee*, which was to carry Secretary of the Treasury William G. McAdoo, and a party of financiers, to the various South American capitals.

The *Washington* was scheduled for overhaul in Norfolk, to last several months, during which her name would be changed to *Seattle* to free the "Washington" name for a new battleship. The *Tennessee*, *Washington*'s identical sister, would later be renamed *Memphis*. Just overhauled, she was considered the best available replacement for flagship of the "Commander Cruisers in the Caribbean," Admiral Caperton's official title. *Tennessee*'s commanding officer, Captain Benton C. Decker, wanting to avoid service in the warm Caribbean Sea, suggested that the two skippers simply swap ships. The idea was quite agreeable to Admiral Caperton, who entertained warm feelings for Father, and wanted to keep him doing what he had been doing so well. The State Department agreed with this analysis, and the Navy Department offered no contrary argument. Thus it came about that a most unusual double "relief of command" ceremony took place in the harbor of Port-au-Prince, and in a few days, now under Captain Decker, *Washington* departed, leaving behind the *Tennessee* under Father's command, flying the flag of Rear Admiral Caperton as the new Cruiser Force flagship. Since the ships were identical in all respects, only the Navy knew the difference.

The Navy Department evidently believed things had somewhat cooled off in Haiti, for the scheduled trip around South America was not canceled. Somewhere it had been decided that for the time being, Admiral Caperton had need for neither his flagship nor his flag captain, who was also his chief of staff and well known for his usefulness in Haiti. Whoever made this decision, in the memorable words of (then) Lieutenant Sims two decades earlier, should have been shot at sunrise, boiled in oil, and then left in the hot sun to contemplate the results of his failure to distinguish between the important and the routine.

22

COALING SHIP

A captain loves his ship, though he may not know how to express his feelings. Lindbergh's "We" was no affectation. The captain is the nerve center for the engines, the guns, the crew, the drills, the discipline, the hygiene, the food, the clothing. He may seem a disagreeable old man: ill tempered, inconsiderate, fault finding, unreasonable. But he does his best to keep his ship efficient, for the honor of the Navy, and his own honor.

Father was of course referring to Charles A. Lindbergh's solo flight from New York to Paris in 1927. He was alone in his plane, which he had named "The Spirit of St. Louis" after the city that had most strongly supported him, and his widely popular autobiographical account of the trip was titled "We." As he made plain, the pronoun referred to himself and his tiny, single-engined airplane.

A captain is never off watch. The watch officer is relieved after four hours on

the bridge, and goes below. But in dangerous weather, or when careful piloting is required, the captain never leaves the bridge. My longest consecutive
period on the bridge was three days (seventy-two hours), but many have
exceeded this. A captain does not feel tired or sleepy until his vigil is ended.

The *Tennessee* left Port-au-Prince in February 1916, bound for Norfolk.
North of Crooked Island Channel in the Bahamas, a heavy gale struck us. But
this was nothing to worry about. We were now in the Gulf Stream with a four
knot current helping us. The wind blew, the rain poured, the sea raged, and
on we steamed. Except for the executive officer, my long time friend Yancey
Williams, I had not previously known the deck officers. We were in the path
of commerce. With these conditions I naturally spent my nights on the bridge.

After leaving Crooked Island Channel we did not see sun, moon, or star
until within a day's run of Norfolk. Having high respect for old Hatteras, and
the rocks to seaward off that dangerous cape, I laid an absolutely safe course.
However bad the steering, whatever the currents, we should be safe. And I
kept our newly installed Thompson Sounding Machine (a wonderful thing,
that; it beat slinging the lead all hollow) going day and night, for one can navigate the waters off the east coast of the United States by taking soundings and
charting them. A rough rule is a fathom of depth for every mile offshore.

Early one morning, by dead reckoning and by soundings, we seemed to be
about thirty miles off Hatteras. The weather continued bad, but my mind was
easy. Every fifteen minutes on the bridge, I received the report of a sounding.

At one o'clock that morning, the soundings suddenly dropped from thirty
to twenty fathoms. I ordered another immediately. The report was ten fathoms. I stopped the ship, ordered an anchor ready for dropping, and got a report
of six and a half fathoms!

"Let go the anchor!" I shouted. "Veer to thirty fathoms! Back both
engines!"

The night was inky black. We could see nothing. I cannot describe the anx-
iety that now possessed me. Only six fathoms of water beneath us, thirty-six
feet, and the ship drew thirty feet! And we were off Hatteras in a gale!

The anchor held, and the ship swung around to the Gulf Stream.

I was nonplussed. I had tested our compasses and knew the error on each
point. How could we be so far from our charted position? But there was the
knock-down argument of six fathoms, which would place us almost on the
rocks. I had boats and winches made ready. Eleven hundred men were in my

keeping, not to mention the ship herself, and depending on what daylight showed us, I might have to face any captain's worst dilemma: we might be unable to avoid taking the ground. We might even have to abandon ship!

The long night hours passed. Sea and wind calmed down; at daybreak the sky was clear. Soon up came Mister Sun: I was never gladder to see him!

There was no land in sight. We lowered and sent out eight boats with an officer in each, each boat to pull in a prescribed direction a thousand yards and to take soundings with the hand lead every hundred feet.

At the same time our navigator Tommy Withers, executive officer Yancey Williams, and I each took a number of sights of the sun. Every boat reported deep water within a thousand yards. And our sights showed beyond a doubt that we were thirty miles off Hatteras. We had picked up a very small, unknown shoal that ships had been steaming over for a century or so! So we hove up anchor and went on our way rejoicing. I reported this to the Navy Department, and a look at a recent chart will show "*Tennessee* Shoal" duly recorded.

Plenty of orders were awaiting me at Norfolk. The secretary of the Treasury and his party, including Mrs. McAdoo (daughter of President Wilson), were to come aboard on the morning of 8 March. There were ten important members of McAdoo's party, as well as two more women accompanying Mrs. McAdoo, and about a dozen assistants, clerks, and stenographers. Necessary arrangements had to be made to provide space for them, and a store of enticing foodstuffs was laid in. Extra stewards to serve the high-ranking guests were assigned to the ship. Secretary McAdoo and his party were to mess (take meals) with me in the admiral's cabin, the assistants in the wardroom. I was given an allowance to cover expenses, and ordered my steward, Watson, to assist in providing everything the guests could possibly want to eat.

The party embarked on a wet and nasty day. After a short chat with McAdoo, I went on deck. There I found a quantity of cases. Wondering what they were, I examined them closely. They were marked "Cognac," "Chambertin," "Mumm's Extra Dry," "Chateau Yquem," "Benedictine," "Gin," "Whiskey," "Port," and so on. While I was looking at the pile a gentleman in a raincoat came up and said, "Captain, this is my private property. I am sure you have a safe place to stow it."

"I'm sorry, sir," I replied, "but Navy regulations forbid any wines or liquors on a naval ship. I must ask you to have all this put ashore at once."

The gentleman exploded with wrath. He shouted at me. He would not send it ashore. I could not compel him to! It seemed that there was little to gain by talking with him while he was in such an angry state of mind; so instead I said to the officer of the deck, "Send for the painter. Tell him to bring some black paint and a small brush. And have a motor launch brought alongside the port gangway."

"What are you going to do?" shouted the irate gentleman.

"I'll paint any address you wish on each of these boxes," I replied, "and will land them on the dock. If you do not give me an address I'll land them without one."

He bolted away, appeared a moment later with McAdoo, and excitedly told him what I had said.

"Are wines and liquors forbidden aboard naval ships, Captain?" asked Secretary McAdoo.

"Yes, sir," I replied, "since 1914, by order of the secretary of the Navy."

Looking at the choleric gentleman, the secretary said, "I judge the captain knows his business," and walked away.

We got under way, passed out through the Capes of Chesapeake, and headed south. At 8:30 that evening, I entered the mess room and handed McAdoo a radiogram reading, "Secretary McAdoo, from Associated Press: We are informed that your party took aboard the *Tennessee* a quantity of wines and liquors in spite of Navy regulations forbidding alcoholic beverages aboard Navy ships. Please state facts by radio."

McAdoo grinned when he read this. He passed it to the gentleman whom I had treated so unceremoniously and suggested that he write the answer. I grinned in my turn when I read what he wrote. My once angry passenger stated indignantly that the *Tennessee* was the driest spot in the world; that no member of the party had a drop with him; that the only liquor on board was in the keeping of the medical officer of the ship.

As Secretary McAdoo wished to investigate the finances of Haiti, our first port was Port-au-Prince. There the party found carriages waiting. We drove to the Caserne, and here a modest though determined-looking Marine major gave the secretary a noisy welcome of nineteen guns. McAdoo lingered a few minutes, conversing. Then the Marine, Major Smedley Butler, approached McAdoo and said, with a sword salute, "Sir, that's all I can give you at the time; but I'll start over if you wish." McAdoo smiled, and left to investigate Haitian finances.

That afternoon we left for Port-au-Spain on the British island of Trinidad. Here, after arranging to receive coal, I left with Secretary and Mrs. McAdoo for the city, five miles away. The secretary's naval aide, Lieutenant E. C. S. Parker, accompanied them. At my suggestion, they took rooms for a couple of nights in the Queen's Park Hotel. I had explained to McAdoo that a naval ship, while being coaled, is decidedly uncomfortable.

In the afternoon the secretary, accompanied by Lieutenant "Alphabet" Parker and me, made an official call on the governor of Trinidad. By making the initial call, the secretary waived precedence and rank. By international agreement, his rank as a cabinet minister was senior to that of the governor of Trinidad. Expressed in naval terms, Secretary McAdoo was a nineteen gun official, and Governor Knaggs a seventeen gun official. In matters of high level protocol the junior is always the first one to pay an official call, unless, as in our case, the senior waives the difference.

So we drove to "King's House" in the beautiful botanical gardens, and there met Governor Knaggs, his charming family, and several of his official staff. I know only two things of Governor Knaggs. One is that on the occasion of our visit to King's House, or rather immediately after, he was guilty of a surprising lack of diplomatic courtesy. The other is that he had a beautiful, and somewhat willful, daughter. Because of her, I forgive him all his sins.

We were presented all around. Amongst others present was a Major Something. I did not catch his name, but became convinced he was the grandson of Mr. Dombey's friend, Major Joseph Bagstock. Another was the Governor's official secretary, who was Sir Sprig Somebody. In the glory of his diplomatic uniform, Sir Sprig put even a Haitian Generalissimo in the shade.

Father had a complete set of Dickens' famous novels, and, I believe, had read them all. Among them was *Dombey and Son*, in which "Major Joseph Bagstock" was one of the principal characters.

And now tea, weak, insipid, and not even hot, was served. There was no "raining upwards" with that disappointing concoction. I was surprised, because I had imagined that the British had learned, in 1773 A.D., that Americans did not like tea. The concoction we were served had no chance of revising that general opinion. This was however a very minor thing when, a few moments later, an uproar of human voice seemed to have broken loose outside. It sounded as if someone were reefing topsails in a gale of wind. Then the doors of the reception room we stood in blew open, and a familiar form, accompanied by a lady whom Americans love, banged in.

"Hello, Governor!" shouted this strangely familiar person. "I'm dee-lighted to see you again! Hello, Mac! I'm dee-lighted to meet you here!"

"How do you do, Mr. President," greeted the governor.

"Hello, Teddy," said "Mac" McAdoo.

"Who's the captain?" whispered Teddy, faintly for him, yet with resounding reverberations.

"Beach," whispered Mac, in unconsciously hurricanic tones.

"Hello, Beach! I'm dee-lighted to see you," shouted Teddy.

Then, blowing a typhoon into my ear, he asked, "Who's the lieutenant?"

"Parker," I whispered back, starting a gale on my own account.

"Hello, Parker!" shouted former president Theodore Roosevelt.

Then, while a general talk followed, Sir Sprig Somebody came to me and said, "Later this afternoon I will return for the governor the call of Mr. McAdoo."

"You certainly cannot properly return Mr. McAdoo's call upon Governor Knaggs," I replied.

"Oh, dear me, that's all settled. The governor has directed me to return Mr. McAdoo's call," remarked Sir Sprig.

"I advise you to tell the governor he's making a serious mistake," I rejoined.

Soon after, McAdoo, Parker and I left King's House and returned to the Queen's Park Hotel. Before long there was a telephone call for me.

"Sir Sprig Somebody, speaking," the caller said. "The governor has considered the matter we talked about and has directed me to return Mr. McAdoo's call."

"Which I've already explained you cannot," I replied.

Mr. McAdoo, of course, was informed of all this. Then Alphabet Parker saw the hotel manager, and gave him specific directions that the latter (so I was later told) rather enjoyed carrying out. Within a few minutes Sir Sprig was in the hotel and was met by the manager, to whom he endeavored, unsuccessfully, to present cards asking they be sent to Mr. McAdoo. But the manager refused to accept them.

"I cannot send cards from you to the secretary of the Treasury of the United States," said he in loud tones. "The secretary of the Treasury of the United States begs to be excused."

This was the beginning, not the end, of the episode. Ex-president Roosevelt was also stopping at the Queen's Park Hotel. And soon after Sir Sprig left, Governor Knaggs drove up in great state and called upon Mr. Roosevelt, who, although a former president of the United States, was at this time only a private citizen.

Some months later I read in a New York City newspaper that Governor Knaggs had been dismissed from the British Diplomatic Service. A newspaper reporter called upon me and said he had heard that the dismissal was due to discourtesy to Mr. McAdoo, and asked for particulars. But for the moment my mind was a complete blank. I couldn't remember anything, and told him exactly nothing.

Going back to our call upon the governor, while there Miss Knaggs expressed a desire to visit the *Tennessee* the next day. "It's impossible," I replied. "We'll be coaling ship tomorrow. You'd get chock full of coal dust."

But she insisted and I capitulated. I always do. And solemnly promised that, coaling ship or not, rain or shine, a boat would be waiting for her at ten the next morning.

A heavy tropical rain was falling the next morning. I could not believe she would come in this deluge. Nevertheless, a steam launch went in for her. And on its return, to my dismay, I saw that Miss Knaggs was in it. And so was Sir Sprig Somebody, and Major Joseph Bagstock, the third.

I rushed down the gangway ladder. "You must come another day," I cried. "This miserable coal is all fine dust, and when the coal bucket is swung over and suddenly opened twenty feet above the deck, the coal dust is instantly saturated with rain water and becomes thick black ink. Aboard this ship, right now, the rain is not water, it's ink."

The vision of loveliness, arrayed in a flimsy white gown, replied, "Pooh! You can't scare me. Come along, Sir Sprig."

The latter looked at his golden aigullettes, his golden stripes, his blazing uniform. First he said he wouldn't; then he said he couldn't. But the governor's daughter was determined that he would. She pulled, and the major, J. Bagstock, sir! Joey B., sir!—tough and devilishly sly—pushed. And all three followed me up the gangway ladder.

And down came the flood of ink. Immediately the black population of the island of Trinidad was increased by one female and two males. I was already pretty black myself, and the day before I had had a desire to blacken Sir Sprig's eyes. But the governor's daughter did a complete job. So I was grateful to her.

Our next port was Rio de Janeiro. Here our financiers were met by distinguished Brazilians with whom long discussions were had. It became evident to me that theirs was not a junketing trip; it was an earnest, far-reaching investigation.

At this point in his saga, Dad left out a story I have always enjoyed. I had pleasure in reproducing it in *The Wreck of the Memphis* (New York: Holt, Rinehart, and Winston, 1966), published (by design) on the fiftieth anniversary of the wreck. En route to Rio de Janeiro, *Memphis* crossed the equator. From time immemorial this has been an occasion for a visit by King Neptune, Davy Jones, and some of their brawny shellbacks, whose mission is to give all "pollywogs" a fair trial for various malfeasances committed prior to this great moment. After their guilt is proven, sentence prescribed, and punishment exacted, the former pollywog becomes a shellback and may forevermore exact equally condign penalties on future unworthy pollywogs. As I carefully described in that book, the presence of Mrs. McAdoo, who insisted on her right to become a shellback like everyone else, created unexpected problems, because even shellbacks are very aware of the limitations of authority. King Neptune and Davy Jones solved everything nicely, however, with a little help from the captain of the ship, who, like all captains, is clothed with extraordinary authority so that he may exercise it wisely. Mrs. McAdoo, after being fairly tried and found guilty indeed, was sentenced to sing "Home, Sweet Home" to the crew that evening, just before the evening movies were shown. From all reports, she had a nice voice, and everyone cheered her good sportsmanship.

A week later we left for Montevideo, where the *Tennessee* anchored five miles from the city. Secretary McAdoo and his party now left. They had work to do at Montevideo, then at Buenos Aires. From there, they were to go by train across the South American continent to Santiago de Chile, and rejoin the *Tennessee* at Valparaiso.

At Montevideo I received a cable from our Navy Department directing me to proceed with dispatch to Valparaiso. We were to put in to Bahia Blanca for coal, proceed through the Strait of Magellan, coal ship again at Coronel, and be prepared to leave Valparaiso with McAdoo at a stated time. To complete this schedule, we obviously would have to go at high speed, and could afford to lose no time anywhere.

Arriving at Bahia Blanca, we found coal barges awaiting us, supplied by the Argentine Navy Department at the request of our Navy Department. We began to take coal on board immediately, and coaled steadily through the night and next day.

Several hours after we arrived I was called upon by a representative of the American ambassador to the Argentine government. His manner was distinctly antagonistic. Said he: "By orders of the State Department, the American ambassador has bought about two thousand tons of coal for you, which will arrive here in an hour or so. I find you are coaling ship from another source. I require you to cancel immediately any contract you have made and take the coal provided by the American ambassador, whose representative I am."

"Thank you, sir," I replied, "but the commandant here has supplied coal enough to fill our bunkers. I am directed by our Navy Department to take this coal and must do so."

The representative of the American minister now became angry. "Your Navy Department cannot do business with a department of the Argentine government. The Department of State does that through its representative, the American ambassador at Buenos Aires. You will take this coal I am bringing you."

I immediately sensed the possibility of a row and resolved to say as little as possible.

"Do you hear what I say, sir?" he shouted. "I am giving you orders!"

To this I made no reply.

"What have you to say, sir?"

"Please express my sincere respect to the American ambassador, and my appreciation of his sending coal for the *Tennessee*. Say that I knew nothing of this, but that I was directed to take coal provided by our Navy Department at Bahia Blanca, which coal, I was informed, would be waiting for me. We have already received several hundred tons. I cannot possibly take the coal sent by the American ambassador."

"You will hear from this," said the American savagely, bolting from my cabin.

And I did. But I wasn't worried any more than I was the time I had broken most of the laws of the Republic of Cuba.

The next morning an Argentine officer clambered over coal barges to the *Tennessee's* quarterdeck. Ordinarily, when an officer in uniform comes aboard, certain courtesies are prescribed. A bosun's mate is there to pipe him over the side; and on American warships there are "side boys," two for a lieutenant, four for a commanding officer, six for a commodore or an admiral. The theory, so ran the naval tradition of the former century, was that after returning from heavy weather ashore, the lieutenant, being young and slight, could be carried by two men; the commanding officer, being heavier, might need four men; and the old commodore, certain to be bulky, would probably need six stalwart men to haul him aboard, carry him aft, and stow him in his bunk.

But this Argentine officer, being spry, had got aboard without side boys or pipe, or even being seen. The rules are off when coaling ship. An orderly brought his card that read, translated from Spanish to English, "Powhatan Page, Captain, Argentine Navy."

I hurried to greet him, and saw, instead of the usual Spanish type of Argentine officer, a man that, except for his uniform, was an American, every inch of him. As we shook hands I said, in English, "How in the world is it that a descendant of Pocahontas is an Argentine naval officer?"

Captain Page laughed. "Of course I am a Virginia Page," he replied. "My father was an officer of the American Navy, but went to Virginia when our state seceded, and was a Confederate naval officer during the Civil War. He was never 'reconstructed,' but came here instead. So, it was natural for me to become a naval officer, and Argentina is my country."

We had a long talk that suddenly became of great interest to me when I told Captain Page of my orders. He informed me that he doubted if they could be fulfilled. He said, "I've just heard that because of some labor questions, within a couple of weeks all the coal mines of Chile will be shut down for two months. All stocks on hand are being rapidly depleted. You will have to make sustained high speed to get to Coronel in time to find enough coal to fill your bunkers!"

This was a most serious matter. McAdoo had to be in Washington 8 May.

The Navy Department never expects excuses or explanations from its captains. It provides ample means for them to accomplish its orders, and will excuse nonfulfillment of the same only after it has been shown that every possible means has been tried. This was the situation now facing me.

As a result, as soon as the last pound of coal was received, with the ship still filthy with coal dust, a tug began to tow the *Tennessee* from the coal dock. The pilot was on board, steam had been raised on all boilers, the engines had been tested, and we started for the Strait of Magellan at the same time as we started to clean up the evidence of our coaling. When clear of the coast, all fire rooms were closed and forced draft blowers started. We brought the speed up gradually, watching for excessive heat in brasses and bearings. But the efficient forced lubrication system kept everything perfectly cool. Soon we were running at contract trial speed, 127 revolutions per minute, or 22 knots (25.7 land miles an hour). I doubled the watches, put coal passers at firing, and sent deckhands to the fire rooms to pass out coal for the fires. And this splendid ship, with never a hot brass or bearing, kept up for three days a speed that test requirements had demanded for only four hours. My heart was jubilant. I loved that magnificent ship, even if later her name was changed and she became a desolate wreck.

I now spent much time studying the sailing directions of the Magellan Strait. As I previously stated, the Navy Department anticipates every possible need a skipper may have, and provides instructions and information in detail for navigating every body of water, and every harbor, in the world. We got out all the charts of the navigation of Magellan Strait. Pinned together, these charts stretched the entire width of the wardroom mess room. And besides the charts were a number of books. I cannot imagine any necessary information was left out.

Williams, Withers, and I made many notes. It was clearly laid down that steam ships never passed through Magellan Strait without anchoring. The reason for this is that in the middle of the strait is a place known as "Crooked Reach," with several miles of twisting and turning, and a lot of wicked rocks. These, with fierce currents, have wrecked many ships. And Crooked Reach had to be passed through during daylight. It was simply too hazardous at night.

As I recall, between the entrance and exit of the strait, there are but three anchorages. One is Punta Arenas, nearest the entrance from the Atlantic. If my recollection is correct, the names of the other two were Beaumont Bay and

Fortescue Bay. All three anchorages were to the eastward of Crooked Reach. Entering Magellan Strait from the east, we would pass them all, in other words, before reaching the most difficult portion of the strait.

The vital need of getting to Coronel in time to secure coal—the fact that my ship would be damned if she didn't, that the Navy Department, if the coal were not received, would fail in getting the secretary of the Treasury back in Washington by 8 May—forced me to a decision I would not ordinarily have taken.

23

THROUGH CROOKED REACH

At eight o'clock in the morning on a day early in April 1916, the United States' ship *Tennessee* was entering the Strait of Magellan. Virgin Cape was two miles or more on our starboard hand. To port was Tierra del Fuego. On either side stretched far-reaching, low banks of white sand. A sad monotony, a desperate worthlessness, seemed to characterize this region. My good *Tennessee* throbbed with desire and the purpose of going. Her engines were now making 132 turns, 23 knots, 27 miles an hour, a speed the contractors had not dared attempt on her trial trips.

But I knew my ship. And I knew my capable chief engineer, Jones, who was carefully watching the thermometers showing oil temperatures in the bearings and brasses, and who would slow down at the first sign of heat above normal. Forced lubrication has done much for safety at high speeds.

To get Secretary McAdoo back by 8 May, we had to reach the Coronel coal mines before they shut down; we had not an hour to spare. And I knew the Navy Department would expect me to use every effort consistent with safety to maintain Secretary McAdoo's schedule. On leaving Bahia Blanca I had planned to take full advantage of favorable currents flowing at high speed through the strait. To get the most out these currents, and maybe save a whole day, required the highest possible sustained ship's speed.

Soon we were shooting through the First Narrows where we encountered the swiftest current I have ever experienced—eight knots. This, added to our own twenty-three knots, was sending us over the ground at the rate of thirty-six land miles an hour; not much, perhaps for an automobile, but a lot for seventeen thousand tons of steel. Indeed, in this swift current, high speed was necessary for safety. On both sides, ashore, were the wrecks of ships that, too slow for the sweeping currents and twisting channel of First Narrows, had left their bones in forfeit. I doubt if any ship has ever swept through the First Narrows with the speed and majesty of the *Tennessee*. Hurricanes of wind were being blown into her furnaces; great columns of smoke were swirling high from her stacks. As to the engines, constant reassuring statements came from Jones.

"Captain," he reported through the speaking tube, "you'd think we had a sewing machine down here instead of thirty thousand straining wild horses!"

The coolest thing in the engine room on that terrific day was the spirit of this young officer. And the time was coming, not many months later, when, in the midst of death and disaster, with boilers exploding about him, this same spirit never faltered.

Our navigation had been carefully studied, with lines on the chart, from the Atlantic to the Pacific, showing the paths of greatest safety. With a small navigating range finder mounted on the forward turret, and with a sextant in hand, the navigator, Lieutenant Withers, was instantly aware if we deviated by even a few feet from our charted course. I felt my responsibilities keenly; but with reassuring reports from Jones, with the navigator constantly alert, and with the ship steering perfectly—there was never a better steering ship—I never doubted for a moment our complete control of the situation.

After several hours of straining effort we passed into the Second Narrows with our favorable current still running strong. The tides swept along the shores as they had swept daily since Magellan dared the unknown. When the boiling current struck rocks and shoals, great volumes of spray ascended like the smoke over a battlefield. And we steamed serenely on, and on.

Early in the afternoon, the southernmost city of the world, Punta Arenas, appeared on the starboard bow. "Captain," asked Withers, "hadn't you better slow down? We should be thinking of anchoring soon."

"We'll not anchor off Punta Arenas, Withers," I replied.

"But, Captain, you must anchor for the night, and there are only three anchorages possible: Punta Arenas, Beaumont Bay, and one other; and Punta Arenas gives a better anchorage than either of the other two bays."

"Of course. But we'll see how much farther we can go."

I had deliberately said nothing to Withers of a determination I had taken, wishing to assume the sole responsibility for it. This was, if possible without risking the ship, to get through the strait without anchoring. To the best of my belief, this had never before been done. The great sustained speed of the *Tennessee*, her reliability, and the swift favoring current, might now make this possible, provided we could go fast enough to complete the navigation of the dreaded Crooked Reach during daylight. I had determined to go as far as the last possible anchorage, and then decide. So, my beautiful ship steamed past Punta Arenas faster than ever any ship had passed that southern city before.

It was bitterly cold; but two suits of heavy woolen underclothing, two pairs of blue Navy socks, a heavy overcoat, a sailorman's "watch cap," and a rubber coat overall, kept me sufficiently warm. Our latitude was about 53 degrees south.

And now we were afflicted with those sudden sharp gales known as "willy waws," with hail and a fine-cutting rain. But we could still see both shores, which was the important thing. The sandbanks on either side had changed to hills; and in the distance, straight ahead, were high mountains.

Some time after three o'clock Withers said: "Captain, we are nearing one of the two remaining anchorages. You should slow down now, sir, if you intend to anchor."

"We'll not anchor here, Withers," I replied.

"But we'll then have only one possible anchorage between here and the Pacific, sir. You know, of course, that no ship has ever gone through the strait without anchoring; and of course you wouldn't attempt to navigate Crooked Reach at night."

"Certainly not, Withers; but we'll not anchor here."

About five o'clock Withers spoke again of anchoring. "This will be your last chance, sir. There is no possible anchorage between here and the Pacific Ocean, and none there. If you don't anchor here you'll have to take the ship through Crooked Reach, the nastiest piece of navigation you can think of, and then run 150 miles through the narrowest part of the strait, and this by night. There will be no lights at all. No ship has ever done this."

"Withers, if we should not anchor, could we get through Crooked Reach during the daylight hours?"

"Why—yes, sir; we're not far from it now."

"I have no doubt of your ability to navigate the ship through Crooked Reach, Withers."

"Nor have I, sir," was the instant reply.

"Is there any reason why we shouldn't run the rest of the way through the strait at night?"

"Captain, look astern at our wake. It's as straight as a string. Look on the chart beyond Crooked Reach. A straight channel, without bends, with forty fathoms right to the shores; and two miles wide at the narrowest place. We know we can depend on the steering and the engines. It looks like a great responsibility, sir, because no ship has ever done this, not even the *Oregon* in 1898. But, with the present conditions I believe it a perfectly safe thing to do."

"All right, Withers, we'll go on. And I promise you we'll be in the Pacific by one o'clock tomorrow morning."

Before six o'clock we were entering Crooked Reach, and our real troubles began. We had to navigate, on a twisting, snake-like course, through boiling currents and between wicked rocks, seen and unseen. The piloting was far more difficult than that for which professional pilots are usually employed, and the chance of salvage, in case of disaster, almost nil. Neither Withers nor I had been through the strait before.

When naval officers do commit faults of navigation it should be remembered that, far from running over the same track time and time again, they are navigating, as we were, in strange and remote waters. Nevertheless, they are held to the most rigorous accountability.

And now, of a sudden, an amazing spectacle was presented. It had been cold, dark, and dreary all day; for two hours we had been pelted by willy waws. Quite unexpectedly the sun burst out, at six o'clock in the evening, with glory indescribable. Ahead and on both sides, hundreds of lofty, cone-shaped, snow-covered peaks reflected its dazzling rays. Roaring through the exit of the tricky passage, we entered what seemed a mighty tunnel. On each side, rising thousands of feet, were steep mountains.

We felt deep in the bowels of the earth. And soon intense blackness settled upon us. But we turned on our eight searchlights, two bearing ahead, and three on each side. We were now on a great highway of smooth water, two miles wide at its narrowest, straight, without a curve or a rock. Danger? None whatever!

And yet, six hours later, when my noble *Tennessee* was safely out in the broad Pacific, with the light on Evangelica Island far astern, my eyes were wet, and I fervently thanked God.

24

SANTO DOMINGO

Oh, the comfort of having a thousand fathoms of water underneath our keel! The security of navigating in a channel five thousand miles wide! A captain has mental ease only when in deep water, far from land.

In a few days we were at Coronel. Here, near the coast, were the coal mines to which we had been directed. They had not yet shut down; but every pound of coal above ground had already been taken away. Only a few employees remained at the mine serving us. For the next week, the *Tennessee* had a disagreeable time of it. It was fetch and carry: a few tons of coal would be mined, sent off to the ship, and in a few minutes we would have it stowed in our bunkers. We lived in coal dust for a week. Finally the bunkers were filled, and we were able to clean the ship and set off for Valparaiso.

Here we picked up McAdoo and his party, and started for Callao, the port of Lima, Peru, where the next conference was to be held. A day out I received a radiogram: "Captain Beach, USS *Tennessee*: Bubonic plague raging at Lima and at Guayaquil. If you go ashore at either place I will quarantine you for a week at Pacific entrance to Panama Canal. Goethals."

McAdoo was much concerned when he read this message. "We have made arrangements for an important conference with the Peruvian government," he said. "It will be extremely unfortunate if we cannot go there. What is your duty, Captain?"

"To carry you where you tell me to go, Mr. Secretary." Obviously this answer caused him deep thought, since it placed the entire decision squarely on him.

Finally he said, "Very well. We'll go to Callao, but please let no one go ashore. I'll go to Lima by myself and try to explain our inability to keep the engagement. It isn't the danger of plague that stops the conference. But a delay of a week waiting for the quarantine to be lifted would prevent my reaching Washington by 8 May."

In two or three days we anchored at Callao. McAdoo, accompanied by his aide, Lieutenant Parker, immediately left the ship. I told Parker to request the U.S. public health officer at Callao or Lima to come on board immediately with his health records. From these I learned that though bubonic plague could hardly be said to be "raging" in Lima, there were some cases of that disease.

In about two hours McAdoo and his aide returned. With them were U.S. Ambassador Benton McMillan, and most of the Peruvian cabinet. McAdoo and Parker each stepped from the accommodation ladder into a waiting bath-tub. The surgeon of the ship, Dr. Robertson, was now major general in command. And he boiled, fumigated, expurgated, and slaughtered any lurking germs that the secretary or his aide may have carried.

Father said nothing about "boiling and fumigating" any of the officials accompanying McAdoo. They may have been immune to the plague, or, more likely, George Washington Goethals, governor of the Panama Canal Zone had not been told of their visit. In any case, they would not be aboard the ship when she reached Panama. McAdoo and Parker would, of course.

McAdoo's report had caused consternation at Lima. The officials there felt that untold harm would be done Peru if it were published to the world that bubonic plague at Lima had prevented this important conference. Emphatic demand was made that it must take place. To my discomfort, the onus of decision was thrown on me.

In accordance with my conversation with Secretary McAdoo, after receiving the report of the U.S. public health officer, and on the advice of our senior surgeon, Dr. Robertson, I had ordered that no officer or man attached to the *Tennessee* should set foot on shore. My order did not include the Secretary McAdoo's party; it was of course immaterial to me whether or not the ship was quarantined at Panama.

McAdoo conferred with the high Peruvian officials who had accompanied him aboard, with the other members of his party, and with Ambassador McMillan, who was indignant that an unwarranted, incorrect, and uncalled for, report of bubonic plague at Lima should stop this financial conference. The cabinet ministers protested with deep feeling against a cruel stigma based on an inaccurate report. They earnestly insisted that there was no bubonic plague at Lima.

The financiers retired for private consultation. Returning, they straddled the principal issue very nicely by announcing that they earnestly wished to carry out the original plan of going to Lima; that personally they had no apprehension; that they hoped the *Tennessee*'s captain would make it possible for them to go; but that they were on a naval ship and felt it their duty to act, in this case, as would any person under the orders of the Navy Department. If the captain would rescind his order they would go ashore; and if not, they would stay aboard.

And now U.S. Ambassador Benton McMillan and the forces of the Republic of Peru fired broadsides, torpedoes, and machine guns at "El Capitan Beach." The still waters of Callao reverberated with the thunders of their indignant, fiery denunciation. Vainly did I protest that I had given no orders to the financiers, who could go ashore if they pleased; and that if the public health officer's report was shown to be wrong, I would go ashore, and permit my officers and men to do so.

I must admit that I spent several uncomfortable hours reading every report of the illness I could find, for I love to please earnest, sincere people, even if they are on opposite sides of a fence. But a naval captain must do what the Navy Department would expect him to do.

We left that evening for Panama. Now, with several days to spare, the ship loafed along. I have never had a more contented time. The weather was fine, mild and pleasant. The financiers, who had been engrossed in their studies, emerged from their rooms and became good fellows.

I have heard that, during the World War, Secretary McAdoo had to provide billions of dollars for our military expenditures and for loans to our allies. I have heard that he was director of all our railways, that he commandeered all our merchant ships. I claim no intimate knowledge of this. But I do claim knowledge of another matter. Mark off a quarterdeck in squares, and I will back William G. McAdoo against the world in a good old game of "Hop Scotch." It was a treat to see the secretary of the Treasury hopping about the *Tennessee's* deck. He won every match.

The sailors adored him and firmly believed that he had once been one of them. I have never known such a complete, beautiful command of nonblasphemous profanity. When he got into action "Mac" was like Niagara Falls. And sailormen regarded him with loving wonder.

One of the financiers was Paul Warburg, a velvet soul. It was a privilege to converse intimately with one so modest in manner, so big in action. The Federal Reserve Bank is his creation. But his real monument will be in the hearts of those with whom he has had close contact.

And there was Andrew J. Peters, assistant secretary of the Treasury, a lovable character; and Senator Duncan Fletcher, Mr. Samuel Untermeyer, Mr. Archibald Kairns, Mr. James Fahey. The ladies in the party were Mrs. McAdoo, Mrs. Peters, and Mrs. Untermeyer. The work of the financiers being done, they were now free, and, I believe, they enjoyed their remaining days on board the good ship *Tennessee*. We reached Norfolk on 8 May. I felt, as this party left the ship, that I was bidding goodbye to dear friends.

I have seen, and hope to be able to find, a wonderful photograph of the *Tennessee* passing through the Panama Canal. Clearly visible are a tall, slender man and a woman in a flowing white dress sitting side by side in a shaded part of the lower bridge. Sailors and officers, dressed in white, were all over the upper decks. It was hot in Panama; all portholes were open, and there was no air conditioning in those days. The interior of the ship must have been like an oven. In the photograph the black "waterline" of the ship is not visible, and the lowest row of portholes, nearly all of them wide open, are unusually close to the water. Fresh water is less buoyant than salt water, and all ships passing through the Panama Canal must take note of this.

Two discomforting things happened at Norfolk. All my veteran watch officers were detached and replaced by ensigns just graduated from Annapolis. These may have been future Farraguts; but at this time not one had ever stood a watch on the bridge without being "wet-nursed" by an experienced officer. The other annoyance was that the name of my beautiful ship was changed to *Memphis*.

Admiral Caperton was now pacifying a revolution in the Dominican Republic. The president, Jimenez, had been deposed by a cigar maker named Arias. But before Arias had had time to do more than issue a proclamation exposing the nefarious acts of his predecessor and proclaiming the unselfish patriotism with which he would serve his beloved country, one of Caperton's captains, Walter Crosley, took him driving into the country. Crosley gave him some good advice; and when the city limits were reached, stopped and said, "Adios, Señor Arias, your course is west-nor-west." His "Excellency" left at a dead run, and was soon back at his trade of making cigars.

While these events were in progress I was ordered to rejoin Admiral Caperton with the *Memphis*. On the trip an incident occurred illustrating a captain's need of eternal, never-ceasing vigilance.

As I have stated, my watch officers were just from Annapolis. Their naval education was by no means complete. I therefore transferred my office and sleeping quarters to the bridge, where there was a bunk I could lie on.

Three or four days out of Norfolk we entered "Crooked Island Channel" for a night passage. There is no difficulty in navigating with careful steering, and lighthouses are not lacking. At the same time, a ship must keep in the middle of the channel to avoid rocks and wrecks.

At eight o'clock I gave the officer of the deck my night order book. This gave necessary information and orders, and particularly the courses to be steered. One of these was, "south by west, nothing to the westward." This was standard phraseology.

One o'clock in the morning, while I was in the emergency cabin examining a chart, I heard the lookout report, "Light ho! White light on starboard bow!" And immediately afterwards I heard my young officer of the deck shout, "Quartermaster, full right rudder! Hard over!"

This would have headed the ship to starboard, to the west and toward land, as rapidly as possible. I ran up the ladder instantly, shouting at the top of my voice, "Steady, Quartermaster, steady! Hold your course, sou-by-west!" The ship had not begun to swing, and the danger was averted. And then, I regret to say, I exploded with fury. My uncontrolled rage utterly overwhelmed the young officer.

"Your order would have put this ship on the rocks in less than ten minutes!" I shouted. "And before that, you would have struck that steamer on our starboard bow!"

When the youngster found his breath, he replied, "Captain, I obeyed your written orders, sir. They told me to steer south-by-west, and *to let nothing be to our westward.* That white light would be to our westward, sir, unless I gave full right rudder!"

"Great God!" I yelled. "Is that all you know?"

"I am doing my best to understand, and to obey your orders, Captain; but this is the first watch I have ever stood alone." And the poor fellow burst into tears.

"My dear boy," I replied, "try to forgive your old captain for his words and manner. They were not deserved." And I said to myself, "If I continue to lose myself this way I'll be worse than Chief Engineer Bobbie Potts ever was!"

We reached the harbor of Santo Domingo where I was glad indeed to rejoin Rear Admiral Caperton. But he was not long with us, for he was promoted to the rank of full admiral and ordered to command the Pacific fleet.

This change, like the one taking the *Tennessee* and Father away from Admiral Caperton for a long trip around South America while things were still troublesome in the Caribbean, cannot be supported in terms of our nation's best interests. As happens in all walks of life, there are times when the bureaucratic obligations of taking an important official on a cruise, or, more to the point, the "rotation" so sacred to the Navy Department, ought to give way to stability of control until the job on the spot is done. All military officers, and (I dare say) most industrialists, would say the same.

Rear Admiral Pond became our squadron commander. He was an officer of strong convictions, always sympathizing with the underdog. He believed that we should not overawe weak nations, nor force them to do our bidding. In a fight he was sure to take the side of the weaker party. He also strongly insisted that officers of his date had far more daring, nerve, and willingness to accept responsibility than those of my date. We thus had constant friendly bantering discussions. Likable, earnest, and true, he was friendly and considerate with everyone, regardless of rank. Soon after he took command, we learned that the parliament of Santo Domingo was about to elect a president.

"Get up steam, Beach," he directed, "we'll leave tomorrow morning for Cap Haitien."

"But Admiral," I protested, "Surely the Navy Department will expect you to be here when Santo Domingo elects a president; of all times, this is the time you should be here."

"What for? To intimidate these free people? To coerce them into selecting a man to please us, not themselves? There's been altogether too much of this intimidation of feeble nations by powerful ones. I believe in building up nations as well as individuals. I have no orders to remain here during the coming elections and I'll go away. And I'll do more for the interests of our country by going away and showing confidence in these good people than by staying here."

Believing that the admiral would displease the Navy Department by doing this, I earnestly portrayed the condition of the country, the banditry by which thieves exhorted contributions from sugar, coffee, cacao, and tobacco growers—the lawlessness and disorder that everywhere existed. Though our government certainly had not given him or Admiral Caperton the slightest indication that it favored any candidate, or wished in any way to interfere in the election, it did wish to prevent disorder and to protect its citizens at a critical time. I urged him to change his decision.

But he was firm in his intention of leaving the next morning. "Bring the charts for Cap Haitien, Beach," he said, "and also for Samana Bay."

Looking at the Samana Bay chart, he remarked, "By George! I'd love to go into that bay, right up to the city of Samana. But it's impossible. There's plenty of water but the channel is twisting and narrow for miles. Just look at it! And there isn't a single buoy. The Atlantic fleet plants buoys, and takes them up when it leaves. Too bad! I'd like to go in."

"Admiral, wouldn't you take a ship in?"

"Without the buoys? Certainly not."

"Well, Admiral, there's no difficulty about that channel. I judge from what you say that men of your date weren't inclined to accept such responsibilities. But there's no trouble about taking a ship in there."

Pond looked at me fixedly.

"Will you accept the responsibility?"

"I certainly will!"

He sent an orderly for the navigator.

"Mr. Withers, look at the chart. Would you be willing to navigate the *Memphis* into Samana Bay?"

"Certainly, Admiral! There's no difficulty at all in that."

"All right, we'll do it," decided Pond.

"Admiral," I remarked, "you may have to change your mind about present-day navigators!"

We took the admiral to the city of Samana and left him there to rejoin us at La Plata two days later. At La Plata, however, while we were returning in a fast steam launch from shore to ship, there was a sudden resounding, rending noise.

"Nobody leaves the launch without the captain's permission!" shouted the coxswain.

No one had a chance to leave it. The boat, which had been literally rent in twain, left us in ten seconds. But the water was calm and warm, and we were picked up in a few minutes. The launch had struck a totally submerged steel plate projecting from a wreck. Naval life has many such incidents.

The admiral came aboard and we left for Cap Haitien. This port has an outer and an inner harbor. So far as I know, the *Georgia* is the only battleship that had entered the inner harbor. But I had been there with a ship bigger than the *Georgia*—the *Washington*—and knew it well.

"Beach," said Admiral Pond as we were nearing our destination, "I suppose you wouldn't care to enter the inner harbor?"

"Why not, Admiral?"

"Well, you've got a channel only thirty or forty yards wide, almost on top of a rocky bluff. Perhaps you think it's too hazardous."

"Admiral, that three-mile channel has hardly a bend in it, and the *Memphis* is the most dependable ship I have ever served in. She steers perfectly. I will go right in unless you stop me."

"I'm glad you will, but I'll not order you to."

We anchored in the inner bay with five hundred yards to turn in. This gave scant room for maneuvering, but I knew I could turn the *Memphis* on her heel within a hundred yards. This may have seemed difficult for a seventeen thousand ton mass drawing thirty feet and almost two hundred yards long; but I knew my ship.

After anchoring at dusk, Pond and I immediately went ashore where my old friend and classmate, Colonel Eli Kelly Cole, was in command of the Marines. Returning soon after eight o'clock we found a radiogram from the Navy Department awaiting Admiral Pond. It directed him to return immediately to Santo Domingo.

"Beach," said the admiral, anxious to comply with the order at once, "we can't possibly leave tonight; the ship hasn't swung a degree; we're heading exactly as when we anchored; the channel is dead astern, and you haven't room to turn."

"Have I your permission to get under way?" I asked.

"Whenever you can do so safely."

I gave orders to warm up the engines immediately, steam having been left on the boilers. Then Withers and I and another officer studied the chart. There were three lighthouses. Their job would be to angle on these lights with their sextants. So long as the angles between them were within certain limits, the ship could not go aground. Getting under way, I handled the helm and the engines, sometimes going ahead with both, sometimes astern with both, sometimes ahead with one, astern with the other. Meanwhile I used the helm to good advantage. I hadn't done this sort of thing four years for Alfred Reynolds without learning something.

Gradually my noble ship twisted around, and in a few minutes we were heading out. Slowly and carefully we steamed through the channel, with searchlights trained ahead and on both sides. In some ways, it was as if we were reliving the last section of our passage through the Strait of Magellan, except that the shores were nearer, and it looked as if we could jump ashore. But out we went, and soon we were in the open sea.

Admiral Pond was constantly on the bridge; but never made a comment until we were well on our way. Then he commended me. "Beach, I thank you. You have nerve and skill. You handled this good ship beautifully."

During our absence the Dominican parliament had elected Dr. Henriques y Carvalhal president. This gentleman, whose personality was impressive, was a physician, an author, and a poet. I saw him every day for a while, and esteemed him highly.

The harbor of Santo Domingo is an open, unprotected roadstead with rolling waves every afternoon. Some thirty miles away is a protected harbor near the city of Agra. We spent a day or two there coaling ship alongside the collier *Vulcan*, while the admiral remained at Santo Domingo.

Because organized bandits infested this part of the country, and we could afford to take no chances, I had a company of bluejackets sleep armed and equipped on the quarterdeck. Sometime after midnight the captain of the collier, known informally as "Whispering Jerry," asked to see me immediately. In stentorian tones (the source of his nickname) he told me that early the preceding morning he had permitted five of his crew to go out in a whaleboat with orders to return by sunset. They had not returned; and he had just been informed that some natives had told a search party his men had been seized and were prisoners in the jail at Agra.

"I'll go for them immediately," I said. I ordered a steam launch and several motor launches lowered; and signaled to the captain of a destroyer anchored near to report to me at once. I told him to steam in after me in order to use his searchlights.

Soon my men were in the boats and we started for Agra, twelve miles away. My plan was to land, march to Agra, locate the jail, and demand to see the Americans confined there (if any), and to know what they were charged with and why arrested. I intended to be courteous, though sure that my trained force of 108 men would be superior to any that could be brought against it. With it all, I doubted the report that these men had been arrested.

At four in the morning the destroyer's searchlights picked up an object in the water. We went over to this object and found it to be the *Vulcan*'s whaleboat, keel up, with three of the men hanging on to it, all completely exhausted. The boat had capsized many hours previously, and two of the men had drowned.

I took the survivors into my steam launch, and directed all boats and the destroyer to return. When we were a half mile from the ship, our launch's boiler exploded, and for a moment there was, one might say, a Hell of a time. The men in the launch, except the coxswain, jumped overboard. Withers jumped into the boiler compartment to do anything he could; I remained with the three exhausted men of the *Vulcan*. Withers was burned a bit, but not seriously.

Another minor incident of Navy life. And sometimes there are incidents of major, tragic importance.

25

THE WRECK OF THE MEMPHIS

The open roadstead of Santo Domingo is unprotected from any southerly or easterly storm; and the West Indian hurricane season was now upon us. Ships that came in for a day or two would keep steam up. We were likely to be in the harbor for months.

Wishing to take every possible precaution at a dangerous anchorage, I talked the matter over with Admiral Pond; and took steps, that, it seemed, would amply protect the ship.

With all due respect to Admiral Pond, himself recently skipper of the older and slightly smaller armored cruiser *Pennsylvania,* and despite his generally good-natured attitude, in this instance he badly failed his duty to the Navy, and to my father. In the discussion mentioned by Father, the big question was how many of the cruiser's sixteen boilers should be kept fired. Father strongly urged four, as Caperton had always authorized, because of the possibility of bad weather in an exposed anchorage. Six were the minimum believed necessary to get under way, but four could be made to do in a pinch, and this was the regular policy under Caperton. Admiral Pond, concerned with economizing on coal, directed the ship keep fires on only two, for auxiliary steam only. It was well known that two boilers could not provide sufficient steam to move the big cruiser, so Father compromised with the special provisions mentioned immediately below. In the ensuing court-martial, he expected Pond to come forward voluntarily in his defense on this point, but when Pond did not do so, he refused his counsel's proposal that he be subpoenaed on the grounds that although testifying was the admiral's duty, it was also his decision to make. As it turned out, the court's adverse decision hung on this very issue, of "not having been able to get under way when bad weather threatened," no member of the court ever having heard of a tsunami, or "tidal wave," as it was then called. In my *The Wreck of the Memphis*, published fifty years after the disaster, I discussed these matters extensively.

I kept steam constantly on two double-ended boilers, and kept four others in immediate readiness, with water at the steaming level, furnaces primed, and a "steaming watch" at their stations day and night. I studied closely the "sailing directions" supplied by the Navy Department. These give specific and detailed information concerning weather, anchorages, storms, and safety precautions in all the harbors of the world. The directions are kept up to date by weekly bulletins.

I had readings of the barometer reported to me hourly, and weather radiograms as received. I also secured daily reports from the weather office on shore. The United States has such an office, or a weather agent, in every port of the world. At these offices weather reports and cable storm warnings may be obtained; and from them, at specified times, daily bulletins are sent out. Storms nowhere come up without some warning. If reports are not available the barometer invariably gives indications. There could be no excuse for being caught unprepared, for the mariner always has many hours of warning. In the terrible hurricane at Samoa in 1889 where four or five German warships and our own *Trenton* and *Vandalia* were destroyed, the ships had a day's notice of the approaching tempest.

On 22 August 1916 I was to entertain U.S. Minister W. W. Russell and Mrs. Russell at luncheon. That morning the weather seemed unsettled, but hardly threatening. At 11:30 I left the ship in a launch to pick up our guests. Returning to the ship with them at noon, I found that the barometer had fallen considerably. I at once ordered steam on the four additional boilers. Just forty minutes later we were steaming out to sea, taking the Russells on an unexpected cruise. But the barometer steadied, then rose; all signs of bad weather disappeared; and in two or three hours the *Memphis* returned to her berth.

This little experience was gratifying, for it showed that no hurricane could burst on us helplessly at anchor. I should have hours of warning, and needed only forty minutes for a "getaway." I rested more easily.

Except for my official report to the Navy Department, what follows is my first written account of the events of 29 August 1916.

That fateful day began pleasantly. Throughout the night the barometer had been high, steady at a little over thirty inches. The sea was calm with no unusual swell. There was no breeze that day, only gentle airs. The weather reports indicated a gale 240 miles south of us, passing to westward. As this could not come near us, it gave me little concern. Wireless reports were wholly reassuring. The crew was busily engaged in preparing the ship for target practice.

At eight in the morning, Lieutenant Shea was brought before me. He was a picture of desolate grief; my heart went out to him. I had known him well at Annapolis in 1908. Since then he had repeatedly been commended by the Navy Department for extraordinary heroism in jumping overboard to save drowning men, and the like. The report against him involved drunkenness on duty. "It's all true, Captain. I haven't a word to say," was his only answer to the report.

Here was a fine young officer, a warm personal friend. But a captain has no personal friends. "Lieutenant Shea, you are under arrest, pending action on charges that I shall prefer to the Navy Department. You are relieved of duty, and will remain below decks."

It was after four in the mornin';
    We 'ad to stop the fun,
An' we sent 'im 'ome on a bullock cart,
    With 'is belt an' stock undone;

'E's reelin', rollin', roarin' tight;
But sentry shut your eye,
We'll 'elp 'im for 'is mother,
An' 'e'll 'elp us by-an'-by.

So goes the chantey. But even I, captain of the ship, could not apply it in this case. One does what one must do.

At one o'clock I allowed a liberty party, consisting of crew members not on duty who wanted to play baseball, to go ashore to a designated playing field, made available to us by the local authorities. We continued with the work of testing the guns and sights for target practice. Withers, who had been ill with rheumatism, relieved the officer of the deck, whose guns needed attention.

At 2:15 the admiral sent for me. "There's to be a lecture on 'Dominican Antiquities' this afternoon at the cathedral," he said. "I'd like you to go with me."

But, though the admiral was insistent, I wanted to work on the target practice preparations, and with real regret, respectfully declined. Shortly before three o'clock Commander Bennett of the gunboat *Castine*, anchored near us, came aboard for a scheduled dental appointment. On my way aft to greet him, I saw Withers, lying in a passageway, writhing in pain. His rheumatism was hard at work. I sent for the surgeon to help Withers; then greeted Bennett, and we went below to my cabin.

At half past three I received a report that the barometer was steady at thirty inches; and just then, his dental work completed, Bennett and I went on deck. Naturally, as a captain always does, I looked around. The weather had continued fine all day with no indication of anything unusual until, glancing shoreward, I cast an eye upon the rugged bluffs three-quarters of a mile away. I examined these bluffs a moment, then ordered the steam launch alongside.

"I'm going to send you to your ship," I told Bennett.

"What for? This doesn't look like hurricane weather to me."

"Take a look at the surf against that bluff. I've never seen anything like it before. I'm going to get out immediately; you'd better do the same."

The suddenness of all this appears from the fact that, until this moment, on this apparently perfect day nothing had occurred to attract the attention of either the officer of the deck or the quartermaster, both of whom were constantly on watch. I was, in actual fact, the first person in the *Memphis* to perceive there was a growing danger.

I called all hands, ordered the ship secured for heavy weather, had fires started on the four extra boilers, had the engines warmed up, and ordered all gun ports, hatches, and other openings closed. I signaled at once to the marine signal station ashore, requesting that the *Memphis* boats and liberty party be stopped from returning.

Owing to the quick, snappy orders of the officers, feverish activity seized everyone aboard. My executive officer, Yancey Williams, was everywhere. Gun ports, hatches, and watertight doors were closed. The boatswain, at the shackle, stood ready to slip the cable.

Yancey Williams reported to me on the bridge: "Captain, the ship is as tight as we can make her. Everything is secured for heavy weather. How soon will the engines be ready?"

"They're going ahead now, Yancey; we'll have high pressure in a minute. Take this glass. Look at the surf against those bluffs!"

"My God!" exclaimed Yancey. "Captain, what is happening? And look at those rollers! Great God, Captain! There's something deadly about to break!"

"Yancey, look directly to seaward. What do you see on the horizon?"

"Almighty God in Heaven! I see a yellow mountain! Captain—Captain! I think it's moving! It's growing, bigger, bigger, *bigger!*"

"Yes, Yancey, it's a mountain of water, a huge breaker headed our way, and it will be on top of us in five minutes! Go below immediately. There's an opening to the main deck not yet closed. Instruct the officers to keep the men steady. We mustn't have a panic."

"Captain!" shouted Yancey as he turned to leave, "this isn't a storm! It's volcanic!"

At this moment Jones reported from the engine room that he had 196 pounds of steam on six boilers. "Very well, Jones. Go as fast as you can without losing your pressure." The time, as then logged, was 4:06 P.M.

My problem now was to steam out into the open sea. Though we were still in calm water, great rollers were already breaking. To my dismay I saw a boat, full of baseball players, heading out of the Ozama River. My message had not been received in time to stop all the liberty boats. On it came, on, and on. Then a huge roller swept over it, and the boat and all in it were gone forever from this world. A hard thing to watch, doing nothing!

I was trying to point my ship to seaward. Lying at anchor, we had been heading northward, toward the shore. I used the helm and the engines at full speed in a desperate attempt to head eight points to starboard to clear a point of land.

But now these heavy, toppling rollers were close to us. I could not slip the cable until we were pointed right. My noble ship had started to swing to starboard, and to starboard was the yellow mountain, now filling the entire horizon, and close at hand!

It struck the ship on her starboard broadside; and it swept the upper decks clean. Boats, chests, awning stanchions, all sorts of tightly secured things were torn away. The starboard side of our superstructure, between our two big turrets, was bellied in from forecastle to quarterdeck.

And now, unbelievable as it may seem, the *Memphis* sank to the bottom of the Caribbean. More specifically, she struck bottom at her anchorage, in the hollow of the huge breaker that had entered the harbor. When this tremendous wave broke on top of her, it covered her completely. This was completely proved; for an American named Baxter, the general receiver of customs, standing on the bluff near the ship, took a series of photographs at this time; and one of these showed only the ends of two masts projecting a few feet above water. Water reached above the smokestacks, poured like an avalanche down those big pipes, and put out the fires in all the furnaces. Steam pressure dropped to fifteen pounds. And now the boilers began to explode. Seven men were killed by these explosions. But for the drop in steam pressure from 196 to 15 pounds, the ship would have been blown to fragments.

Jones would not leave his post until all the fire rooms were cleared. I have heard captains praised for being the last to leave a wrecked ship; but what about the chief engineer, who, standing in darkness, scalded by steam, with boilers popping about him, is the last to leave his Hell?

As the mountain of water threw the ship on her beam ends, a hail of missiles filled the between-deck spaces. Mess tables and benches, pianos, practice shells, chests, human bodies, hurtled through the air. Several men were killed by these flying objects.

Meanwhile, I had jumped, or been thrown, from the bridge to the inside of the framework of the cage mast (an "inverted wastebasket"). The ironwork of this mast provided a shelter that saved several lives; but my orderly, who stood beside me when we were overwhelmed, and may have helped push me inside the steel lattice-work, was never seen again. I found myself lying face down inside the wastebasket, flattened out, with tons of water pressing upon me.

But my ship, almost tight, had remaining buoyancy, and struggled upwards. Soon we survivors were breathing air instead of water.

I think five following mountains of water struck us. Twice again we went under. But, while burying us under water, each huge wave picked up my big armored cruiser like a chip of wood and hurled it toward the shore. Soon we were grinding on the rocks in shallow water.

At 4:45 P.M. we landed on a clump of rocks in twelve feet of water. There the ship is today, listing slightly to port, on an even keel, fore and aft, not more than a hundred feet from the bluff.

In 1937, special equipment finally began to work on the Memphis's old bones, and there is nothing now left of the ship, except perhaps some rusting scrap iron too far buried to be worth recovery. Interestingly, the company that finally was able to dismantle the ship's strong hull was reportedly owned in Japan. Her great steel plates were sent there, re-smelted, re-machined, and built into Japanese warships. In this form, she came back to us from the enemy during World War II.

Much had happened in the preceding thirty minutes. Forty lives had been snuffed out. A great warship had been destroyed. But in her death agonies the noble Memphis had saved 850 lives. Sunk repeatedly, she rose repeatedly from the depths of the Caribbean Sea. Knocked over on her port beam, she righted herself. Though her boilers exploded, she remained intact and preserved most of the lives in her keeping. With her outer bottom torn open in a hundred places, she still remained buoyant.

And her officers and crew were worthy of her and of the Navy and of the country they served. As later investigation proved, while men and heavy objects were being hurled about decks (the distance from side to side was seventy-six feet), while boilers were exploding in the fire room, and with men being killed all about the ship, there was no sign of panic, no demoralization.

Yancey Williams went from deck to deck inspiring officers and men with his own glad, cheerful courage. Besides the killed, 204 men had been badly injured. It was a badly battered Yancey when I next saw him. No matter how cheerful and courageous a man may be, how good a seaman, he is likely to be hurt when catapulted seventy-six feet across the deck of a big ship!

Up on the bridge I could only surmise what was happening below. The men about me were as steady and as quiet as if at church.

But during this wild convulsion we saw one heart-gladdening sight. The gunboat *Castine* was slowly creeping out. She had only two boilers and was able to get under way quickly on the one then steaming. I saw her buried a dozen times and thought her sunk; but up she came. All honor to Bennett; by his fine seamanship, his correct judgment, his steady nerve, he saved his ship.

As soon as the *Memphis* had settled on the rocks close to the bluff, I had a 9-pound sounding lead heaved ashore, where it was eagerly grabbed by soldiers and Marines from nearby Fort Ozama, and some civilians as well. To the heaving line we tied a heavy hawser, which was hauled ashore. On this we rigged a "breeches buoy."

Meanwhile I had given the order, "All hands abandon ship!" The hatches were opened, and up poured the men, under perfect control by their officers. Details were sent to search every part of the ship to make sure that none was left below.

Men were now being sent over the breeches buoy. I had the wounded sent first; then the sick, and arranged for their care on the bluff, where now there were thousands of anxious watchers, many of them Dominicans. I learned later that Dr. Carvalhal, newly elected president of the Dominican Republic, had personally come to the scene and had directed that all available automobiles come there to shine their headlights on our working parties handling the various breeches buoys as they got into operation.

I received a report that the lower decks had been searched and that no one remained below. But finding that I could be absent myself from the deck, I directed a quartermaster to get two lanterns and to follow me while I personally examined the lower decks, wishing to take no chance of leaving some helpless man below. I inspected every space that I could get into. I had quickly reached every part of the main, gun, and berth decks; and felt sure that these decks had been perfectly cleared. They were free of water.

The engine and boiler rooms I could not enter, because their ladders all led into water. I descended to the port "wing passage," leading fore and aft some three hundred feet between the engineering spaces and the side of the ship. This was filled with water up to my neck. Holding my lantern high, I started to walk forward. It was intensely dark except where the lantern cast its beams a few feet ahead. I reached the forward end of the passage and then turned sharply to the right, passing forward of the fire rooms to the passage on the opposite side. Owing to our list to port, the water was not quite so deep on the starboard side. So far I had seen no sign of life. But as I turned to wade aft, I was astonished to see, perhaps a hundred feet ahead, a light also moving aft.

"Hello!" I shouted. "Who are you? Come here!"

The man with the light heard me and turned; we approached each other.

"Shea!" I called out. "What are you doing here?"

"Captain, a lot of men were hurt while the ship was bouncing about. I assisted in sending up some who needed help. After that I thought I would go through the two lower decks to make sure that none were left. I know I am under arrest and not allowed to perform any duty; but I hope, Captain, you will consider what we have been through and will overlook this breach of arrest. Please, Captain, do not make matters worse for me."

"Shea," I replied, "mountains of water have poured over this ship within the last hour and have carried innumerable things into the sea. Among things forever lost were all papers relating to your arrest. They will never be found. And here, in this flooded passageway, I officially restore you to duty."

I later learned that when matters had seemed their worst, Shea had been magnificent in controlling the men and keeping them busy.

At just eight o'clock the breeches buoy from the *Memphis*'s bridge made its last trip to the bluff. The New York papers said that "Captain Beach was the last to leave the ship." This was not wholly correct. It is certainly the captain's duty to be the last to leave a wrecked ship—not a mere sentimental duty. But he also is honored for it. I felt that the crew of the *Memphis* had been so perfect in maintaining the naval tradition that one of them should share this honor with me. Chief Electrician Erskine and I left the ship together on the last trip of the breeches buoy.

After *The Wreck of the Memphis* was published, I learned for the first time about Emeterio Sanchez. The picture that was sent to me, taken right after the disaster, was of a scrawny, ragged fisherman, but he had once been a commander in the Dominican Navy, and many of the survivors of Dad's old ship made sure I knew his story. It was a little late for that book, but not too late for me to do my best to repair the omission in later ones. In its 1998 re-issuance by Naval Institute Press, I included the following words in the new introduction: "He had dived into the boiling water around the base of the cliffs where some of the men from her capsized motor launch were struggling; being a good swimmer and well acquainted with the area, he succeeded in saving at least three of them." By some accounts, he saved five lives in all, one after the other. His photograph is now on display among the *Memphis* memorabilia, where it is also stated that Sanchez "received a pension of forty dollars a month from the U.S. government in gratitude for the saving of American lives."

So far as I have been able to discover, however, no such pension was ever awarded. Whoever announced it, no doubt meaning well, was apparently unable to deliver. Years later, when Emeterio's widow, by then in penurious circumstances, asked for aid from the U.S. government, she was refused.

Everyone involved is now dead (except myself, elected by the dwindling number of survivors, now all gone, as "Honorary Captain" of the *Memphis*), and omissions or mistakes of the past cannot be rectified. They can, however, be remembered. Santo Domingo newspapers recorded Sanchez's brave assistance in our hour of need, and a street in the city was named for him. Pertinent information now resides in a place of honor in Millington, Tennessee, a suburb of Memphis, where our Navy has a great installation. May this tiny bit of recognition, although it can no longer benefit him or his wife, at least partly assuage an old obligation.

Inclusion of this little notice in Father's autobiography is in partial payment of the debt I'm privileged to honor for him in all the ways I can.

26

COURT-MARTIALED

Within ten days a court of inquiry composed of Captains Hood, Hughes, and Pringle met at Santo Domingo to investigate everything connected with the disaster. They spent two or more weeks there, and then proceeded to Norfolk. It took them thirty days to complete their inquiry. My court-martial followed, which took three days. All this time was necessary for complete investigation. If there was anything not thoroughly looked into by the inquiry and the court-martial, I do not know what it was. The guidance of the Navy has been built up by the work of these courts. I know of nothing more thorough, more unprejudiced. The facts ascertained by such investigation serve to guide officers for the future.

I was brought to trial before a court-martial on six specifications, as follows:

1. That I did not keep sufficient steam on the *Memphis* to get under way at short notice.
2. That I did not immediately proceed to secure the *Memphis* for bad weather on the first appearance of bad weather.
3. That on the appearance of bad weather I did not immediately light fires on additional boilers.

261

4. That on the appearance of bad weather I did not immediately shut and secure gun ports and hatches and deck openings.
5. That I had not anchored my ship in a safe anchorage.
6. That I had not sent ashore for weather information.

Upon reading these specifications of offenses charged against me, I of course understood that these, in the judgment of the Navy Department, were the things I should have done. And in the same instant I also realized that the court to try me was certain to find, by the complete evidence that existed, that upon the appearance of bad weather I had immediately secured my ship for heavy weather, lighted fires in additional boilers, and secured gun ports, hatches, and deck openings; that I had anchored my ship in the exact place recommended by the Sailing Directions; and that I had sent ashore to the weather office for weather information.

I also realized that the whole thing depended on the judgment of the court with reference to the first specification. It could be proved that the ship's engines were turning over within forty minutes from the time I had personally noticed the appearance of bad weather. The real question before the court, and in fact the only one, was whether "short notice" meant forty minutes.

The last five specifications were found not proved, and of them I was found not guilty. The court found me guilty of not being able to get under way upon short notice. This, I judge, meant that to be able to get under way upon short notice a ship must have steam up on sufficient boilers to get under way without raising steam on additional boilers. I bow to and accept this definition and this decision.

But note that this was precisely the basis of the conversation with Admiral Pond, in which the admiral overruled Father's request to keep steam on four instead of only two boilers. Note also that under Admiral Caperton four boilers steaming were the routine. It would seem to me, now with eighty-five years' hindsight, that Dad's defense should have made more of this point.

The court therefore sentenced me to a loss of twenty numbers in my grade of captain, which meant that in seniority of rank, twenty captains junior to me would pass ahead of me.

In the official publication of my court-martial, the Navy Department said:

The members of the court spread upon the record the following unanimous recommendations to clemency:

In view of his previous excellent record; and in view of the fact that he took extra precautions which, in his judgment, would have met the requirements of any contingency; and in view of the fact that the extraordinary conditions that arose so quickly were not only unprecedented but could not be foreseen, and came with only slight warning; that apart from the fact that he did not have steam in sufficient boilers to get under way immediately, he took every measure which could be taken to insure the safety of his vessel, we recommend the accused in this case to the clemency of the reviewing authority.

Action of the Secretary of the Navy:

The Department has given careful consideration not only to the record of the foregoing trial of Captain Beach, but also to the unusual circumstances out of which this trial arose (the wrecking of the U.S.S. *Memphis* off Santo Domingo City on August 29, 1916).

The only portion of the specifications found proved by the Court consists of the allegation that Captain Beach failed to keep sufficient steam on his vessel to get under way "on short notice."

The records of the Department show that Captain Beach has served in the Navy for over thirty-two years, during which time he has maintained a spotless record. His reports on fitness are conspicuous on account of the zeal and careful and efficient manner in which he has always performed his duty. The efficient manner in which he has done so has always met the highest approval of the various distinguished officers under whom he has served.

As shown by the recommendation to clemency, his actions on the occasion of the disaster were sufficient to impress the members of the court-martial which tried him and inspire them to spread upon the record the above quoted impelling and unanimous recommendation to clemency.

The proceedings, findings, and sentence in the foregoing case of Captain Beach are approved, but in view of the recommendation to clemency and the previous excellent record of Captain Beach, the loss of numbers is reduced to the loss of five numbers in his grade.

Josephus Daniels, Secretary of the Navy.

Some time later I received a letter from the Navy Department stating that upon further review of the circumstances it had been established that no hurricane had taken place. The waves rolling into the harbor must have had a seismic source for which there could not have been forewarning; therefore, the loss of five numbers was removed; and I was restored to my original place on the Navy list.

The complete text of this letter is printed in *The Wreck of the Memphis*, page 299.

But all of this, however important to me personally, was really unimportant. The big comforting fact, the fact that has made me glad, was that in a convulsion of nature rarely experienced in world's history, my noble, splendid ship, *Memphis*—in the face of overwhelming, destroying force, though herself destroyed, yet by the soul of the U.S. Navy which built her and which had guided and controlled her on the day of her destruction—saved all but 20 of the 850 lives on board at the time. Twenty more lives were lost in the liberty boat returning to the ship.

I do not use the term "the soul of the U.S. Navy" lightly. I use it seriously and earnestly. Naval officers had designed that ship; had ordered every rivet that was driven; had made the drawings of every detail of machinery and hull; and the ship had been built under the immediate supervision of naval officers. The officers and men on board had been trained for their duties by officers of the Navy under Navy Department direction. These officers had inherited the traditions and experiences of our Navy from its beginning in the year 1775. And the men on board the *Memphis* on 29 August 1916 had maintained these traditions by their own conduct and actions. For these reasons I believe I can justifiably say that the *Memphis* on that sad day represented, structurally and personally, the soul of the U.S. Navy.

Of course I knew that I was finished as far as any future naval career was concerned. And so, naturally, great was my surprise when, a few weeks later, I was ordered to command the naval torpedo station in Newport, Rhode

Island, one of our most important naval stations. I hurried there. On arrival I telephoned the commandant of the district, Admiral Sims, that I had been ordered to report to him for this duty but that I was minus the necessary formal reporting uniform; it had been destroyed with the *Memphis*.

"Hell, Beach," replied Sims, "come over in your undershirt and drawers." Which was quite like Sims, but despite Sims' invitation, I was a little better dressed than this when I arrived at his office.

Before long war was declared against Germany. The Newport torpedo station received orders to build hundreds of torpedoes; and many hundreds more came in from ships for repairs, overhauling, and testing.

A torpedo is the most intelligent, most obedient, inanimate thing in the world. It contains twenty-six hundred different machined parts. It will go in the exact direction it is pointed. If it does not hit, it is because it was not pointed correctly. If it hits an obstruction, like a log in the water, it will glance off; but it is certain to resume its original course. The gyroscope, making sixteen thousand revolutions a minute, rebels if the torpedo is not going in the direction it started. Its rebellion consists of tipping its axial direction of rotation, and it is so connected that this tipping pulls the rudder in the right direction to restore it. The torpedo also has a depth control mechanism, so that it will travel on the surface, or submerged, as desired.

———————

I fear that Father waxed a bit over-enthusiastic in his description of how well our torpedoes performed. Anyone who served in World War II, and especially in our submarine service, will eloquently and angrily describe how poorly they worked. Their depth control was terrible, the mechanism that caused them to explode on hitting the target had not one but two things wrong with it, and sometimes they ran in a circle, with devastating results to the submarine that fired them. Three of the torpedoes fired by USS *Trigger,* in which I served more than two years of the war, circled upon us, and two of them exploded. But because of faults in the exploder design, they did not explode near enough to cause fatal damage. Otherwise you would not be reading this book!

———————

Because of the requirements of superfine workmanship, the machinists employed in the torpedo's manufacture must be highly skilled, and then must receive special training. The gyroscope had to be machined to a fineness of one five-thousandth of an inch. Men capable of this work received special appointment as torpedo machinists, with proper pay for their extraordinary skill.

Because of the orders for large numbers of torpedoes, I put in an urgent request to the Navy Department for additional torpedo machinists. And soon a party of twenty-odd men reported, having been sent from Washington. Also, at the same time, I received a mandatory order from Assistant Secretary of the Navy Franklin D. Roosevelt that I was to appoint these men torpedo machinists, and pay them at the highest rate paid men for this rating. Which I did. And at the end of ten days I had discharged each and every one of them.

And then came an indignant letter from Franklin D. Roosevelt. He had wanted to help me. He had made special earnest efforts to send me torpedo machinists. I had treated his efforts with contempt; instead of showing a proper spirit of doing the best I could with the material he had sent me, I had thrown it all away. This was not the spirit that would bring victory, he wrote.

But I had expected something of this kind, and was prepared. In my reply, and in my defense, I sent a history of each of these so-called torpedo machinists. Several had been policemen in Washington, several had been gardeners in parks, several had been soldiers, some had been firemen, clerks, teamsters, or watchmen; but not one of them had ever handled a machine tool of any description.

I ended my letter by saying it was quite impossible, no matter what orders the Navy Department might give, to impart to these men the knowledge and skill required of torpedo machinists. That it would be treason in me to allow one of them even to touch a torpedo. And that it would be as unreasonable in him to expect a single one of these men to exhibit the skill of a torpedo machinist as it would be to tell a man who had never seen a violin or heard a note of music to pick up a Stradivarius and play with the skill of an Ole Bull.

Ole Bull (1810–1880) was a famous Norwegian violinist and composer of the nineteenth century.

And then came as kindly and friendly a letter from Franklin D. Roosevelt as a worried naval officer could have wished for. I always did like the Roosevelts, even if Teddy was a Republican.

During the war our naval strength in personnel shot up from about fifty thousand officers and enlisted men to over half a million. Of course it was impossible to obtain men of skill in the grades they were, sometimes, shoved into. But the good ones rapidly became familiar with, even expert in, their duties. There were always, close at hand, officers and Navy-trained men, and I believe everyone serving in our Navy at this time, enormously increased as it was, was fully imbued with the Navy spirit. In time of war greenhorns soon catch on. To show how desperate we were for experienced officers, however, at one time, in Newport, the battleship *Massachusetts* came in, safely and carefully through the twisting channel, under the command of a volunteer lieutenant whose only previous naval experience had been gained in the Michigan naval reserve.

Lieutenant Bellamy's story provides another example. Assigned soon after the war began as the legal adviser of the commandant of the naval district, Bellamy was about thirty years old, by profession a lawyer, practicing in New York.

One time I said to him: "Bellamy, how did you happen to enter the Navy and become a lieutenant?"

"It was this way," he replied. "When war was declared I wanted service and did not intend to be drafted. So I came to Newport to enlist. The morning I arrived I met a friend who was in a bluejacket uniform. 'What are you?' I asked. 'Quartermaster, third class!' he answered. 'What does that mean?' 'I haven't the least idea,' he replied. 'I intended to enlist as landlubber and so told the recruiting officer; but he said why don't you enlist as quartermaster third class? I told him I was willing, so here I am, a regularly enlisted quartermaster third class in the U.S. Navy. But I haven't yet learned the meaning of the words.'"

"So," continued Bellamy, "when I went to the recruiting officer and he asked me what I wanted to enlist as, I replied: 'Quartermaster third class.' He looked at me and said: 'Is there any reason why you shouldn't ship as an ensign?' 'No reason in the world that I know of,' I answered. And, to my amazement, I actually found myself an officer."

I must hasten to remark that these things were in the confusion of the first days after war was declared; soon, when first enlisted, men were carefully examined for their experience and capability, then quickly employed where best fitted. And as far as Bellamy personally was concerned, it was a privilege to serve with him. Whatever experience he may have lacked he had the Navy spirit, was a quick learner, and was remarkably intelligent.

A guard of 108 naval reserves was sent to me. They had been recruited entirely from eastern universities. Among them was "Cupid" Black of Yale, "Charlie" Barrett of Cornell, Gerrish of Dartmouth, and dozens of others famous in football. They were commanded by a lieutenant. It was soon evident that these college boys were having a lot of fun with their commander, some of it not at all funny, in fact, some verging on insubordination. So I investigated the lieutenant's history. He was commissioned a volunteer lieutenant because he had been a mate in the merchant service. For nearly forty years he had been on coal barges, towed between Norfolk and Boston. And I soon learned that he could neither read nor write. Clearly, he was not the man to command these fresh college lads, and besides, he made the Navy look ridiculous. So I got rid of him, from that assignment, anyway, and got him placed where his special talents were better utilized. And so, by the way, were those of my college athletes.

Our torpedo station, situated on a small island in Newport harbor, was crowded with buildings. And crowded with workmen. My job was to carry out the orders of the Navy Department, which were coming in faster every day. I also spent hours every day in the different shops, where we now had forty-four hundred employees.

Besides building torpedoes we were loading warheads, depth charges, and mines. We took special precautions against the ever-present danger of explosion, which was always present, and I worried that great loss of life might thereby result. So I gave earnest effort to drill everybody immediately connected with explosives in each and every safety precaution of the many laid down in the Navy regulations. Naturally, there were daily accidents—in a manufacturing program as big as ours, under the tremendous pressures of the war, they were unavoidable—but none in explosives, except for one time, of which more later. Despite my constant fears, I'm sure our extra effort to achieve safety in our handling of explosives achieved good results.

It was not all work. I formed pleasant friendships in Newport. Soon a battalion of Marines was sent to me. I had felt the need of seasoned soldiers because we had more than a thousand torpedoes in storage. So now I slept easier at night.

One of the college boys was Thomas Fortune Ryan, the third. I do not know how well he did in college; I do know he became quite skillful in peeling potatoes. And there were lots of them to peel. Sometimes he was detailed as a night sentry, and I did worry if he was up to that important job. And also, at times, Thomas Fortune could call at my quarters to spend an evening with my lovely young niece, Ethel, who was visiting me.

Ethel Schneider was the daughter of Father's sister. Father had an older brother, John, and a younger sister Mary. Mary became the wife of T. F. Schneider, a prominent Washington, D.C., architect, and had three children, Ethel being the youngest.

One summer day, nearing dusk, a barge full of tri nitro toluol, better known as TNT, was towed to the torpedo station and left there. It could not be taken over to Rose Island, the naval magazine to which I had banished all explosives except those being actually worked on, because the workmen had left for the day. It could not be properly and safely stowed there until the next morning. So I ordered that the barge be secured and a sentry posted.

At 7 P.M. I received a call telling me that the sentry on the TNT barge had been found smoking. This angered me more than only somewhat. To light matches, smoke cigarettes, or do anything involving fire near a stock of TNT was absolutely criminal! The thought of all the possible consequences appalled me.

"Relieve him immediately! Put him under arrest, and bring him to my quarters," I ordered.

Shortly afterward I saw three men approaching my quarters, one small, slight figure between two great strapping fellows. And I instantly knew the small one was the culprit. He positively cringed as he came along. Then I saw it was Thomas Fortune Ryan, the third. I was in a fury. I didn't care a hang whether he was a good potato peeler or the grandson of a billion dollars. But the fact that he was lighting matches on a barge holding one hundred tons of TNT, endangering the entire stock of torpedoes of our country except those on board ship, and the lives of everyone at the torpedo station and in the city of Newport, caused some cell in my brain to explode.

I met the three as they were ascending my steps and I let drive; in violent language I denounced Thomas Fortune Ryan, potato peeler, U.S. Navy, with a flood of overwhelming reprimands. And as I paused for a fresh start, Thomas

Fortune, in trembling voice, said, "Captain, is Miss Ethel in? I have brought two of my friends to call upon her."

Then an eighteen-year-old fairy blew in. "Why are you scolding poor Tom so terribly, you big goose?" the fairy demanded.

And just at this time three more men came marching up, two of them Marines, armed with pistols on their belts and menacing rifles on their shoulders.

"Sir," reported one, "here is the sentry found smoking on the TNT barge!"

"Lock him up in the brig in double irons for the night," I directed, making no further remarks, but having an uncomfortable feeling that perhaps Ethel was right.

The Marines now guarding the torpedo station gave me great comfort. I believe it is a general consensus that there are no better trained soldiers. Every generation of Marines has inherited inspiring traditions, and every generation adds to them. War can be declared only by a joint resolution of both houses of Congress, but Marines can be sent where they are needed, which, among other things, means anywhere American interests are threatened. This can be done with or without congressional action. So, since 1775, the Marines have constantly been sent to scenes of trouble. They travel light, in small numbers, but everywhere they go they are heavyweights.

They practice daily shooting at targets. Their discipline is admirable. Marines are specially trained to understand orders exactly as given, and to carry them out exactly as received. Basically, this is an excellent criterion, but once in a while strange results can happen. When a Marine obeys orders, he is supposed to be an unreasoning automaton. He is expected, and heavily trained, to do precisely as directed; but this gives his officers the added responsibility of being absolutely certain that whatever orders they give him are exactly complete and correct, and fully understood.

I will give a couple of examples of this. As already stated, we were loading explosives into warheads and depth charges. I had fenced off a walk leading to the buildings where this was done. I gave orders to Colonel Huey, the Marine commanding officer, to post sentries at the entrance to this walk with instructions to allow no person to pass unless his name was on a special list of those so permitted, a copy of which I personally handed to him.

A few days later I started to enter this walk. Immediately a Marine, with rifle at "port h'ahms," barred my entrance.

"You may not pass, sir," he said.

"What are your orders, sentry?" I demanded.

"To allow no one to pass whose name is not on my list. Your name is not on the list, sir. You cannot pass!"

"Do you recognize me?"

"Yes, sir. You are Captain Beach, the commanding officer of the torpedo station."

"What orders have you about the commanding officer of the torpedo station?"

"To obey at once all orders he may give me."

"Then I order you to permit Captain Beach to enter this walk."

The sentry immediately swung to one side, went to "present h'ahms," and called out, "Pass, Captain Beach, by order of the commanding officer of the torpedo station!" I couldn't fault him. He had done everything exactly right, even though he must have thought the whole thing was slightly ridiculous. It was really my fault for not having put my own name on the list I gave Huey, but it gave us a little mirth when we recalled the incident. The following is another instance.

Huey and I were determined that no German should possibly gain access to our torpedo station and destroy our big stock of torpedoes. This did not seem to us a needless precaution. A couple of months before we had entered the war, a German submarine suddenly came to the surface in Newport Harbor and its captain, Hans Rose, paid an official call on my immediate predecessor as commanding officer of the torpedo station. Then he put back to sea and sank two or three ships right outside our harbor! For this Hans Rose will never be forgotten. He was an innovative naval officer, although maligned by the press at the time for bringing the European war so close to our shores. Still, he is gratefully remembered by our Navy for his fine action, later in the war, of sending out a radiogram announcing that he had sunk the American destroyer *Jacob Jones* and giving the latitude and longitude of the location. This enabled many of her crew in rafts and boats to be rescued by other members of her squadron.

Hans Rose survived World War I by many years, and has always been fondly remembered by our Navy.

By this time, German submarines were on our eastern coast; our cruiser *San Diego* had been sunk, and so had numerous merchant ships. A captain as

daring as Hans Rose might have made a night raid on our station. It was something to think about.

Originally the *California*, the renamed *San Diego* was one of the slightly
smaller predecessors of the *Memphis*.

After sunset, one could not walk far on the torpedo station grounds before
hearing a sharp cry: "Halt! Who goes there?" And close at hand would be a
Marine with an automatic gun in his right hand, pointing upward, but ready
for anything.

One blowy night in March 1918, a fierce fire broke out in one of the buildings. The fire alarm was sounded, and men from their barracks started running
out to get the fire apparatus. But they were stopped dead in their tracks. They
did not have the countersign. Fire or no fire, the sentries would not allow the
men to pass. It did not take Huey and me long to remedy this state of affairs,
but it was another lesson to both of us.

This story is still told in Newport.

Several months after I arrived at Newport, a British naval officer, Lieutenant
Commander Mock, was sent there. Mock was an expert in gunnery matters.
He told me he had entered the British navy as an enlisted apprentice, later he
had been warranted a gunner, and afterwards received a commission as an officer of the Royal Navy.

A great, and very secret, invention had been made by a man named
Brown, a Massachusetts electrician. By this time the German submarine
was a deadly menace. This invention, similar to the "influence exploder"
installed in our submarine torpedoes of the Second World War, made it
nearly certain that the magnetic field of a submarine boat running within
a hundred feet of a planted submarine mine would explode the mine; and

at this distance the blow from the explosion would sink the submarine.

Again, Father is merely repeating what was reported to him. The World War II torpedoes, designed and built at Newport and using such an exploder, were a fiasco. Perhaps the "magnetic mine" exploder was simpler and therefore performed better. Under Dad's supervision, many tests were performed on the magnetic mine, until he was confident it would work as designed. Would that the same care had been used on the secret torpedo exploder! Details of both mechanisms are (unnecessarily) still on the "secret" list.

I was given directions to load 125,000 bursting charges for the mines our Navy was to plant between the Orkney Islands and the Norway shore. This secret invention was only known at the torpedo station by Mock, two other officers, and me. We had the parts of the exploding mechanism so made, and so assembled, that no one could have suspected what it really was.

Mock had been told of this by our Navy Department and asked to inform the mining department of the British Admiralty, by cable, in guarded words, what was projected. But the result of Monk's cablegram was a cable to him of stinging language. The mining department of the British Admiralty thought he had gone crazy. Then, for some reason, the Royal Navy decided to send one of its regular line officers to see what we were doing, and as a result I was directed to meet a British officer, Lieutenant Commander de Salis.

Mock and I were at the landing when de Salis came to the torpedo station. I was instantly indignant at his behavior. He was offish in manner to me. He did not even shake hands with his brother officer, Mock.

"I've come to see and test your wonderful invention," he said.

"We're all ready," I replied. "I have prepared for your inspection five submarine mines. We'll plant them where you wish. The exploding mechanism is in place, likewise ready for inspection. The mines are not loaded with TNT, however, but with sand. We will have a submarine run by between them, and later pull them up for you to see whether or not the fuses have exploded."

All of which was done, the sneer never leaving the face of this contemptuous English aristocrat. But when, after our run, we pulled up these mines, something else exploded. And that was de Salis. When he took a look at the exploded fuses, all five of which had functioned correctly, he gave a yell, grabbed Mock, and embraced him. He couldn't control his wild joy.

"We've got 'em now!" he shouted. "We've got 'em now!"

De Salis remained with me for a month. I have not known a more modest, gentle soul. He said one time, "In our mining department we were all worn to an edge by the sinking of our ships. There seemed to be no possible protection; we were being destroyed. We were furious with Mock's cable. We thought him a fool. That accounts for my manner when I first came here, and for which I most truly apologize."

The mines were intended for the North Sea mine barrage, planned to keep U-boats far distant from vital British harbors. A few submarines were actually sunk in the barrage, but the many thousands of mines we participated in laying in the North Sea proved to be extraordinarily difficult to remove after peace was signed.

27

ARMISTICE

One morning while my chief clerk, John P. Sullivan, who was also my dear friend, and I were discussing something in my office, a wild roar suddenly filled the air. It seemed as if our building was being shaken. The long feared explosion had happened!

Sullivan and I ran as fast as we could out of the office to our loading houses, or magazines, half a block away. At this moment the air was full of flying debris. Sullivan got there first, and, taking a look, without stopping he turned and ran back. I had plenty to do helping to pull some live and thirteen dead men out of that mix-up.

While I was engaged in this, doctors, nurses, friends, priests, ministers, and ambulances began arriving. I had been so occupied with what I was doing that I never thought to send for any of these and had not given a single order to do so to anyone. It had not been the worst accidental explosion in the world, but bad enough. A moment's carelessness on the part of a single person who should have known better, and paid for it with his life, had heavily damaged a part of our munitions loading building. But the next day I was a hero, receiving the commendation of the Catholic Archbishop, the thanks of the city of Newport, a vote of commendation from both houses of the legislature of the state, for my instant thoughtfulness at a time of death and disaster.

Dad had done one very significant thing that greatly minimized the damage: he had required, from the beginning, that stored munitions be located on Rose Island, fairly far out in Narragansett Bay, where shock from explosion of a smaller amount at the torpedo factory would not endanger the far greater amount in storage. This, too, is still remembered in Newport.

The amusing part of this tragic event was that everybody at the station and in the city of Newport knew that Johnnie Sullivan had telephoned the hospitals, the fire departments, priests, and ministers. He had sent scores of messages: "Explosion at torpedo station. Captain Beach says, 'Do this or that at once.'"

And soon a court of inquiry assembled at Newport to investigate this disaster. A searching examination followed. The orders I had given were reviewed. My own daily inspections, the training and instruction that everybody connected with handling explosives had had, were investigated. One would have judged that I had ever kept in mind the belief that danger of an explosion was imminent, and had used every means within my power to avert such a catastrophe. And indeed I had, as the court's report showed.

Some weeks later, while I was giving a luncheon to friends, an orderly brought an official letter to me. There was lots of fun and laughter in that crowd.

"What is it, Beach? Are you up for another court?" called out one of my guests.

"You're a ribald bunch," I returned. "You don't seem to realize I'm a hero! But Josephus Daniels knows it. He says so in this letter."

"Read that letter, Johnnie Sullivan Beach," shouted someone.

And in the midst of the laughter I read aloud the report of the court of inquiry and the secretary of the Navy's favorable comments thereon. By the time I reached the end of the comments, interrupted constantly by amusing and laughing remarks, I was in a high feather. Mr. Josephus Daniels had stopped suddenly, but I was unable to stop. I was going too hard and too fast; and, without change in voice, I continued with wild eloquence.

And from my husky basso went up a mighty roar
That rumbled in my dining room, and rattled on my floor;
That struck poor Stanford Moses and hit the Newport mat,
For I, like mighty Casey, was advancing to the bat.

With sonorous impressiveness, I pretended to continue to read: "Now, therefore, I, Josephus Daniels, secretary of the Navy, by order of the president of the United States, do appoint Captain Beach to be admiral and commander in chief of the Navy. And I do hereby charge all officers and men of the Navy, wherever they may be, from the Aurora Borealis in the far distant north to the Primeval Chaos in the extreme south; from the farthest meridian of the Celestial Sphere in the East to the last rays of the dying sun in the west, to be obedient to his orders as supreme admiral of the Navy, by doing all manner of things—"

But shouts of mock indignant mutiny stopped me; and in a moment's pause, my dear mother, nearing four score years of age, and taken from me only a few days later, cried with radiant happiness, "I always knew that, some time, my boy Ned would be a great man!"

I was instantly filled with contrition. It seemed as if I had been making fun of this loving saint. So I said, "Dear Mother, that last part was just in fun. I wasn't trying to fool *you*."

Then she looked at me with indignation. "Well," she said, "I knew all the time there was much ado about nothing!"

This was greeted by noisy approval.

"You struck out that time, just like mighty Casey did," laughed one of my friends.

This little incident is typical of the fun that naval officers have when off duty and relaxed. And, no matter what their ages, they are boyish in their fun. I know of no other set of men closer in their thoughts.

Several months after this, at the close of a dinner party in Newport, the host announced that he had engaged a mind reader to amuse us, and introduced "Professor" Calder, reputed to be an Egyptian. The guests were placed in two lines, facing each other. "I will ask of each of you to think intently on some subject, and I shall try to think what you are thinking of," said the professor.

The first person he approached was Colonel Packenham, the British military attaché in Washington.

"You are thinking that your first name is Hercules," remarked the mind reader.

"That's exactly what I chose to think," returned Packenham. "Now look here, mister, don't you ever look into my mind again!"

Exclamations of amazement greeted Calder's guessing as he went down that line.

A momentous secret had come to me that day. A letter from an admiral in Washington informed me I had been selected to command the battleship *New York*, flagship of the American Battle Squadron of the British Grand Fleet. The letter added that this, for the present, was confidential.

Before long Calder stood in front of me. He looked at me, then shut his eyes. In a moment great beads of sweat seemed to be on his face. Then he said, "You are thinking that you are going to relieve Captain Hughes."

Hughes was skipper of the *New York*, and was one of my classmates at Annapolis. That was exactly the thought I had chosen. I have thought of this incident many times since, and it is quite beyond my powers to imagine just how this man had been able to look into my mind.

In September 1918, I reported to Rear Admiral Hugh Rodman, commander of the American Battle Squadron, then anchored in a great basin, Scapa Flow, in the Orkney Islands, north of Scotland. Scapa Flow was the operating base of the greatest armada of warships ever gathered together. Assembled there were fifty capital ships, battleships and battle cruisers, averaging more than thirty thousand tons displacement, armed with guns of 12-inch caliber and above; also assembled were scores of cruisers, hundreds of destroyers, submarines, oilers, colliers, ammunition ships, as well as provision and refrigerating ships.

Scapa Flow was protected on all sides and had only one entrance that, except when a ship was entering or leaving, was kept securely shut. Besides having ample room for anchoring this whole great fleet, there was plenty of space for great gun target practice. Another advantage was that Scapa Flow, at that time, was beyond the limit of German air attack. It was ideal for an operating base. And, reciting this, I have exhausted all the good things I can say about it. It is certainly the most dismal, most uncomfortable, most unattractive, and most everything else that is uncomplimentary, of any place I have ever seen.

> The days were cold and dark and dreary,
>   It rained and the wind was never weary.

Not once in the three months I was at Scapa Flow, or cruising in nearby waters, did I see sunshine. It was always foggy or rainy. Though the thermometer ranged between 45 and 50 degrees, while I was there I felt colder than in good honest zero weather. And the sea was always in a muss; if it wasn't kicked up by a strong wind from one quarter, it was certain to be nasty because of a strong wind from some other direction.

However, I thought more of those things later. Spirit and interest were high. We were at war. German battleships were less than a day's steaming away; and in every heart there was expectancy that they might come out into the North Sea at any moment.

As part of the British Grand Fleet, we were under the general command of its commander in chief, Admiral Sir David Beatty. But of course we carried our stars and stripes, were directly under the orders of Admiral Rodman, and our interior ship discipline was entirely ruled by our own Navy regulations.

On an average of once in two weeks Admiral Rodman took his ships out for a sweep in the North Sea, the Irish Sea, or wherever he was directed to go. These short cruises lasted for perhaps a week. British squadrons were also, at the same time, sweeping these northern seas. I much admired the clearness and conciseness of Admiral Beatty's orders.

At this time the only entrance and exit of German submarines to the Atlantic was to the northward by way of the Orkney Islands. Each of Admiral Rodman's battleships was attacked at least once by submarines. The New York was attacked twice while I was on board. But torpedoes missed more often than they hit.

While in Scapa Flow our ships were kept busy at drills and target practice, shooting at a target being towed, the distance of the target generally being about six miles. Its speed, the direction it was being towed, and its exact distance had to be determined by the ship that was shooting. I believe it correct to say that our battleships shot faster than the British battleships, and that our marksmanship was better.

This was due to the fact that our turrets were controlled by electric power, while the British ships had turrets operated by hydraulic power. Also, our methods of obtaining distance, speed, and the direction in which the target was being towed were distinctly superior to the British methods at that time. This meant better hitting ability.

While at Scapa Flow, all ships were required to be ready to leave at short notice, within an hour, two hours, or four hours, according to the signal of the commander in chief. But I judge that Admiral Rodman agreed with my court-martial; that short notice meant "immediately."

I do not believe a battleship could have been more efficient in every respect—officers, crew, guns, engines, and equipment—than was the *New York* at the time I relieved Captain Hughes of her command. And I also believe the other battleships of Admiral Rodman's squadron were each at the top notch of efficiency. I have repeatedly seen him take his squadron in close formation and steam at eighteen or twenty knots for twelve to twenty hours at a time, day or night, in good or foul weather, rain or fog. Under some conditions of bad weather some captains might feel this a serious responsibility even when traveling alone. With five super dreadnoughts, averaging thirty thousand tons displacement each, with but three hundred yards of water between the stern of one ship and the bow of the ship following, a hundred mishaps were possible each minute. But no mishaps ever occurred. Like my poor old *Memphis* only two years before, though in a very different way, that squadron surely represented the soul of our Navy. The ships were all designed and built by Navy Department orders. And officers and men were trained and fitted for their duties by Navy customs, orders, and traditions.

But, besides thorough training, much experience, and determined character, there is another item of great importance and of great influence upon the effectiveness of a navy squadron: the ability and the spirit of its commander. When a commander has won the complete confidence of his officers and men, that complete confidence is an important part of the squadron's efficiency.

It was my judgment at the time, and is today, many years later, that the American Battle Squadron of the British Grand Fleet, in 1918, could not have been more efficient, more certain to do what it was expected to do. I do not believe that any officer or enlisted man of Admiral Rodman's squadron would have wished any other admiral in the Navy to lead him into battle.

Admiral Rodman had been with the British Grand Fleet for nearly a year. Every day that we were anchored in Scapa Flow, British admirals and captains came on board the New York to call upon him. And, in accordance with U.S. Navy customs, I greeted these visitors, the admiral also being present at the gangway to greet admirals when they called. In this way I met personally with many British officers of high rank.

It was quite evident that Admiral Rodman had inspired not only their high respect, but also a warm friendship for himself. They liked him personally.

I can vividly recall a day when a party of admirals came on board, and remained for several hours. One had many gold stripes on his sleeves indicating that his rank was "Admiral of the Fleet." At lunch, sitting next to this admiral, whose comments on nearly every subject were quite interesting, it was hard for me to realize that this was George V, King of England. Here he was, surrounded by intimate personal friends, quite at home, and apparently a kindly, intelligent, warmhearted gentleman. He had, in fact, been an officer in the Royal Navy until the unexpected death of his older brother made him heir to the throne. But had a stranger been present this day and told to pick out the king, with nothing to guide his judgment except the way these men treated each other, he would have had no clue to help him. I did not once hear the king addressed as "Your Majesty." Quite certainly, everyone present was full of deference, and even reverence for him in his heart, but there was no occasion for an outward exhibition of this. I judge that the British know how to treat their kings; and, except in cases of ceremony and on public appearances, try to let them be natural human beings. On the other hand, we Americans are inclined to imagine they go around wearing crowns and clothed in ermine, with everybody kneeling as they pass.

One day at dusk, while the New York was steaming in Pentland Firth a sudden bang was heard, and the ship quivered with a heavy shock. We had certainly struck something hard. The starboard engine raced and was shut down. As we had thirty-three fathoms of water beneath us it was evident we had bumped into something and had lost our starboard propeller.

A few days later the New York was dry docked at Rosyth. The three blades of the starboard propeller were gone. Two hundred feet forward of the propeller, the ship's bottom had been driven upward from twelve to twenty-four inches. British officers all said that, without question, we had collided with a submarine, and had undoubtedly sunk it. Well, perhaps.

To go to Rosyth we left our squadron, steaming with the port engine. We had eight British destroyers guarding us. At one o'clock in the morning, my executive officer, Commander Theobald, and I were together on the bridge. During a pause after some casual conversation, he said in a matter of fact tone, "Captain, I think it will miss us!"

A white thread of water was on our starboard bow, and this white thread of air bubbles, the exhaust from the engine of a torpedo, was rapidly approaching, followed by two other lines of white bubbles. Three torpedoes in all had been fired at us in a "spread," a long narrow "V" originating at the firing point, the submarine, in other words. We maneuvered radically to avoid the advancing, slightly diverging, tracks of the torpedoes, and the eight destroyers went into rapid action. They chased toward the source of the bubbles, dropping depth charges, but the submarine gave no evidence of being hit. I am inclined to believe that in future naval warfare, between torpedoes underneath, and bomb droppers overhead, battleships will have a hard time.

How right Father was! And change will be even faster now, with the advent of an entirely new sort of war, ushered in when the World Trade Towers and the Pentagon were attacked on 11 September 2001.

I spent many anxious hours traveling at eighteen to twenty knots in dense fog, day and night. They would have been anxious had my ship been traveling alone; being in squadron formation didn't make them less so. "Never mind about ships to the rear, Beach," directed the admiral. "Go full power astern if necessary. All the ships astern will keep out of our way."

One night, in a blinding fog, I found myself right on top of a great ship. For a few seconds it seemed as if we were certain to hit her. The instant I saw her, I jerked the telegraphs of both engines back to "full speed astern." The "collision" signals, with their deafening screams, resounded through the ship. On the bridge we could hear and sense watertight doors throughout our great battleship flying shut. Our suddenly backing engines, revolving full speed astern with thirty thousand horsepower (only reciprocating engines could handle that sort of instant, emergency reversal), shook up the New York—and our fifteen-hundred-man crew in their hammocks—as I never imagined a ship could be shaken.

I waited for the crash, recognizing, in the tiny space of time, that we had stumbled on the Olympic, the slightly older sister of the Titanic that, for the past six years, had been lying at the bottom of the Atlantic somewhere south of Iceland. Then, as I saw the stern of the monster draw past the New York's bow, I heard a quiet voice beside me say, "Beach, you didn't touch her. You missed her by three feet. Good night." Admiral Rodman had run up on the bridge in thin pajamas and bare feet. He certainly belonged to the "Don't Worry Club."

Another of my occasional anxieties was the captive blimp, tied to the ship by a wire cable, which was a thousand feet up during daytime. It had two observers in its basket, with telephones and telescopes. All flagships sent blimps aloft when cruising, but when a gale struck us, the blimp was hauled down. And whenever near to the ship, the wicked way that blimp dashed about; the mad speed with which it swept across the quarterdeck, was not comfortable to watch. But our blimp never had an accident.

There was attached to the New York a British officer, Commander Money, to advise about signals, maneuvers, customs, etc. On the afternoon of 9 November 1918, he and I were on the bridge when Beatty's flagship, the Queen Elizabeth, hoisted a "general signal" for all ships. This signal was: "The Germans have surrendered! Mend Clothes!"

There were whoops of joy bottled up in that signal. But I was mystified. "Great Scott, Money!" I exclaimed. "My socks are all darned, buttons are sewed on shirts, pants are patched. I have no clothes to mend!"

"Oh," returned Money, "during the Napoleonic wars our Navy ships were fighting, or preparing for fights, all the time. We had two hundred sea battles, and won all but five of them. After every fight our men were always ordered to 'mend clothes.' It has become a traditional way to announce an 'all hands' holiday."

Admiral Beatty took the British Grand Fleet to the Firth of Forth, 250 miles or so south of Scapa Flow and a far more hospitable place for a fleet full of terribly bored and lonely men. One morning at the mast a fine looking soldier in neat Canadian uniform was before me. On his coat were hung different medals, several indicating distinctive good service.

"Sir," said this man, "my name is Butler. In 1915 I was quartermaster in the Navy serving aboard the American destroyer *Cassin*. I deserted and enlisted in a Canadian regiment and have been fighting in France for three years. Our American congress has passed a law giving pardon to all Americans of the Army and Navy who deserted to fight in an Allied outfit, if they report back for duty. They are to be restored to the rank they held in our service. I give myself up, and request restoration."

"Orderly," I directed, "tell Commander Theobald I need him at the mast."

A moment later I said, "Commander Theobald, did you command the *Cassin* in 1915?"

"Yes, sir."

"Do you recognize this man?"

Giving the man careful scrutiny, Theobald replied, "This man's name is Butler. He was a first class quartermaster aboard the *Cassin* and deserted in 1915."

"Butler," I now asked, "are you still in active service with Canadian troops?"

"Yes, sir."

"Is this request made with the knowledge of your Canadian officers?"

"No, sir."

"I'll restore no one who comes to me in the uniform of one of our allies!" And I returned to my cabin.

Several hours later I was again called to the mast. Before me was a filthy dirty man. He was dressed in foul dungarees that looked as if they had been used to swab up bilges.

"Sir," said this man, "My name is Butler. In 1915 I was serving aboard the American destroyer *Cassin*, and deserted to fight with the Canadian army in Europe. I report to you for duty and ask to be pardoned and restored. Commander Theobald can identify me."

Theobald solemnly identified Butler. And then I solemnly restored him without asking questions. But, judging by the crowd that had gathered about the mast, I have always believed that those dungarees were borrowed aboard the *New York* and specially prepared for the occasion. I hope the Canadian government will forgive me for helping one of their fine soldiers to desert.

Several days later, a warship flying the German flag emerged from the fog that hung over the Firth of Forth. She carried the German admiral, Meurer, who had come to inquire of Admiral Beatty the details that would govern the prospective surrender of the German High Seas Fleet. I have never seen a written account of this meeting between Beatty and Meurer. One of the British officers who was with Beatty at the time told me the story I now relate.

To understand the attitude of the British officers, one must appreciate that there was intense feeling against the Germans. This feeling dominated their thoughts. There was indignation because of the tactics of the German submarines, the execution of Miss Cavell on charges of spying for Britain, and of Captain Fryatt. Most important, however, was the burning, overwhelming, bitter recollection that twice the German High Seas Fleet had fought the British Grand Fleet, and twice the Germans, after inflicting heavy damage, had got away when Britain's overwhelming naval superiority should have destroyed them. At Jutland, the last great battle, the British suffered considerably greater loss in ships and men than the Germans. By consequence, even though it was the German fleet that departed the scene of battle and ran for home, many German historians, citing the disparity in loss, claimed a tactical victory for their side. England had been looking for another Trafalgar, and this, of all insults, the British Navy could never forgive.

Captain Charles A. Fryatt had been awarded a gold watch for ramming and sinking a German submarine that had surfaced in accordance with the "cruiser rules" to permit his crew to get into lifeboats before their ship was sunk. Fryatt neglected to throw it away when he was later captured, thus leading to his identification and subsequent execution for not obeying the rules when the submarine had given up its security to comply with them.

After Dewey had defeated Montojo at Manila in 1898 he sent Montojo a kindly personal message. Togo called on the defeated Russian admiral, Rojestvensky, in a Japanese hospital in 1905. When Cervera, hauled out of the sea at Santiago, was brought aboard our *Iowa*, he was greeted with all the honors of his rank, and with much personal affection because of his magnanimity toward the Americans who had so daringly sunk the old collier *Merrimac* in the channel entrance to Santiago in their failed attempt to bottle up the Spanish fleet in 1898.

But in November 1918, the British had no kindly feelings toward the

Germans. When Admiral Meurer with his officers reached the quarterdeck of the *Queen Elizabeth,* there was no welcoming by noisy buglers, no marines at "present h'ahms!," no beating of drums, no band. The deck was almost deserted. An officer met the Germans, touched his cap, and said, "Please follow me." He led the way to Admiral Beatty's cabin.

This was the manner, also, in which U.S. officials greeted the Japanese delegation that came to surrender aboard the *Missouri* in 1945. Emotions were similar, though the reasons differed. Pearl Harbor was still a strong memory.

Here was a long table behind which a number of British officers were standing, the youthful appearing Beatty in the center. These bowed their heads courteously, but there was no hand shaking. Then all were seated, and the British gave necessary information and instructions to the Germans.

After several hours occupied in this way, Beatty said, "We will have a recess, Admiral Meurer. I have provided refreshments for you and your officers. This attendant will conduct you."

In a cabin a bountiful meal had been prepared. A table was loaded with hot meats, vegetables, beer, and wine. After the Germans had entered, the attendant closed the door to the cabin from the outside. The British were unwilling that any British sailor should act as servant or attendant to the Germans.

On 20 November Sims, now a four-star admiral, with several of his assistants, came on board the *Texas,* sister to the *New York.* This made her the temporary flagship of the American Battle Squadron, and Rodman moved over there, too.

And at two the next morning the British Grand Fleet got under way in a thick fog, squadron by squadron, and steamed out to meet the surrendering German High Seas Fleet. That so great a number of leviathans of the sea, in thick fog and with heavy tides running in a cramped space, could get under way and leave port without mishap of any kind, is complete proof of the high efficiency of the ships of the British Grand Fleet.

The fleet traveled in two lines, each squadron bunching its own ships. At ten o'clock Beatty sent radio signals to all ships. The fog had lifted, leaving a heavy mist, but through the mist, the High Seas Fleet was seen to be approaching.

Squadrons counter-marched and now three long lines of ships might have been seen heading toward the Firth of Forth, the middle line composed of German ships. During that return Beatty was taking nothing for granted. Every gun of his fleet was fully manned, ammunition was ready, fingers were on triggers. In the collective mind of that fleet there was, amongst the British, a strong wish that there might arise occasion to use the guns, and bitter knowledge that this hope would not be realized.

We of the American Battle Squadron were the only happy ones in that great fleet. We were full of joy, while strange as it may seem, the British were filled with heartbreaking, bitter disappointment. They had been expecting "der Tag," the great battle they thought was inevitable, that would wipe out all the doubts of Jutland; and of even this they were now being deprived. Rationalize it as they might, supine surrender could not take the place of the new Trafalgar they had been living for.

After we anchored, a number of British admirals and captains came aboard the *New York*. Since May 1916, they had been living in hope that the terrible disappointment of the battle of Jutland would be wiped out. This hope was gone. In my cabin British captains met and gave way to their feelings. One of them actually wept. This was not the way they had hoped to destroy the German High Seas Fleet!

28

AFTER SCAPA FLOW

It has now been twenty-three years since the events described in the fore-going chapter. A few years afterward I retired from active duty in the Navy with the rank of captain and have since then concentrated on raising two sons and a daughter to be good Americans.

Father's last service was as commandant of the Navy yard at Mare Island, California. Originally titled "Epilogue," he wrote this final chap-ter in late 1941.

At the time of the surrender of the German navy, we of the American Battle Squadron were very much surprised. We had been brought up in the tradition of John Paul Jones, who fought on to victory when all seemed lost, and of James Lawrence, who, knowing indeed that all was lost, lying wounded and in pain, thought only of his country's honor. The possibility that the great German fleet, which had shown its dogged courage at the Falkland Islands and fought so brilliantly at Jutland, would simply surrender without further test, had not occurred to us. It might have occurred to Admiral Beatty and other British officers, who doubtless knew German psychology better than we did. As we now know, while most high-ranking German naval officers probably wanted a great, final, battle, their crews mutinied and refused to fight.

That the outright surrender of the German High Seas Fleet was a bitter disappointment to everyone in the British navy is, however, well established. As one British officer expressed it to me, "We should have sunk them, every one. That is the only kind of treatment they understand!" We Americans thought this attitude extreme. The Germans were excellent seamen, and they had built an outstandingly good navy, though smaller in size than England's. At Jutland they had proved, ship for ship, that their ships were superior to the British warships.

The Royal Navy had reason to hold them in very high respect, and it's difficult to find justification for the British officer's hate-filled remark. There had been no perfidious "Pearl Harbor." Perhaps the officer quoted had fallen victim to England's own anti-submarine propaganda.

For us in the American Battle Squadron, we felt it had been a challenge to best the German High Seas Fleet, and we were, in the main, completely convinced that we had forever ended the menace of German aggression. Henceforth there would be peace on the sea, and we hoped on land as well. We sailed home with happy hearts, in a sea free of lurking submarines, our ships a blaze of lights. We had won our Armageddon. We had fought for the greatest cause ever conceived by mortal man, and we had won. We had made the world safe for democracy. Forever.

But what then? We Americans, and the British, and the French too, though in a lesser degree, proceeded to give the greatest demonstration of mass stupidity imaginable. Flushed and enthusiastic, we ourselves did our Navy more damage than it has suffered in its entire history, and I include Pearl Harbor. Only men like me, who had grown up from young manhood in the Navy, could see and appreciate the enormity of what was happening. When the Navy cried to Congress for funds, for even barely enough to maintain itself at fighting efficiency, it was not listened to. To keep at the peak of form, any navy must have constant improvement. It must have an orderly building program. Only thus can it stay abreast of scientific developments. Only by constant improvement can it keep from sliding backwards.

Between 1922 and 1941 we built no battleships, and only a few cruisers and destroyers. True, in the late 1930s a few good ships began to be built—but it takes four years to build a battleship, even if you have the designs, facilities, resources, and building supplies already to hand.

As this is written, the United States is reeling from the unexpected attack of the Japanese. The extent of the damage at Pearl Harbor has not yet been announced. I feel perfectly safe, however, in saying that more ships were sunk by the Treaty of 1922 than were damaged by the catastrophe at Pearl Harbor, because in 1941 we did not even have that many battleships in our Navy. We are now building them quickly, it is true, but our new ones are not built yet. Thus do old mistakes carry their influence into the future. Thus does the past control the future.

Building all these magnificent battle wagons, however, would have been a mistake. They were already long past their prime usefulness, as Pearl Harbor demonstrated. The real mistake lay in trying to hold on too long to the familiar past. Father himself, earlier in this autobiography, predicted that with bombs overhead and torpedoes below, future battleships "would have a hard time."

Present reports indicate that the old *Baltimore* may have received a mortal wound on 7 December. No longer seaworthy, she was little more than a hulk, maintained only for scrap and possible sentimental value, in a back channel at Pearl Harbor. I hope she diverted some Japanese bombs or torpedoes from a more valuable target. She fought in the forefront of our battle line forty-three and a half years ago at Manila Bay, and Darkest Africa notwithstanding, I'm proud of having participated in that historic fight. I hope she did take a bomb or two that might have hurt us more somewhere else. If so, she may have rendered us one last and useful service.

Which brings to mind the ultimate purpose of this book. Like the poor old *Baltimore*, I am now too old for active naval service. My thought has been to leave a record of our Navy as a living, breathing organization of men, different from other men only by the fact that they chose the Navy for their careers, instead of business, the arts, or one of the professions. The one thing the men of our Navy have been bred to is the ideal of never giving up while there is a job to be done. The Japanese warrior thinks being killed in battle for the emperor is a sure passport to heaven, and the Germans and Italians risk death because Hitler implacably forces them to. Our men fight, not for death, but for freedom. They have always fought for it. They will never cease to fight for it, until freedom is assured—and not then, either, for such absolute assurance can never be. It is up to Congress and the people of our country to ensure that they do not fight—and die—for nothing.

I lay no claim to omniscience. In 1922, like many others, I also thought war was a thing of the past, at least for a long time to come. I therefore retired from the Navy to become a professor of history at Stanford University, where I never got over the pleasure of watching so many bright young faces attentively drinking in every word I said, and hurriedly copying them all down on paper, so as not to forget them. And when I gave examinations, I never got over being astounded at how little they all knew! Mr. Ernie Nevers could certainly play football, however, in spite of his appalling lack of appreciation of the military principles involved in Stonewall Jackson's campaign in the Shenandoah Valley. And I have to admit that every time he made a touchdown I forgot about Stonewall Jackson.

And so I have finished my story. Lately, I have come under the domination of a most despotic admiral, who always makes me wear an overcoat when I go out for a walk, and even insists on my wearing a cap in the house, so I won't catch cold in my bald head. Our two sons are respectively in the Navy and Army, and so is our daughter, who has become a "Navy Wave," thereby ranking about even with her two older lieutenant brothers. The only people left to obey my orders are a collie dog, who takes walks with me every day and thinks I'm wonderful, and a ridiculous cat, who is very insubordinate.

————————

And from the son, in 2002, it is necessary to point out that Father left out one important thing: he told nothing at all about his tour of duty as commandant at Mare Island Navy Yard. Its greatest product, so far as I'm concerned, was construction of the magnificent fleet flagship

California, more than thirty-five thousand tons of battleship majesty. Dad was in charge of her launching, and, though it has fallen on hard times, we still have the wonderful scrapbook Mother so laboriously kept of those halcyon days. I'll never forget *California*'s terribly diminished condition—badly damaged, her mud-streaked sides showing how far she had sunk—as I saw her from the deck of the submarine *Trigger* as we entered Pearl Harbor in early 1942. More than anything else, this brought home the true facts of the war we were in.

As a small boy, my memories of Mare Island are few. The place always represented Navy shore duty to me, and on our few visits there after Dad's retirement there were some things that fixed themselves in my mind. Most prominent was the tremendous pile of steel plate that had been accumulated for building the *Montana*, a battleship a third again bigger than the *California*, and for which Dad laid the keel. As already noted, construction of this ship was canceled on the shipping ways, and this was just as well, considering that she was already so far behind the times.

In 1922, a bit more than three years after his arrival at Mare Island, Father submitted his retirement papers. His total naval service had lasted nearly thirty-eight years. As he has already mentioned, he then became a professor of history at Stanford University, and culminated his working career as city clerk and assessor of Palo Alto.

————————————

INDEX

About the Authors

Edward L. Beach Sr. graduated from the U.S. Naval Academy in 1888 and retired from the Navy in 1922 at the rank of captain. As secretary-treasurer of the U.S. Naval Institute, he published the first edition of *The Bluejackets' Manual* in 1902. He saw action in the Spanish-American War at Manila Bay, and in World War I he commanded the battleship *New York,* flagship of the American Battle Squadron. He later became a professor of history at Stanford University. Thirteen of his books were published before his death in 1943.

Edward L. Beach Jr. graduated from the Naval Academy in 1939. During World War II Captain Beach participated in the Battle of Midway, and his submarines conducted twelve combat patrols that sank or damaged forty-five ships. A highly decorated officer, Beach received the Navy Cross and two Silver Stars. After a number of postwar assignments, Captain Beach served as naval attaché to President Dwight Eisenhower from 1953 to 1957. In February 1960 Beach began his record-breaking voyage in the nuclear submarine USS *Triton,* which circumnavigated the earth submerged in sixty-one days. During her nearly thirty-one thousand mile journey, *Triton* set a speed and endurance record that stands today. In May President Eisenhower presented Beach with the Legion of Merit. Captain Beach retired from the Navy in 1966. In addition to a brilliant naval career, Beach wrote novels, memoirs, and naval histories, works that earned him numerous literary awards. Among his books is the bestselling *Run Silent, Run Deep.* In honor of both Captains Beach, the home of the U.S. Naval Institute in Annapolis, Maryland, was named Beach Hall.